Cosmic Journeys

My Out-of-Body Explorations with Robert A. Monroe

Cosmic Journeys

My Out-of-Body Explorations with Robert A. Monroe

Rosalind A. McKnight

HAMPTON ROADS
PUBLISHING COMPANY, INC.

Cover design by Mayapriya Long
Cover art by Lisa Podgur Cuscuna, Index Stock Imagery
and Steven Barnes, Index Stock Imagery

For information write:

Hampton Roads Publishing Company, Inc.
134 Burgess Lane
Charlottesville, VA 22902

Or call: 804-296-2772
FAX: 804-296-5096
e-mail: hrpc@hrpub.com
Web site: http://www.hrpub.com

If you are unable to order this book from your local
bookseller, you may order directly from the publisher.
Quantity discounts for organizations are available.
Call 1-800-766-8009, toll-free.

Library of Congress Catalog Card Number: 98-73918

ISBN 1-57174-123-2

10 9 8 7 6 5 4 3 2 1

Printed on recycled acid-free paper in Canada

Dedicated to:

Bob and Nancy Monroe,
whose love and devotion to each other have spilled over into The Monroe Institute, making it what it is today and in turn transforming thousands of lives . . .

Nancy Lee (Scooter) Honeycutt McMoneagle,
Nancy's daughter, whose radiant personality, brilliant mind, and executive abilities have positively affected many lives through her dedication to the work of The Monroe Institute over the years . . .

Laurie A. Monroe,
Bob's daughter, whose loving and sensitive nature, combined with her excellent management skills, confidently carries the Institute into the twenty-first century . . .

George Durrette,
Bob's forever-faithful silent partner and my good friend always . . .

Melissa Woodring Jager,
my wonderful friend and teacher, and Bob's confidante and trainer, who for several years helped to transform lives through her Gateway Voyage training sessions and continues to do so through her dedication to the joys of living and Baba . . .

Other Very Special Monroe Institute Servers:

☆ The other Honeycutts (Nancy's children)—talented artist Cindy, who is dear to my heart and taught me a lot while I worked with her at the Monroe Packing Shed; Penny, the stand-up comic who is now a trainer; and Terry (A.J.), my movie buddy and now Institute executive . . .

☆ Helen Warring, a Monroe Institute legend and my spiritual mentor . . .

☆ Paul Andrews, my special friend, who successfully managed The Monroe Institute on the West Coast for years . . .

☆ The many dedicated trainers, some of whom are Karen Malik, Ann Martin, David Mulvey, Bill Schul, and Chris Lenz . . .

☆ Bob's other Explorers, who ventured out, as I did, into cosmic dimensions . . .

My Invisible Helpers—My Angels,

who have reached across the cosmos to make these amazing journeys possible and who have given me the following affirmation that I repeat regularly as I swirl around in God's radiant energies: *"I am light, manifested in love, expressed in joy, joy, joy!"*

ACKNOWLEDGMENTS

I express heartfelt gratitude to David McKnight for his professional editing skills and the hours he pored over my manuscript.

☆ To his wife Mary, who was always behind the scenes cheering me on.

☆ To Eleanor Friede, my agent, who is the best of the best.

☆ To Darryl Doran, who gave me a computer system long before either of us knew why.

☆ To Ramona Morgan, a Gateway participant, who, in 1985, was the first person, besides Bob Monroe, to strongly encourage me to write this book.

☆ To Ed Pierson, giver of the best advice I have ever had.

☆ To my niece, Patrice Lynn, and my good friends, Shirlee Olesen, Betty See, Lucille Williams, Martha Ambrosi, David Hagerman, Pat Foreman, Andy Lee, Patty Summers, Joe Heddings, Raven Campbell, and Michael Millner, whose continuous enthusiasm and support for my work kept me going (and keeps me going).

☆ To Ann McKellips, a professional in the field of writing, who encouraged me with her high regard for the book.

☆ To Jim McKellips, whose computer expertise made the process of producing a manuscript seem simple.

☆ And last, but not least, warm hugs go to the skilled and talented staff at Hampton Roads, who make me feel like an important member of an extended family!

CONTENTS

To Use Such Greater Energies and Energy Systems . . .

Also, I Deeply Desire Assistance [and] Wisdom . . .

I Ask Their Guidance and Protection . . .

New Beginnings . . .

FOREWORD

Cosmic Journeys is a true account of actual sessions that were conducted in the research laboratory of The Monroe Institute beginning nearly forty years ago. Material from many of these Explorer sessions became the foundation for the residential programs held at the Institute, including the world-renowned Gateway Voyage.

The Monroe Institute was founded by Robert A. Monroe, author of *Journeys Out of the Body, Far Journeys,* and *Ultimate Journey.* The work of the Institute today is the result of the many people who collaborated with Bob during these formative years in the exploration of human consciousness. Many educators, psychologists, physicists, psychiatrists, engineers, and physicians were instrumental in the growth and support of the Institute. Rosalind McKnight is one of these early Explorers who volunteered time and curiosity of spirit to venturing, with Bob's guidance, into other, nonphysical dimensions.

In July of 1985, Bob himself encouraged Rosie to publish this record of her experiences. He wrote to her,

> *Rosie, if you wish to submit the material independently, by all means do so with my blessing. We've been friends for a long time. You've helped me and the Institute through the years in whatever way you could—and when it seemed you needed help or whatever, I've tried to be here.*

This is a warm, inspiring, and fascinating book that illuminates a wide range of issues. Rosalind McKnight's profound experiences will bring to life a clarity of perception and a sense of the greatness that is beyond our everyday life. You will feel the incredible energy and the dedication of the Explorers' research through this author's insights and unique expression. You will feel the depth of Bob's inquisitive mind as well as the expression of his heart and soul in this book.

It is with heartfelt gratitude that I write this introduction for Rosie. I thank her deeply for her invaluable participation in the history of the Institute and for the many Explorer sessions that assisted us in furthering the understanding and exploration of human consciousness. It is truly an outstanding tribute to the work of The Monroe Institute and Robert Monroe.

Bob would have been proud of this account and very appreciative of everything that went into bringing it to fruition.

Laurie A. Monroe, President
The Monroe Institute

I Am More
Than My Physical Body . . .

1

TRANSFORMATION

It was Friday afternoon. I walked in the door from work, tired and hungry as usual, to the telephone ringing off its hook.

"Where have you been?" my good friend Melissa demanded.

"I told you I was doing some temporary work. Remember?"

"That's right; I forgot! I've probably left you six messages to call me back," she replied.

"I just got in and haven't even checked them. What's up?"

"Bob died this morning at nine o'clock," she said so quickly that I almost didn't understand her.

"Bob who?" I asked.

"Bob Monroe!" she said with an intonation that implied, "Who else?"

"Oh, wow," I said as I slid down onto a chair in disbelief. "He's taken his final out-of-body journey! When's the memorial service?"

"Next Friday."

"Let's see," I mumbled out loud. "Today is March 17, so that puts the service on the twenty-fourth." Then a light went on in my head. "Melissa, did it dawn on you that Bob died on St. Patrick's Day?" I asked.

"I've been so busy calling people that I didn't give St. Patrick's Day much attention," she replied.

"Isn't it an amazing coincidence that Bob died on St. Patrick's Day when 'Patrick' was probably Bob's all-time favorite nonphysical friend?"

"You're right," Melissa said. "Patrick probably did more to help Bob get over the fear of death than all of his out-of-body trips combined!"

"Thanks for your persistence in calling, Melissa. I have to go. My cats are staring at me with starved looks in their eyes. See you!"

As I hung up the phone, the reality of Bob's death began to sink in. I got an empty feeling in the pit of my stomach. Then I remembered my very intense belief that when Bob finished his third book, *Ultimate Journey*, he would probably return to his lab work, which he loved, and just take "the journey." But I didn't think he would take it so soon after the book was written. Only a few months had stood between the 1994 publication date of the last book of his trilogy and his departure on March 17, 1995.

All week long my mind was clicking into a "life-review" mode, with experiences I had with Bob flashing involuntarily across my mind. Our relationship went back 24 years, to 1971. That was a landmark year for both of us, because so many things happened that would create the setting for what was to come. Bob had recently married Nancy Penn. He had just published his classic book, *Journeys Out of the Body*. His Whistlefield Research Laboratory was appropriately renamed the "Monroe Institute of Applied Sciences" (now called The Monroe Institute).

And after two years of marriage, David McKnight and I had moved from the New York City area to the Shenandoah Valley of Virginia, where David took a position with the Virginia Community College system. David and I were from Ohio but had met in New York City at Union Theological Seminary, where we were both working on our Master of Divinity degrees.

The biggest thing about 1971, however, was that Bob and I met. What was created through the combination of our energies would read like a science-fiction novel—almost too amazing to be true. But a fact I learned in my experience with Bob is that truth is indeed much stranger than fiction.

The drive into the 600-acre Monroe Institute complex has always given me goose bumps. I was with Bob and Nancy when they first drove onto the property. When we got to the top of the hill where the training center now stands, we were awestruck. I got a Shangri-la feeling as we viewed the layers and layers of mountains for the first time. The one in the fore-ground, Roberts Mountain, was once part of the Roberts fam-ily farm. It was as if it was just waiting for Bob to arrive!

Time rolled back as I drove up the road to the Monroe Institute on the afternoon of Bob's memorial service. The day was crisp, with a very special atmosphere. A recent cold front seemed to give the blue sky extra depth. A breeze blew my silk dress gently as I stepped out of my car. A young man was direct-ing a steady flow of cars into efficient rows in the field beside David Francis Hall, one of the Institute's main meeting facilities.

Not being alert to signs that had been put up to direct peo-ple, I walked into David Frances Hall and down the stairs, ex-pecting the room to be filled with people. I was surprised to find the room empty, but very elaborately decorated for the recep-tion. Around the room were pictures and memorabilia of Bob and Nancy's life. A large picture of them seemed to pull me directly to it. The reality of Bob and Nancy's passings hit me as I stood there staring at their picture. I had missed Nancy's memo-rial service two years before. Tears began rolling gently down my cheeks as I absorbed the presence of their powerful energies in the room.

A voice from behind me broke my silent communion with Nancy and Bob. "The service is out on the hill behind the building," a lady said as I swung around, startled. She pointed to the basement patio. "You can go through these glass doors. You might as well sign the guest book now, because there will be a long line after the service."

I thanked her and walked through the doors. I looked at the book where several people had already signed, and slowly wrote, "Rosalind McKnight—ROMC." ROMC was Bob's code name for me. I had been one of his longtime Explorers. I felt a sense of pride, mixed with sadness, as I signed off for the last time.

The mesmerizing view again caught me as I walked out of the shadow of the building. Chairs were set in rows facing the moun-tains. Some people were milling around; others were seated. I was so deeply caught up in my thoughts that I wanted to avoid small talk with friends. So when I saw an empty spot toward the back of the seating area I slid unnoticed onto a black metal chair that wobbled as I sat down.

For about ten minutes I absorbed the magic of the moment. Then a hush came over the group. The service was about to start. I took a closer look at the program in my hand: "A *Celebration for Robert Allan Monroe, 1915-1995.*" I turned the program over, and there was Bob's "Affirmation." As I started reading it, I was startled by the sound of Bob's voice as it rolled out of a loud speaker beside me: "*I am more than my physical body . . . .*" It was the familiar audiotape of Bob reading the affirmation. As the taped message continued, I sensed Bob's living presence swirling up over the crowd, as if in flight above us, while the echo of his voice seemed to reach out to Roberts Mountain to include it in his final benediction.

The affirmation Bob's voice was reciting had always been used in his Explorer and other training programs. Almost everyone at this celebration of Bob's life had repeated the affirmation many times before, as I had. But the power and reality of the message struck deep within me at that moment. Bob, now fully in his more-than-physical body, gave the affirmation renewed meaning as it connected with that more-than-physical reality of my own being:

> *I am more than my physical body. Because I am more than physical matter, I can perceive that which is greater than the physical world. Therefore, I deeply desire to expand, to experience, to know, to understand, to control, to use such greater energies and energy systems as may be beneficial and constructive to me and to those who follow me. Also, I deeply desire the help and cooperation, the assistance, the understanding of those individuals whose wisdom, development, and experience are equal to or greater than my own. I ask their guidance and protection from any influence or any source that might provide me with less than my stated desires.*

With The Monroe Institute affirmation as a framework, we turn to the amazing story of the incredible journeys I took with Robert Monroe as we explored dimensions beyond physical reality.

2

THE LABORATORY

As I came around the corner onto West 67th Street, I could see Rosemary talking to the doorman of the apartment building where I had roomed with her for the past few months. I did a New York-style double-park in front of them, and the doorman and Rosemary brought my luggage to the car. "I'm going to miss you," Rosemary said as we placed the luggage in the trunk.

"David and I are really going to miss you, too," I said as I closed the trunk. "This city has served us well these past seven years. But once we get settled in Virginia, we probably won't be eager to come back for a while. So, you'll just have to come and visit us."

"I'd love to come to Virginia," Rosemary remarked as we walked around to the side of the car. "In fact, I have a friend there whom I'd like to visit. He also moved from New York. Everyone's abandoning me!"

"Rosemary, don't make me feel guilty about leaving," I said as I hugged her. "You'll just have to release Manhattan and move to Virginia yourself! Have I met your friend in Virginia?"

"I don't think so," Rosemary replied. "But I know you and David would appreciate meeting him. His name is Robert Monroe. Most people call him Bob. He's a very unusual man. He has just remarried, but I haven't met his new wife, Nancy."

"It would be great if we lived close to the Monroes since we know almost no one in Virginia," I said as I waved a driver around my illegally parked car. "Where do they live?"

"In a town called Afton, Virginia. And I have no idea where it is," Rosemary replied.

I opened the car door and pulled out the Virginia map. "We might as well hold up traffic a little longer," I chuckled as I spread out the map on the hood of the car.

"Okay, let's see where Afton is in relation to Bridgewater," I muttered as I looked for the city listing. "Yes, here it is, one finger-joint away! Wow, that's not far at all. Probably less than an hour's drive from Bridgewater."

"Well, that settles it," Rosemary exclaimed. "I'll come!"

"I'll be there sooner or later," she called as I drove away. Through my rear-view mirror I saw her waving as I turned off 67th Street onto Broadway and headed toward the Lincoln Tunnel. It would be my last drive out of Manhattan as a New Yorker.

After a short time in the little town of Bridgewater, we moved to Oak Hill Farm in Mount Solon, an old rural community nestled next to the mountains. I had seen an ad for a farmhouse renting for $100 a month. Being used to New York City rents, I thought it had to be a misprint—or that there were no windows, electricity, or indoor plumbing!

When David and I rounded a bend in the road and viewed Oak Hill Farm for the first time, we were astounded. There, sitting elegantly on a hill, was my picture of a lovely southern mansion, with two-story pillars and a huge oak tree in front. Other beautiful trees surrounded the house, which was on 22 acres of gently rolling hills. This idyllic farmstead became ours for the next seven years and the rent never rose above $100. The house did, by the way, have windows, electricity, and running water—as well as thoughtful, attentive landlords.

When our friends in New York City learned about our newfound treasure in the country, entertaining a steady stream of visitors became a major activity.

One day the phone rang and a voice said, "Sooner is here. When can I come?" I was elated to hear Rosemary's voice.

"Our guest room is yours whenever you arrive."

"What about the weekend after next?" she asked. "I'm going to rent a car and drive down."

I was thrilled. "I'll get directions to you in the mail today, Rosemary!"

"Great," she said. "And I'll call Bob and Nancy Monroe to see if we can visit them while I'm there."

When I hung up I realized that our absence of a social life had been almost as challenging as our environmental adjustments. Social contacts were very important to David and me, and our few months in Virginia hadn't given us enough time to develop a circle of friends. Actually, I was feeling a sense of loneliness and isolation. The thought of meeting some new friends with mutual interests was exciting.

It was a crisp November day in 1971 when Rosemary, David, and I drove over Afton Mountain for the first time. When we arrived at the Monroe's estate—"Whistlefield Farm"—we passed a prefab building and circled around a lake before arriving at the main house.

As I stepped out of the car, the view was so breathtaking and awe-inspiring that I temporarily lost my sense of reality. A favorite scene in the deep reservoir of my fantasies is that of layers of mountains towering on the horizon. From the time I was a child growing up in the flatlands of central Ohio, I would transpose low-hanging clouds into an image of endless mountain ranges. Gazing upon such scenes always gave me a feeling of déjà vu. And here, in real life, were the mountains of my dreams! Goose bumps rose on my neck as I sensed something very special about the energies of this setting. Was it a premonition that on this stage my future would be played out?

As we moved up the walkway, Bob stepped out on the porch. He and Rosemary hugged each other warmly, obviously old friends. Then Rosemary turned to introductions. My first impression of Bob has always remained with me. He had a rare mystique that completely set him off from other people. In a casual, gentlemanly manner he held the door, inviting us to come in and make ourselves at home.

Bob's wrinkled attire presented a sharp contrast to his wife's stunning appearance as Nancy walked in from the kitchen to greet us. The two of them were always the odd couple as far as dress was concerned. Nancy was the perfect southern hostess, and dinner in their formal dining room was more than we had expected for our first social visit in Virginia.

When we moved to the living room after dinner, Bob looked at Rosemary and commented that a book she was featured in was doing quite well since its publication earlier that year.

David and I looked at the two of them in a quizzical manner, and Bob began to chuckle and relate the story of their first meeting.

"Rosemary, wouldn't you agree," Bob asked, "that our meeting could probably be listed in the *Guinness Book of World Records* as the most unusual first meeting ever to take place?"

"Absolutely, Bob. But I didn't plan to sit on your lap the first night you visited my apartment!" Rosemary continued in mock irritation. "I simply forgot that that chair was assigned to you for the evening."

"What a way to treat a first-time guest!" Bob replied in a teasing manner. "However, it was good you sat on my invisible lap, Rosemary, because that made it much more evidential when I reported my out-of-body visit to your apartment. It actually turned out to be one of my most successful and humorous experiments. That's how you earned your own special niche in *Journeys Out of the Body*."

Rosemary's face was aglow as she said, "You really blew me away, Bob, when you called later that night and described my apartment, the number of people in the group, where we were sitting, and how we were dressed, as well as the fact that I'd mentioned working at a cancer hospital—and, of course, that I sat on you!" Bob leaned over a coffee table and picked up a copy of what would someday be a classic in the field of out-of-body travel. He autographed the book and walked across the room, handing it to Rosemary. "Even though you may already have a copy, I want you to have this one from me. You earned it. I want to thank you again for being willing to use your group and apartment for one of our out-of-body experiments. You were quite brave to offer, since I hadn't even met you when we set up the experiment."

"Thank you, Bob. It was quite exciting to finally meet you in-the-body!" Rosemary replied. "Your friendship has always meant a lot to me. When I read the report of the experiment and then learned that it went into your book, I was a little embarrassed that my posterior faux pas was put in print for posterity." Everyone laughed as Rosemary continued, "But I always meant to ask you, Bob, how did it feel when I sat on you?"

Bob chuckled as he said, "Well, your action sure added a lot of weight to the experiment."

David was captivated by the conversation and asked Bob when he first started going out-of-body.

"I began to 'go' out of my body in the fall of 1958," Bob replied. "And I might add that no drugs or alcohol were used to precipitate the event."

"Did you have many other happenings as exciting as the 'Rosemary Event'?" David asked.

"My book is full of them," Bob continued. "But the time I woke up in a body that was laid out for viewing in a funeral home was my most frightening experience. And you'd better believe I didn't stay around for the viewing! I didn't even look back to see what the body looked like." Though the experience may have been frightening to Bob at the time, he was far enough away from it to view it humorously. We were all laughing as Bob interjected, "Well, I'm not going to tell you more. You're going to have to buy the book, David. And I'm completely out of copies. When we get them in, they disappear as quickly as I do when I leave my body. Since you live across the mountain, why don't you order one at your local bookstore? The publisher is Doubleday."

"I'll do that on Monday," David replied, as he wrote the information in his pad of perpetual notes. "But you can talk about the nature of the work you are doing here at Whistlefield, can't you, Bob?" he asked, putting his notepad back in his shirt pocket.

"Of course," Bob replied with enthusiasm. "We have just changed our name from Whistlefield Research Laboratories to the Monroe Institute of Applied Sciences. The best way for you to learn about our research is to come over to the lab and let us hook you up so you can personally experience what we do here."

We were all so excited about the possibility of learning firsthand what Bob was doing that Rosemary volunteered to come back again in January. So we set a tentative date for our laboratory experience. Rosemary arrived in mid-January and David and I were happy to see her. At Whistlefield, we pulled into the parking lot surrounding the prefab building we had passed on our first visit. We had no idea at the time that this was the first laboratory of the Monroe Institute of Applied Sciences, soon to be recognized worldwide.

Bob greeted us at the door and immediately took us on a tour of the facilities. The chalet design and layout of the building gave the impression of walking into a laid-back ski resort. Bob escorted us through the living room, with its iron stairway circling up into the Institute library loft, past a kitchen and offices, and on down a hall toward the laboratory itself.

As we walked down the long hall toward what Bob referred to as his Control Room, I noticed a change in the atmosphere. I felt tingly all over. The atmosphere was charged with very unusual energies. I couldn't analyze or understand my feelings. The air felt electrified as we moved down the hall.

We peeked into three experimental chambers Bob pointed out as we walked by. He didn't pause to tell us what these rooms were for, because he seemed eager to get to the Control Room. In pied-piper fashion, we kept pace behind him.

I was pulling up the rear of our group, and by the time I walked into the Control Room, Bob was in his chair, twirling knobs. It reminded me of a scene out of *Star Trek*. I was so awestruck that if Bob had announced that the Monroe Starship Enterprise was ready for takeoff, I would have gone along without batting an eye—in fact, I would have been one of its most eager passengers!

I carefully watched Bob's face as he continued flipping switches and pushing buttons as if he were indeed preparing for takeoff. I was so mesmerized that he startled me when he suddenly swung his chair around and asked which of us wanted to go into one of the experimental chambers for a session. We all eagerly volunteered.

"Bob, is there a name for these booths?" I asked as we walked back down the hallway toward them.

"These experimental chambers are called CHEC Units," he replied.

"What does CHEC stand for?" I asked.

"Controlled Holistic Environmental Chamber," he said.

David chimed in, "I think Bob is giving us a fancy name for a room with no outside interference."

"You got it," Bob said as he motioned each of us into a unit. I heard Bob greet someone in the hallway as we examined the water beds we would be lying on. One of his lab assistants had just come by at the right moment. I heard Bob ask him to wire us up for the experiment, and then Bob headed back to his Control Room.

I was sitting nervously on the side of my water bed when I heard the technician say something to David and then close his door. As he came to my door, which was still open, I was flippantly thinking: Perhaps in good, *Star Trek*-style, they're going to beam us up into another dimension. Little did I know how accurate my thoughts were on this momentous occasion of getting wired into CHEC Unit 2 for the first time.

I was prepared to lie down when the lab technician asked me to take off my shoes so that he could attach electrodes to the toes of my left foot. He did the same to the third finger of my left hand. Then he placed electrodes behind my ears. I made a mental note to ask Bob what these wires were all about—if and when we got out of these eerie booths! New experiences can elicit fear, and I wasn't exempt from this sometimes unwanted emotional monitor we were born with to keep us out of trouble.

The technician put a set of headphones on me and asked me to lie down on the water bed. He placed a microphone directly in front of my mouth. My nervousness inspired a multitude of anxious thoughts and questions. I wondered what I would do if someone yelled, "Fire!" while I was wired into this soundproof room. I managed to relax somewhat in spite of my apprehension and the equipment that was attached to me. My pulse quickened when the technician walked out, closed the door, and left me alone in that silent room of total darkness.

I lay there anxiously awaiting what would happen next when a tone sounded in my right earphone. Bob's voice broke in, announcing, "You are now hearing a tone in your right ear. If you are not hearing a tone in your right ear, please turn your headphones around." Mine were on correctly.

As I became more and more relaxed, an ocean-surf sound rolled gently into my ears and moved back and forth inside my head. It was a strange feeling that I had never experienced before. As the sensation of movement became more prominent, it began to feel as if a slow-motion tennis game were being played inside my brain.

When this energy movement subsided, I went into a deeply relaxed state. The soothing quality of Bob's voice, along with the intoxicating sounds, seemed to do a job on my nervous system. I could feel every cell in my body applauding this opportunity to relax after several days of entertaining our New York guest.

The next thing I remember was Bob saying, "And now you are back, wide awake, alert and full of energy." It took me a few seconds to figure out where I was. I thought, Good heavens, I flunked my first experiment!

Then Bob announced over the microphone that when we were ready we could leave our CHEC Units, but he suggested that we take our time coming back. I took him at his word. Don't know how long I lay there before I got up. I was thinking that my body was more relaxed than it had ever been in my life. I wasn't sure what sounds Bob had put in my ears, but my body certainly reacted favorably to them.

By the time I got out of my CHEC Unit the whole crew was having coffee at the opposite end of the building. I followed their laughter. When I walked into the living room, my other two exploring companions, David and Rosemary, were talking excitedly about their experiences. As they talked, Bob nodded knowingly as if to say, "Yes, that's a typical experience people have."

David beat me to the question when he asked Bob what the electrode feedback told him about us.

Bob looked at him and in a teasing tone said, "Let's see how smart you are."

"Try me," David replied.

"Well, what is an EEG apparatus?"

"Doesn't that register brain-wave patterns?" David asked.

"Yes, we of course have electrical patterns in our brains," Bob replied. "And I can look at my EEG instrumentation and read what your brain is telling me about your body's activity. But I'll wager you don't know what an EMG machine is."

"Watch your step, Bob," I cut in. "You are challenging a magna cum laude graduate of Harvard, with a major in psychology. I'm sure he's retained some of his hard-earned knowledge."

I saw a gleam in Bob's eye; he was a person who always acknowledged credentials.

David quickly replied, "Actually, I don't know what an EMG is."

Bob, with something of an "I got you" tone in his voice, told us that the EMG is a muscle-tone apparatus that registers pulse rate and body voltage.

Then Bob turned to me and said, "The machines very clearly told me that you went sound asleep."

I was stunned and embarrassed. I didn't think anyone would know I'd fallen asleep if I didn't say anything. My face turned beet red. Needing to find some excuse other than my tiredness, I said, "But Bob, it was those crazy sounds that you rolled around in my brain that did it. I have never had anyone play slow-motion tennis in my head before. What in the world were those sounds?"

Bob had a satisfied look, telling me I had asked the right question. "I've been experimenting with a new sound system to help subjects stay awake," he announced.

"Well, I sure bummed out on that one," I said.

"I'm still working out levels and frequencies," he continued. "You are a perfect subject if you're willing to come back. I'd like to do a series of sessions with you."

"I'd be happy to. David and I decided that I get to stay home and be a 'kept woman' while he works. I haven't been able to stay at home since my Dad supported me." Everyone chuckled as I excitedly continued, "I have the time and would love to come, even on a regular basis."

David nodded, happy that I had found something both to get me out of the house and to keep me out of trouble.

Bob went on to tell us about his research. "The sound you heard comes from a binaural-beat-frequency stimulation that sets up a Frequency Following Response, or FFR. It holds the subject in a certain state of consciousness between wakefulness and sleep for extended periods of time."

"How does it do that?" David asked.

"By controlling the brain wave frequency," Bob explained, "we can help the subject relax, stay awake, or go to sleep. It takes hundreds of hours of testing responses while I adjust pitches and look for changes in the monitoring instruments. And I'm always looking for volunteers to help me develop and perfect this sound system."

David looked at me, and then said, "She'll be a good test subject, Bob, because she loves to sleep! If you can find tones that keep her body relaxed and her mind awake—for any period of time, you'll really be onto something."

"That's exactly what we're striving for, Mr. Magna Cum Laude. How did you guess?"

"No guessing needed; it just seemed logical," David replied, mimicking Bob's teasing tone.

Bob got more animated as he went on. "Now, let me tell you what we've discovered about our FFR sound system. We use headphones to isolate one ear from the other. When we send a different sound pulse to each ear, the right and left brain hemispheres act in unison to produce—that is, they 'hear'—a third signal, which is the difference between the signals in each ear. For example, if you hear a sound measuring 440 hertz in one ear, and a sound of 434 hertz in the other, the signal your whole brain will generate will be 6 cycles per second—the difference between 440 and 434."

"So 'hertz' means cycles per second?" I murmured, trying hard to understand.

"Yes," Bob continued, "but it's not an actual sound that is generated. It's an electrical signal that can be created only by both brain hemispheres acting and working together. The hemispheres synchronize, and we call this process 'Hemi-Sync'—which is short for hemispheric synchronization. Once learned, your brain can retrieve this newly learned Hemi-Sync signal on its own at any time. In our normal waking state, both sides of the brain are usually not synchronized; they are not working together. So, Hemi-Sync is like putting a new program into your brain so that both sides function together."

"Are these binaural beats, as you call them, ever encountered in nature?" Rosemary asked.

"Usually not," Bob said. "Beats are rarely encountered, because in nature, sustained pure tones are rare. But beats do abound in mechanical devices. This is a part of what noise pollution is all about. I'm sure you have flown, haven't you, Rosemary?"

"Oh, yes," she replied. "I just got back from Egypt."

"Did you ever get a funny feeling in the pit of your stomach when the jet engines start up?" Bob asked.

"I always do," Rosemary replied.

"Well," Bob continued, "jet engines operating at slightly different speeds can produce a very strong beat, often recognized only as a feeling in the pit of the stomach."

"Well, that's a relief," Rosemary said with a sigh. "I thought I had a fear of flying. I wasn't even aware of why I got that feeling in my stomach."

"Two blowers running at different speeds in a house or apartment can set up the same Hemi-Sync effect," Bob added. "Uncontrolled beats of different frequencies can be the cause of a lot of stress in overpopulated areas. That's why I am experimenting so avidly. I'm striving to come up with Hemi-Sync sounds that are conducive to human growth and the fulfillment of potential. Beats can be used to our advantage when frequencies are determined precisely."

David interrupted with much interest: "So this newly generated signal of 6 hertz, or 6 cycles per second, creates a new brain-wave form."

"Exactly," Bob said.

"Can the subject's consciousness state be altered by merely changing the sound pattern?" David asked.

"Absolutely," Bob said. "People go to ashrams for years to learn to meditate. But we can put them in the same meditative state in minutes by using our Hemi-Sync process."

"So, Bob," I asked, "when the sounds move back and forth, what kind of cycle makes me feel as if someone were playing slow-motion tennis in my head?"

"When the beats are very infrequent," Bob replied. "When they're fewer than about 3 cycles per second, you will experience the sounds as moving back and forth in your head, as you express it."

"This is revolutionary," I exclaimed. "And it's exciting for us to meet you at the beginning of your experiments, Bob. Who knows where this might lead?"

Bob smiled and reached to shake my hand. "I'm glad to have you on board, Rosie. This could be a long-term relationship. We have a lot of work ahead of us."

"When do we start?" I asked.

"We'll have to wait until spring before we can work together on a regular basis," Bob said. "I've been invited to Esalen at Big Sur, California, to conduct a weekend workshop using our new methods and techniques. So we're getting ready for that. We haven't done anything like this before. The workshop is in March, so give me a call the first of April."

My mind was racing as we drove back over Afton Mountain. Little did I know then what I was getting myself into. Or I should say, little did I know then what I was getting myself *out of!*

~3~

EXPLORERS

My first April in Virginia was exhilarating. As I came to the top of Afton Mountain and started down the steep incline on my last lap to the Monroe lab, my foot automatically hit the brake at a "scenic view" sign. I parked my car at the overlook and wondered if I should pinch myself to make sure I was still alive and in my physical body. The view was so breathtaking that for a moment the thought crossed my mind that perhaps I had actually died and gone to heaven.

I got out of the car and stood on the stone retaining wall. The song, "On a Clear Day You Can See Forever," ran through my mind. Miles and miles of rolling hills, flatlands, miniature dwellings, curved roadways, and spring-blossomed trees seemed to whisper messages of beauty and joy as they spread toward the horizon in the sweeping scene below my tingling toes.

Exploring has been an innate part of my nature. Travel and other forms of adventure have always been at the top of my list of priorities. In my fifth year, when our family of eight moved to Eichelberger Avenue in Dayton, Ohio, my first act was to climb to the top of an old windmill to find out how far I could see. The exploration came to a rapid halt when my father's firm voice demanded that I retreat, very slowly, back down the rickety steps. When my feet landed safely on solid territory, I received my first reprimand for being such a fearless explorer. But the uncomfortable swatting of my posterior didn't even begin to dampen my adventuresome spirit.

I was still high with excitement about the view when I met Bob at the door of the lab.

"I thought you had forgotten about our appointment," Bob said as I followed him down the hallway to the Control Room.

"I'm sorry I'm late, Bob. But I just had to stop and see the view on the top of Afton Mountain."

"That's a gorgeous view, to be sure. But let's see what kind of view you will get from inside your head," he said as he began twirling knobs and flipping switches.

My eyes got as big as saucers as I watched with fascination. I do not have a technical mentality, and I had no idea what this Control Room was all about. I didn't hear anyone walk into the room, but felt a presence behind me—and turned to see John, Bob's lab assistant, standing there.

"John, you can wire Rosie up in CHEC Unit 2, where she was before," Bob directed as John motioned for me to follow him.

"Before you leave, Rosie," Bob said, "I just want to mention that I'm adding something new to this session. I have an affirmation that I used with the group at Big Sur in California, and I would like you to use it at the start of our sessions. I'll read it to you and let you repeat it after me this time. When you come out of the booth, I'll give you a copy to take home so you can memorize it for our future sessions. This is an experiment that I'm mainly trying out on you for now."

"Great," I replied. "I'll gladly do whatever you suggest."

When John closed my CHEC Unit door, I wasn't as nervous as I had been on my first visit, and the darkness was beginning to have a familiar feel. Then sound overrode my other senses as marvelous tones began to pour into both ears through my headphones. In a gentle voice, Bob started reading the affirmation one sentence at a time: "I am more than my physical body . . ." I repeated each line of the affirmation after him as he continued. Then he asked me if I could hear the tone in my right ear.

"Yes, I can, Bob," I replied.

When he asked if I could hear the tone in my left ear, I felt as if my voice were trailing off in the distance.

Then Bob gave me instructions to give him verbal feedback about what was happening. This was the focus of Bob's research. He could tell from his instruments what was happening in my body, and he could get a readout on my brain waves. But he couldn't tell what was going on in my mind.

It was like a dream research lab. The researcher can tell when a person is dreaming, but not *what* he or she is dreaming. The same was true in The Monroe Institute laboratory. Bob could always detect when something was happening—but he did not know what was happening until I told him. So we had a buddy-system setup. No matter what happened, we were always to keep verbal contact if at all possible.

I had made it a point to get a good night's sleep the night before. Now I found myself getting more and more relaxed, but I was determined not to fall asleep this time. Then everything began to feel weird in my head. I was going through what I later referred to as a "thick state of consciousness." That was the best way I could even begin to describe it: my energy felt thick and heavy. When Bob asked me how I was doing, my voice even sounded thick and heavy to me as I slowly answered, "I'm doing fine."

Then I went into what seemed to be a black-out period, which I later interpreted as my consciousness changing gears. When I came out of this blackout state, I experienced a new level of awareness. I felt a sense of detachment from my physical body. My physical heaviness had disappeared. Indeed, I suddenly experienced my consciousness as existing *outside* my physical body.

I don't remember looking back and seeing my body lying there as some people do in out-of-body experiences. Nor did I notice a "silver cord" trailing behind me, as others have experienced when leaving their bodies. But I was intensely aware of feeling more free than I had ever felt in the physical body. My mind also was very clear. I felt as if I were pure energy, as if I could move anywhere instantly, just by the mere thought of being there.

I suddenly had a strong sense of presence with me. Immediately, two forms of "light" appeared. I began to feel waves of energy being directed toward me. I knew intuitively that this was some kind of support system, but I didn't know what it was.

From the instruments in the Control Room, Bob knew that I was in an out-of-body state. In a quiet and gentle voice he asked, "Can you tell me what is happening?"

I began to describe to Bob what I was experiencing. (I pause to note here that Bob and I have the same initials—for Robert A. Monroe and Rosalind A. McKnight. So in all transcripts of our recorded conversations, "RAM" was used to indicate Bob's words, and "ROMC" became my official Explorer designation.) The following is my first report of what I experienced, in answer to his query.

ROMC: "I feel relaxed and far away. I am very comfortable. There is a coolness coming in around me. Two beings are taking my hands. They are helping me, giving me security, and talking to me. They are going to take me to a certain level; and on the way I will go through a dark area. They have put a kind of blindfold on me and are communicating without words that when I get up to this other level, it is going to be a lot lighter. I am to wear this blindfold as I work my way up. Now I am experiencing a floating feeling, as if I'm gently bouncing on a cloud."

(At this point my new "light friends," holding my nonphysical hands, began moving me away from my physical body. I realized that they were actually helping me out of my body, and would then lead me to their level, a dimension of which I was consciously unfamiliar.)

RAM: "Can you communicate with these people?"

ROMC: "Yes. They seem very gentle. Both of them are holding my hands to help me out of the body. They seem very warm, and I feel good about them."

RAM: "Ask these people what their relationship is to you and to me."

ROMC: "Okay . . . (pause) They communicate that they are on the same consciousness level that I am on. I have been with them on an unconscious level in the sleep state. And now we will continue our work in a conscious state."

RAM: "Ask them what we can do to help you improve this communication."

ROMC: "Exactly what you are doing is the right thing. I must take it slow and not be afraid. This is important in getting started."

RAM: "Ask them if they have any special messages."

ROMC: (pause) "They answer that they would like to take me out of my body and to another level. They also would like to communicate back through this vehicle."

RAM: "Ask them what name or names we can use so that we can renew such communication."

ROMC: "They say that names would stand in the way, as they are in a different dimension than that of the earth. They will always be with me when I am ready to work with them. A name would block communication."

RAM: "Ask them what other procedure would be a good one to follow at this time."

ROMC: "They would like to do some work in helping me to get in and out of the body, until it feels more comfortable. They are working on the physical aspect, and would like for me to do some deep-breathing exercises to assist in the process."

RAM: "Are there any instructions for these exercises?"

ROMC: "Yes . . ."

Instantly an amazing thing happened. Instead of perceiving these instructions as coming from the light beings, I simply began experiencing the exercises I was to go through. I told Bob that they were going to take me through the exercises step-by-step. Human breath and the breathing process seemed to have a great deal to do with the transition between the physical and nonphysical dimensions. At this point, I perceived my "light" body to be directly over my physical body. What was more strange was that a third dimension of my self was observing my other two bodies going through this process!

I began explaining to Bob that I was being instructed to build an "energy balloon" around my physical body using a breathing technique. I was instructed to visualize myself in the middle of a very large balloon, and to experience my physical body as floating lightly in the middle of this balloon. Then the beings instructed me to feel the energy circling around my physical body as I slowly breathed in and out. I was to build the energy balloon with the energies of my own breath. As the breathing process took place, I would experience myself floating gently in the middle of my energy balloon.

After relaying this to Bob, I began actually experiencing the energy encircling me. I felt myself getting lighter and lighter. From a third dimension, I saw my light body floating up out of my physical body, and from the second—light—dimension, I experienced it. My light body looked like a glowing yellow balloon, with a dark background behind it. It was almost like viewing an object moving into outer space.

When I reached a certain point in the breathing process and my light body began floating above my physical one, my two glowing friends stepped in and took me by my "light" hands, and moved me further away from the physical level. Suddenly, I was no longer an observer of this process, for my conscious awareness shifted from outside to inside my light body.

So much was happening to me that I was unable to analyze or evaluate it at the time. I was merely having these experiences and describing them as they happened.

When Bob asked me if there was anything else the two light beings would like to discuss, I instantly perceived the purpose of our communication. I knew that throughout our series of sessions they were going to take me to different levels. Levels of *what*, I didn't know. I was simply to take one step at a time and follow their guidance.

Trust, and dispelling all fear of the unknown, would be crucial for me in these journeys. I knew at a deep level that these explorations were of major significance, and that my ability to report my experiences back to the earth plane was a vital part of the mission. On a personal level, I knew that these sessions would be important for my growth as I broke through to new levels of awareness.

Suddenly, my light friends told me it was time to return. My first journey was over, and they were asking me to move back into the physical level of reality. I told Bob what was happening, and he instructed me to come back slowly when I was ready. He suggested that I count myself back to my normal state of physical consciousness. As I came out, I again experienced the "thick" state, like shifting gears back down into low. I counted slowly from ten to one. Then my eyes popped open, and I felt wide awake and alert.

I don't know how long I lay there thinking about what had happened, as one does with a dream upon awakening. As I moved further away from the experience, it grew less clear in my memory. While I was in the nonphysical dimension, the physical one was unclear and hazy. Now that I was back in the physical realm, the nonphysical universe was indistinct—part of being back in the "thick" state of consciousness. It was somewhat like coming out of a dream—except that my nonphysical experiences had seemed much more real than a dream.

After I lay there quietly for awhile, Bob asked if I would like to listen to some music while I was "coming back" into my normal state. I agreed, and he put on a gentle jazz recording that very quickly centered me in my physical body.

When I came out of the CHEC Unit, I was amazed to see that it was dark outside. I had lost all track of time. It seemed that I had been in the CHEC Unit for about 20 minutes. But when I passed the clock in the hallway, I realized I had been in the session for nearly two hours! The effects of leaving the physical time/space dimension boggled my mind.

Bob was still concentrating on his instruments when I stepped into his Control Room. I could tell by the energy in the room that he was excited by what had happened. Since he was experiencing my journey as it was taking place, even if secondhand, it was as new and revealing to him as it was to me.

He turned to look at me, and his eyes gleamed with excitement. When he asked how I felt, I realized that I was tremendously energized by what had happened. In fact, I felt as if I were floating a few inches off the floor!

Another result of our session was that I was extremely hungry. Bob was also hungry, having put as much energy into the session as I had. He suggested that we drive to his favorite restaurant atop Afton Mountain. This would give us a chance not only to satisfy our appetites, but also to talk about what I'd experienced. I was game; David had to teach a college class that evening, and I wasn't expected home for dinner.

When the waitress asked for our order we weren't ready; we had been so busy talking we hadn't looked at the menu. As I began examining the menu, I suddenly became aware of a man standing beside our table.

"Fancy meeting you here," the man said as he slid a piece of pie in front of Bob.

Bob pulled the pie toward him and picked up his fork as he said, "It's good to have a friend in the kitchen. Rosie, this is George Durrette, my part-time manager at Whistlefield. George, this is Rosie McKnight."

George and I nodded to each other as Bob went on to say, after swallowing a bite of pie, that he had been trying to get George to quit his job as kitchen manager at Howard Johnson to work as a full-time manager for him.

"But Bob, if I quit my job here you wouldn't be able to test our specials directly from the kitchen any more," George said proudly, retying an apron string that was slipping down his waistline.

"I can get my favorite pie anytime, George. But I can't get my work done at Whistlefield without you," Bob replied with a pleading look. "And by the way, George, Rosie is the latest addition to our Explorer Team."

George extended his hand and said, "It's a pleasure to meet you, Rosie. Welcome to the team!"

After George excused himself to get back to work, I looked at Bob and asked what he meant by an Explorer Team.

"Oh, yes," Bob said. "I forgot to mention that you have just joined a group of elite regulars at our research laboratory. I put a lot of people through the lab. But only certain ones are selected to work with me as Explorers."

"Wow, Bob," I said. "After falling sound asleep the first time, I feel lucky that I passed the test my second time in the booth."

"You not only passed the test," Bob replied. "You get an A+ for your performance today. You're a natural Explorer. I was amazed that you went so deep in only your second session. I didn't expect that. My main goal during today's session was simply to find some electronic frequencies that would at least keep you awake. As it is, I think we have the potential of being longtime Explorers together."

As Bob talked more about his Explorer Team, I realized that he was somewhat secretive about his other Explorers. He didn't want us to meet each other because he did not want us to compare notes. But he couldn't help telling a little of what was going on with the other Explorers.

Our visit to Ho Jo's became a regular event after each Explorer session. I learned that there was a husband-and-wife team, Explorers TC and JCA, who came once a week for their sessions. TC was a physicist and seemed to have a very different type of session than his wife, who was a social-services executive.

TC was unable to report experiences while they happened. He would go through the experience, come back and report it in detail to Bob, and then go back to see what else was happening—or to try to get an answer to one of Bob's questions. His information was much more technical than mine, perhaps because he was a physicist. His wife, JCA, had the ability to report events as they took place, just as I was able to do.

One night during our Ho Jo's outing, Bob began talking excitedly about SHE, a female Explorer who worked in a very unique way. A guiding energy came through SHE, identifying itself as Miranon. Bob explained that Miranon usually talked with him while SHE was venturing out into the nonphysical universe. Miranon and Bob had some grand dialogues, but SHE never gave details of her own personal explorations when she returned to her body.

During one session SHE got so far out that Miranon became concerned, and had to excuse himself to go after her! Bob waited for fifteen minutes, with real concern, to learn what was happening. When Miranon returned, he said that SHE was enjoying her new freedom so much that she was debating about whether to come back into the physical realm. He told her that she had to come back, since that was part of her contract with her physical world. She soon returned to her physical body, much to Bob's relief.

I asked Bob about the guiding forces, and whether they were common to his Explorers. He explained that everyone who traveled to levels outside the physical realm ran into some type of guiding force. One Explorer might interpret the guiding force as a presence. Another might be guided by a voice. Still another Explorer might see an energy form similar to—or different from—the ones I saw. A guiding force might appear first in a robe and later as pure light, explaining that the robe was only necessary because the Explorer expected some type of physical form.

Titles or names did not seem to be important since these guiding energies operated in their own ways without regard to how they were interpreted or what they were called. An Explorer might refer to the energy form as an angel, Jesus, a guardian, an inner-self-helper, a guide, a higher self, a control, a universal consciousness, an invisible helper, a super ego, or a guiding voice. It really didn't matter. What we name them from our physical perspective seems to have nothing to do with the nature of the guidance.

"Bob, this brings up an important question," I said. "If a person doesn't know about or even believe in guidance, is it still possible for the guiding force to get through to them?"

"Absolutely," Bob said with a chuckle. "Knowing about or believing in out-of-body travel doesn't determine whether a person goes out of the body or not. I had never heard of out-of-body travel when I first started having my experiences. I didn't have to believe in the experiences to have them. I just had them—and I truly thought I was losing my mind.

"Let me tell you about a scientist friend of mine whom I talked into having a session in the lab once," he continued with animation.

"My friend was willing to be hooked up in the lab because I used a technical and scientific approach. Even though he started out as a reluctant subject, he really got into the session. Now here was a man who believed in nothing beyond the physical realm. But during his session he described himself as being guided into a dimension quite foreign to the one with which he was familiar. He encountered beings of a different nature, and when he came to the realization that he was on an unidentified flying object, apparently from another dimension, he freaked out and came back into his body instantly."

The scientist's rapid reentry into the physical realm was clearly precipitated by fear. Fear can have a positive protective purpose. But when misdirected, fear can also be a deadly enemy of the human race, a blockage that can keep us from being fully human and fully alive.

Bob said with a faraway look that the scientist was so shocked and confused by his experience that he refused to come back for another session. "He didn't believe in guidance, out-of-body travel, or UFOs, so how would it be possible for his reality to handle such an experience? The way he handled it was to deny that it ever happened. It's a shame that his scientific mind didn't have a desire to explore itself."

After about a year of Explorer sessions, Bob decided to bring his Explorers together for a "Fly-In" one weekend. I was fascinated to meet those I had heard about. Bob's purpose was for all Explorers to go out-of-body and have a "rendezvous." Two Explorers did bump into each other in a nonphysical dimension. But I didn't have any dramatic happenings that weekend—except for meeting the other Explorers. And meeting them in the physical world was as exciting to me as meeting them out-of-body!

Looking back, I realize that my "Invisible Helpers" had a specific plan laid out for our research and explorations, and Bob's weekend rendezvous didn't fit into that agenda.

Bob always called me a real trooper because I had no fear of moving into new and untapped zones. As our exploring sessions continued, the out-of-body phenomena became more and more intriguing. Like Bob's mystery scientist, I was having all kinds of unusual experiences. Our sessions became increasingly fascinating because we had no idea where they would lead, and we were always surprised by the results.

I began to realize as the sessions unfolded that they were designed from a higher level than I myself could understand. There was a progressive pattern in the explorations and Bob and I were more than eager to cooperate with the planned events.

~4~

INVISIBLE HELPERS

When you have a good team, you can accomplish anything. I was soon to learn that I had an amazing team of Invisible Helpers. They were obviously familiar with human psychology, having decided to assign just two light beings to work with me during the first session, and then to bring in others when I was more familiar with the process. Either they didn't want to overwhelm me with too much to comprehend all at once, or they wanted to see how well I would work with Invisible Helpers. Or both.

I need to clarify here several of Bob's technical terms that apply to the session that follows. As Bob experimented with and created various levels of Hemi-Sync sounds using his binaural beat and Frequency Following Response systems, he was able to create specific inner states—"focus" states—to which he gave numbers. A great deal of experimentation lay behind the technology, and the states he was able to induce were the miracle of his extensive research. They are as follows: "Focus 10," in which the mind is awake but the body is asleep; "Focus 12," in which a person has expanded awareness; "Focus 15," in which levels of "no time" are reached; and "Focus 21," in which one moves into other energy systems.

When I got settled in the CHEC Unit one day in an early session, Bob ran through the preliminaries, concluding with having me repeat my affirmation mentally and letting him know when I was finished. Then I went into my usual exercises as the session began.

RAM: "Reel time: 28 minutes."
ROMC: "An energy pattern is building up around me, and

45

I am ready to work with some energy inside this compact energy ball. I am told to build a bar of energy to cleanse my physical body and get out all impurities, starting with my head."

RAM: "Very good. Do it carefully and thoroughly."

ROMC: (pause) "I've finished. I'm ready to continue."

RAM: "Now let your whole self move into this state of expanded awareness we call 'Focus 12.' Let yourself move into 12 with the method you have learned."

ROMC: (pause) "At '12' I went into a relaxed state—almost unconscious. It is a very relaxed state. I felt the presence of someone. This presence seems to be waiting for me to go into a more deeply relaxed state. I felt the energy balloon begin to rise and float. I was floating inside; I got the feeling that my physical body was going to let go of this energy balloon with my energy body inside, and that it was going to float on out into a weightless atmosphere. There is an energy presence, or maybe more than one energy presence, here working with me. And they are going to . . . I'm not sure what they are going to do."

RAM: "Ask them what they are going to do next."

ROMC: "Okay. I sense the presence of four helpers with me, including the two who were with me the last time. They are standing around me, and I have a very good feeling in their presence. They're here to keep me balanced and work with me in the body, and out. A fifth presence, an energy being, is now with them. They're going to try some experiments with my energy body. This last energy being is going to work through my body and implant energy. It's like a yin and yang energy."

RAM: "Would you like to do this?"

ROMC: "Yes. The energy being wants to project a ray of light into my energy body while I am going through this very relaxed state. Let's see what happens. Now I am watching and experiencing at the same time." (pause)

"The four helpers lifted my body out, and I felt light and really good. The light ray that was projected into my energy body was energizing and protective, and had a lightening effect on my body. Then I sensed that the energy being was talking about how they would experiment by using my body as a transmitting set between dimensions—and that I will be able to step out. They talked a little about that before, but I just saw how it will happen. I will be able to step out and be with these helpers—and still be able to observe, if I would like to. I got the feeling that I could stay and listen, or I could do some exploration. They are very warm, friendly helpers."

RAM: "Do they want to do any other experiments now?"

ROMC: "They would like to use the light beam to communicate through my vocal cords, and I am to observe."

RAM: "Okay. Do what they suggest and see what happens." (pause)

ROMC: (in a different voice) "I am speaking through these vocal cords. I would like to speak to this young lady as she observes what is taking place. The physical body is seeming to heat up very rapidly. Sometimes it will be in a cool state; at other times it will be in a heated state. The molecules of the energy body, which are working through her physical body, are vibrating at a more rapid rate. Therefore, at this time there is a feeling of heat surrounding the body. I am going to show this young lady how it will work with the energies of her physical body, and protect and keep it in its most pure form while I work through her."

RAM: "Thank you for your care in working with her."

ROMC: "I am going to change the level within this body, from the heated state to the cool state. The balloon of energy which she has built up around her can be rapidly changed for various purposes. I want her to be aware of how we work with the energy levels. She will experience a coolness. I want this young lady to experience the various energy sensations, so that she will understand and know how I will work, and how we will work together. We will cool the molecules that surround and fill this body. It is being experienced at this time."

RAM: "Go with the flow, and report back what is happening."

ROMC: "The young lady will understand what is happening when we project light into her energy body which you might call her 'soul.' There will be a feeling of warmth. As she gets relaxed and begins to float above her physical body, she will experience the coolness, and a feeling of complete security. These will be the physical experiences from level one—of the heat state—to the second level of the cooling-off stage, where she will feel light and airy and relaxed. At this point she will be able to go out to explore. Where she explores will be decided when the time arrives."

RAM: "That's fine."

ROMC: "We will work on these levels first, as we have done before, with the breathing and the building of the energy balloon around her body. Then she will know that she is going gently out of the body but will always be in complete control. She is always there to observe and to speak at any time—or can even choose to step into other dimensions. There will be those who will help her into these other dimensions. While this is taking place, we will bring information through these vocal cords, but it will take time. As she learns and grows, it will improve."

After a pause the voice again directed itself to Bob: "It is a privilege to be working with one such as you. You have been a guide to many souls who need to be released into greater knowledge areas. This is a special experiment in creating knowledge connections. It could not be done were it not for you—with the knowledge you bring, and with the great light and confidence with which you surround the whole project that you are working on."

RAM: "Thank you for your kind words."

ROMC: "As you know, there are numerous dimensions of knowledge; knowledge can be understood from many perspectives. We will tune into knowledge from multidimensional levels. I am working at this time on a dimension within the consciousness of this particular being. As the dimensions of her awareness are opened, I will work fully and freely on a level of consciousness of greater light. I have others working with me who will communicate as we reach different dimensions and levels."

RAM: "We will look forward to working with the others you speak of."

ROMC: "At this time, I am able to tap into a particular level of consciousness of this dear being who is allowing us to work with her. I can work on many levels of consciousness, and there are more beings who will come with knowledge from other levels. We will not say 'higher' or 'lower.' They are light dimensions. As we break through into the various levels, it will become easier to bring through knowledge. I am working now on the level where this entity is at present, but we will work together through various levels."

RAM: "How do you work with these levels?"

ROMC: "I will always be the one to communicate first, to help open up various states that she must experience to get her into the level where communication can take place effectively. I will always be the one who will begin, because I am in touch with her first dimension; from that level, there will be an opening up into other dimensions."

RAM: "How can we get in touch with you?"

ROMC: "We exist outside of earth time. Your communication is a thought-form, and the thought can be the signal. Just think that you are ready for the communication process to take place. If all situations are right, we will be able to communicate immediately. You are doing the perfect performance for this particular body—because it is very important for this soul to feel confident, and in this most relaxed state."

RAM: "Are there others working with her as well?"

ROMC: "Yes, there are others who are working with her. I speak in terms of 'we,' because each time that I come, we come as a group. There are others who are the assistants, and who will always be there to bring the energy levels up, and to work. We say that you are doing exactly what is necessary to help the situation to be in that perfected state whereby the energies can be released into other levels of consciousness."

RAM: "Thank you. I'm glad to know that I'm doing the right thing."

ROMC: "You are doing just what you can, and that is important. You are helping this dear soul to be able to open up into other dimensions—and you are doing it in a wise manner. She is very comfortable. We're creating the energy around her with movement, and this keeps an energy flow. Now there is a cool flow around her, keeping her relaxed.

"We will move out of her energy area now. Each time that she works, she will work in a special energy area. The area, and the energy, is built up through her own internal circles of energy or energy systems, and from her own base. And now we will help her to come back fully into her own body. It is a privilege. Thank you, dear friends."

After a pause, ROMC speaks in her own voice: "I feel very relaxed. I've been observing everything. It's interesting. I was standing right here with the four helpers, observing, listening, and learning."

Throughout the many sessions that I did with Bob over the next eleven years, my Invisible Helpers were always there guiding, directing, and evidently planning the sessions ahead of time, even though there is no "time" as we know it in their dimension. They said that they were working with me in the body and out. I have come to realize that they have been with me since I first placed my tiny foot upon this planet.

I can look back and remember many times when they were there guiding and directing me, especially when I was in trouble—which was not infrequently. The important message here, of course, is that we all have guiding forces working with us, whether we realize it or not. And a great many people, of course, are aware of the existence of such help in their lives, frequently at key—and unexpected—moments.

Often these unseen helpers are called angels. My Invisible Helpers are my angels. I can remember a song from my childhood that spoke of "angels watching over me." It said, "One is at my right hand, one is at my left hand, one is at my right foot, one is at my left foot." These words seem literally true to me, for my personal life has been affected dramatically by the guidance and help of angelic beings of light—my Invisible Helpers.

I never really thought about what we look like to these kind helpers from another dimension—until something quite strange happened in the lab one day. Bob and I tried to stick to our schedule of regular sessions, though it was difficult at times. Bob seemed to love the Explorer sessions more than anything else he was doing. I was always amazed at how patiently he would wait for my responses during the sessions. Sometimes I would get into the "thick state," and instead of coming out on the other side, would fall asleep. I always felt it was easier to be an Explorer than to do his job of monitoring the sessions. But he treasured his role even when nothing seemed to be happening.

On one occasion when I had to miss our scheduled meeting, I called to let him know that I wouldn't be coming that day. When I arrived for our next session, Bob asked me to come into his Control Room and sit down. He had a grin on his face and a twinkle in his eyes.

"What's up, Bob?" I asked.

"You'll never believe what took place the day you missed your session."

"What happened?"

"A female psychologist from the Washington area dropped by for a visit that day, wanting to learn more about our work. I spent several hours that afternoon showing her our methods and techniques. But I could tell that she was still skeptical about the program. I finally decided it might help her if she experienced some of the Hemi-Sync patterns for herself."

"So, you put her in a booth?"

"I sure did—yours!" Bob replied, shaking his head in disbelief as he recalled what happened next. "She agreed to try—but fully expected that nothing would happen. And as skeptical as she was, I was doubtful myself."

"Well, what happened?" I asked, finding it hard to contain myself.

"She had been in the booth about five minutes, listening to the Hemi-Sync sound on the earphones, when her voice came through the intercom speaker."

At this point Bob pressed a "play" button, and the tape of their session began.

PSYCHOLOGIST: "There is someone else in the booth with me."

RAM: "Are you sure?"

PSYCHOLOGIST: "Of course I am sure. As a matter of fact, there are four of them."

RAM: "Are you sure there are four?"

PSYCHOLOGIST: "I can perceive them very clearly. There are two at my feet and two at my head."

RAM: "What are they doing?"

PSYCHOLOGIST: "They are trying to lift me out of my body, if you can believe that."

Bob hit the "pause" button and turned to me, saying, "Suddenly, I knew the answer as I looked up at the clock. It was ten minutes after five on Wednesday afternoon—the exact time of your regular session. And the same booth. I couldn't keep from laughing, and was about to explain to the psychologist what was happening, when I thought better of it."

Bob hit the "pause" button again, and the dialogue continued.

RAM: "What are they doing now?"

PSYCHOLOGIST: "They have stopped trying to lift me out of my body. And they are arguing."

Stopping the tape again, Bob laughed. "I really had difficulty keeping a straight voice!"

RAM: "What are they arguing about?"

PSYCHOLOGIST: "The four want to lift me out. And now there is a fifth that is arguing with them that they should not."

RAM: "Do you want them to?"

PSYCHOLOGIST: "I don't think so. Now they have stopped arguing and they are going away. So, I guess there is no problem."

RAM: "Well, just relax a bit and I'll get you out in a few minutes. Are you comfortable now?"

PSYCHOLOGIST: "Oh, yes, I am fine."

I was amazed. And Bob and I began laughing so hard we could hardly talk.

"What did she say when she came out of the booth?" I finally asked.

"Well," Bob replied, wiping tears from his eyes, "I left her in the booth for a few minutes, and the instrumentation showed she was relaxing into a light sleep. After a brief time I awakened her, and she came out very refreshed. But she was obviously bewildered by the experience—and she made a valiant attempt to stay skeptical!"

"So, did you tell her about my sessions?"

"I did," Bob replied. "I showed her our session schedule with your appointment for that afternoon. Then I played a recording of the 'lifting out' technique of one of your sessions."

"What did she say to that?" I asked eagerly.

"She was almost speechless," Bob answered. "She seemed actually stunned, and left here very puzzled and preoccupied. But her skepticism had dissolved somewhat—at least temporarily."

"Did you hear back from her?" I asked.

"No, and I don't expect to," Bob replied, still laughing.

"I don't blame her. It must have been a shock for her to meet five spooks on her first visit to the Institute!"

Bob was chuckling as he continued. "Can't you just picture the dialogue among your helpers? One says, 'This is her.' Another one says, 'No, it isn't her.' A third disagrees, with, 'I'm sure it's her.' A fourth helper says, 'She doesn't *feel* the same.' Then with the encouragement of a fifth helper, all of them realize at once, 'Oops, wrong one!' and drop her!"

We were now laughing so hard at this imagined scene that my sides hurt. Finally I said, "Bob, I thought the helpers were all-knowing since they are from a higher dimension than ours.

Do you suppose they have certain limitations in perceiving, just as we do with them?

"Obviously," Bob replied. "They must see us as some kind of energy form, just as you see them as indistinct 'light' beings."

"Wow, " I said. "That's incredible. I had never thought about how they must be perceiving me. To them my real body would be my soul or light body, the part that's like them. That may be what they see. So, I'm actually a soul that takes on a physical body. Cool!" I added, "Do you suppose they arranged this whole incident to teach us something?"

"If so," Bob replied, "they obviously have a good sense of humor! They've indicated clearly in your sessions that the physical body is an illusion here when you're born, and gone when you die."

"And where are the billions of beings that walked this planet before us?" I pondered.

"They're in their real bodies—their soul bodies," Bob replied. "Your helpers are trying to teach us to see things from the perspective of true reality, not our illusion."

"You know, Bob, we really do have everything turned around here on earth. We look at the physical world and call it 'real' when it really isn't, and we look at the spiritual dimension and perceive it as unreal, equally erroneously. Perhaps this is what Paul meant when he said, 'Now we see things through a glass darkly, but then face-to-face.' When we're in our 'thick' state of consciousness, our daily life mode, things of the spirit are unclear. But when we perceive from our 'soul-body mode,' it *is* like seeing face-to-face."

"That makes sense," Bob replied. Then he turned around abruptly to prepare for our Explorer session. We had gone from hilarious laughter to philosophic musings and back to work in a short time. Our sessions normally triggered deep conversation, since we were continually challenged with new thoughts that arose from them.

As Bob started switching on his Control Room instruments, he interjected, "I do want to add that it's difficult for us to change what we were taught to believe. Our science has taught us that only what we can see and measure is real. What you don't see, feel, or touch doesn't exist. These Explorer sessions are truly opening my eyes to a different way of perceiving. Let's see what they have to say today! Get into booth 2, and John will get you wired up—even though you seem to be 'wired up' already."

5

COMMUNICATION

RAM: "Reel time: 23 minutes."

ROMC: "I heard a voice that said, 'We are working on a delicate wavelength and want you to pick up this dictation.' I am to report as it comes through. As I repeat the words, the energy keeps flowing, and they are able to continue the contact with this flow."

RAM: "Just relax and go with the flow."

ROMC: (speaking for the helpers) "It is important to use this flow to build up the energy level. The voice is a special energy. We want to describe the different processes by which and through which there is communication. The basic form of communication, which is the mind, is on a wavelength that is on a very high rate of vibration on the earth level."

RAM: "Is the communication the same between humans as it is when we talk with you?"

ROMC: "The communication that takes place between the minds of those who are in the earth atmosphere is on a wavelength that is different from the communication that takes place from the levels beyond the earth atmosphere. There are various levels of energy. That is what we want to discuss."

RAM: "What are those levels?"

ROMC: "In the earth atmosphere, thought radiates from the human mind at a certain rate of vibration. Thoughts are energy, and as they come into being they are immediately dispersed into the atmosphere. Thoughts are powerful, and are at an extremely high frequency. They are limitless in their ability to travel and penetrate, and can affect the earth level in many different ways."

RAM: "How does it work?"

ROMC: "Within the human system, there are several levels of consciousness. They are the physical, etheric-substance, emotional, mental, and spiritual levels. These five levels control the many points of energy throughout the physical system. The key to the effectiveness of this energy system is the way in which it is utilized. The effectiveness has to do with the ways in which the mind is trained."

RAM: "How is that?"

ROMC: "Humans are taught what to think instead of how to think. Basically, there are no limitations in the physical universe. The mind that is taught what to think is taught belief systems with limitations. Therefore, there are limitations. This is the power of the human mind. It becomes what it thinks itself to be. This is why it is so important to re-educate the human race to the full potential of the human communication system."

RAM: "What is the full potential of the human mind?"

ROMC: "Humans who are taught how to think would discover that the human mind is capable of traveling into the depths of every type of universe, to tap into all knowledge that exists. At the base of every human system is the very principle of universal knowledge. Every cell in the body is a pattern of the whole, and is a universe in and of itself. All knowledge exists therein. Every human system is capable of tapping into that source, which is its very being. When this knowledge is understood, the human mind and human soul are then freed to explore the depths of all possible universes, which are all within."

RAM: "How does the body relate to the mind?"

ROMC: "The body is in no way a boundary. It is just an encasement—a storage place for the human system to energize. But there is one important factor to take into consideration. All systems must be 'go.' Thought, or emotional levels, can in and of themselves block the communication flow. When everything is synchronized and flows freely, the mind can function at its various levels, opening up new vistas in human consciousness."

RAM: "How does out-of-body travel fit into the overall scheme of things?"

ROMC: "Out-of-body travel is a term used to describe the manner in which the energy body, or soul, can function in the other dimensions of its own being. The freedom to move into other dimensions has to do with vibrations of the overall system, and this varies, depending on the balance of energies."

RAM: "How can we tap into these levels of knowledge?"

ROMC: "There are different ways in which souls can tap into various levels of knowledge. It is important for each person to know that his or her vibratory rate is completely different from any other's, just as all fingerprints are uniquely different. Each soul has its own soulprint and special form of communication."

RAM: "What are the levels of communication?"

ROMC: "One level is the sending out of thought. Thought is an energy more real than your physical body, because every thought you have goes somewhere. You think of a person, alive or deceased, and they pick up the thought instantly. Thought can travel into all levels inside and outside of time."

RAM: "It certainly makes one stop and think about thinking! In fact, it gives relevance to the assertion, 'I think, therefore I am.'"

ROMC: "Yes, indeed. Another level of communication is the receptive, where, when all energy systems are 'go,' communication is picked up on the mental wave-level from the time and timeless dimensions. The timeless are the dimensions from which we communicate. It is hard for humans to understand timelessness when they are locked into time."

RAM: "This is why you tell us that we are merely to think about communication with you, and you are there?"

ROMC: "Exactly. There are one-way and two-way communication systems. We on this dimension are able to pick up rapidly all that happens on the earth plane because we are on a higher vibration than the earth level. Those on the earth level who vibrate on a rate close to that on which we function can tune into our dimension readily."

RAM: "So, what is your purpose in communicating with us?"

ROMC: "It is our basic purpose to get the communication through to the earth level that there are no limitations in your dimension, other than those that you put upon yourselves. This is the important basis of the training you do at your Institute. You make it possible for people to get into the free flow of their own existence, and to explore the limitless boundaries of higher universes, which actually are all within each being.

"This concept is difficult for humans to understand, since you are locked into 'spatial' concepts, as well. In reality there is no time and no space. A special flow of energy is released when you work on the assumption that there are no limits in the human communication system. Those who are able to freely get into the flow of their own existence are able to get into this limitless level of communication that exists outside of what you consider to be time and space."

RAM: "What about death on the earth plane?"

ROMC: "Souls who are in the flow of their own higher attunement know that there is no death. Death is merely a word created in the physical language to describe something not understood. Therefore, death is merely a word that describes an experience. Death, in itself, is not a reality. Death can best describe those souls whose systems are at a stopping point, a level of stagnation."

RAM: "Is anything in the universe ever really destroyed?"

ROMC: "Those who are in the true flow of higher energies know that nothing is destroyed. There is no beginning and no end, because there is no time and no space. That which we see and touch, including our human loved ones, vibrates into and out of the earth time/space level of consciousness. Because we cannot see or touch something does not mean that it does not exist. Death is only transformation from the physical to the etheric-substance body. Therefore, the word 'death' is a separate entity in itself, created and used by humans to describe the hidden mysteries of existence. Death is not a mystery for those who are in tune with their own life flow. Death is just another beautiful life experience."

RAM: "Thank you very much. It would be helpful if you could explain to us the transformation that takes place when the physical body is no longer inhabitable. What happens at that point?"

ROMC: "When this process of transformation takes place, it is a shifting of basic energies from the physical home base into the energy levels of the etheric body. The soul will go into the dimension of its highest vibratory level."

RAM: "Are there souls that don't get out of the physical realm?"

ROMC: "There are souls whose energies shift into the etheric body, but whose mental or emotional levels, or both, keep them in the physical realm of vibration. These are souls whose mental or emotional vibrations are at the rate of the earth vibrations. And because they are locked into certain earth-level concepts, or emotions, they stay in this earth-level of consciousness until they are able to release the special thought-forms that confine them. These are considered to be 'earthbound' souls—or ghosts, as you call them—because of their attachments to the physical energies of the earth."

RAM: "So, do all souls have guiding forces that work with them the way you are working with this energy?"

ROMC: "Absolutely. Our purpose is to work on all levels to release souls into the higher level of their own freedom."

RAM: "Explain further what you mean."

ROMC: "There are certain universal principles on which the human communication system functions: Like attracts like. You are what you think. There is no God that punishes.

"There is a built-in system, which operates on basic laws, that controls the human energies. There is a God-force in the universe, the highest energy, the highest consciousness level of existence, constantly working to guide you back to your true natures. There is no *before* and no *after*; these are merely confining concepts, or thought-forms, manifested in the earth realm of existence to create the illusion of time. There is only *now* in the reality of existence."

RAM: "What about life after death?"

ROMC: "When you speak of life after death, this is a misnomer. If one is dead emotionally, mentally, or spiritually before the physical body is dropped, that same consciousness level will still be in operation in that soul upon transformation. We continually work with all souls to bring them into their higher level of transformation. Hell is a state in which souls are locked into levels of stagnation. We will work with all souls from the earth plane until they come into their highest level of light transformation. There is only life. Your life in the body is the same as your life out of the body, or after death."

RAM: "So, you are saying that I am more than my physical body in that I am always alive somewhere?"

ROMC: "Certainly. One can live in the timeless level of reality within the body as well as out of the body. That is why we are saying that there are no limitations, even while in the physical body.

"Now we must step aside, dear friend. Continue in the mode in which you are presently working—namely, to help souls to become freed and released into the higher natures of their own being. Thank you."

RAM: "Thank you very much for coming and sharing. (pause) Count yourself back down slowly, and let me know when you're back." (pause)

ROMC: "I'm here."

RAM: "How do you feel?

ROMC: "I feel great!"

RAM: "Where were you when this dialogue was taking place?"

ROMC: "I was right here with my Invisible Helpers. It was so fascinating that I had to stay here and listen, even though I could have gone out exploring elsewhere."

Interestingly, at the beginning of this session I saw a "tape" with words on it flowing by, and I received the impression that I was to read the words as they moved across my vision. But after the session got under way, the energy seemed to increase and I wasn't aware of seeing and reading the tape any longer.

This session was very powerful. We didn't realize how strong the energy was until we got outside. Bob describes the event in his book, *Far Journeys* (p. 49):

> *When we got into our cars parked outside some twenty feet from booth 2, we found that the batteries were dead in all three cars. They jump-started quite easily, as it was a summer night, and stayed in charge afterward. Cars parked on the other side, or sixty feet away, were unaffected. Thus, we learned we had better not park too close to booth 2 during certain experiments.*

This situation actually happened several times because we would simply forget to park far enough from booth 2 only to find our car batteries dead upon leaving. As Bob stated in *Far Journeys*, "Exactly why this took place and still does so—we don't know."

Because I Am More Than
Physical Matter, I Can Perceive
That Which Is Greater Than the
Physical World . . .

6

MORE THAN PHYSICAL MATTER

My Invisible Helpers spent many sessions preparing me for our journeys into other dimensions. They taught avidly and worked endless hours of earth time on my energy body. In order to move freely into other dimensions my energies had to be clear, so there was a lot of cleaning up to do.

One day when I was driving to the Institute for my session I had the feeling that something very special was about to happen. My energies were exceptionally high. Little did I know that I was about to launch upon my first major journey. Apparently my helpers, in their master plan for me, had determined that on this day I would come to understand clearly that I was more than physical matter.

It seems they wanted to impress upon me that the material world in which we live is merely a "reflection of the real world," as they termed it. They chose to put this point across by launching me on a very strange journey of reality distortion, so that I would indeed learn how abstract and unreal life in the physical realm is. And when I say they "launched" me on this unusual journey, I mean just that.

As I got hooked into my CHEC Unit, I was feeling such excitement and anticipation that I found it difficult to relax—until the soothing sounds of ocean waves came through my earphones. I mentally repeated the affirmation, and it wasn't long before I went into my level and moved through the thick state.

As I mentioned earlier, sometimes I would get stuck in this state—and simply fall sound asleep. This was always embarrassing, with Bob waiting patiently in his Control Room for something to happen. After a period of time, he would say in a gentle voice, "Is anything happening?" As often as not I would reply groggily, "I don't think so"—and continue sleeping. I rationalized by convincing myself that at these times I needed sleep more than anything else. Perhaps I did.

Sleep, however, was not on the docket for this particular session. Suddenly, I felt a great surge of energy, as if I were literally being launched into space. This incredible burst of energy left me breathless and speechless, and I was unable to report anything to Bob until my pace slowed. It seemed as if I was moving rapidly through a dark tunnel. Strangely, it also seemed as if I was standing still. It was a paradox of simultaneously feeling movement and nonmovement.

Then, just as suddenly as my launch had occurred, I was suspended in a space of absolute stillness and isolation. An eerie feeling came over me, and I knew then what it would be like to be the last person on earth!

I desperately wanted to believe that my Invisible Helpers were with me, but they certainly didn't make themselves known. I seemed completely lost in an endless space. I experienced a sense of separation from all my earthly support systems.

Those few moments of absolute isolation seemed like an eternity. Then I realized that my Invisible Helpers had guided me into this particular space and experience for a reason. They wanted me to become aware of my need for detachment from the earth energies. This space was like a cleansing center to prepare me to enter a very different dimension.

At this moment I had a vivid memory of an experience I'd had one night while sleeping. I remembered moving out into the expansiveness and darkness of outer space. I felt called toward the unknown, and to the stars beyond. But at the same time I was frightened—even petrified—because I was being drawn away from any familiar territory. Had this nighttime experience been a preparation, designed by my Invisible Helpers, for my present state of lonely separation from all I knew?

As I was just beginning to resign myself to this new feeling of naked isolation, I suddenly experienced some kind of energy capsule starting to surround me. Like a protective shield, it replaced my feeling of abandonment with a sense of security. I realized that this unique pod had been formed around my energy body by my Invisible Helpers, both to protect and to prepare me for a "higher octane" transportation mode. Without it I knew that I simply was not capable of the journey about to take place. A great surge of energy suddenly radiated within and around me. I could feel that I was very much running on "high octane" and was ready for whatever was next.

My Invisible Helpers did indeed have a sense of humor. Having found myself encircled by an energy space capsule, I began making voice contact with Bob back in the CHEC Unit. As I brought him up-to-date, a helmet with a "12" on it floated before my eyes and was placed on my head. I sensed that it was a symbolic gesture.

As I described it to Bob, I heard a chuckle from the Control Room. We both realized it was an indication that I was in Focus 12—and was ready to "helmet up" for an important journey. By this time my space capsule was becoming extremely cozy, and all my attention began to focus on my immediate surroundings.

The next thing I knew the energy changed. My capsule was changing direction. I looked out, and there it was—an incredible view of planet Earth from outer space. Suspended below me, it looked no bigger than my own space capsule. Then we picked up speed and began moving toward that distant, tiny ball known as planet Earth. Light, dark, and radiant colors were shooting out from it in all directions. I realized at once that, viewing it from another dimension as I was, I was actually seeing the earth's aura—or energy form.

It seemed as if I was, in fact, seeing the "spiritual body" of the earth. My helpers were clearly showing me that the earth was indeed a living entity—that it, like me, is more than physical. At the same moment I could see planets shining in the darkness beyond, and I remembered that the earth is but a tiny atom in an immense system of bodies, each with its own spiritual body.

As we continued moving closer to the earth, the radiating, colored lights surrounding it became more and more prominent, emanating in every direction. I wondered what my Invisible Helpers were going to do with me next, and assumed they would drop me off on our way through the earth's atmosphere.

"On our way through," however, took on literal meaning: We went right through the earth's surface, the way a neutrino penetrates solid matter as though it didn't exist. I wondered if I had been transformed into some kind of subatomic particle, or if I was traveling on a ray of some type. The thought occurred to me that our etheric energy bodies probably consist of particles more subtle than any known atomic or subatomic particles that make up our physical plane.

As we penetrated the earth's surface, it became dark. Then we moved through levels of color like the spectrum of the rainbow. Next, we were in an area of molten lava. I sensed the outside of my capsule growing very hot, but I knew it was a secure cocoon around me.

Much movement was now taking place on the outside of my capsule, but I was experiencing a strange sense of weightlessness, timelessness, and stillness within it. It was as if two time zones were touching, but that the time zone in my capsule and the one I was traveling through were at opposite ends of a spectrum. I perceived that the earth was on a much slower vibration than my speeded-up light vibration; paradoxically, the earth's lower vibration seemed like movement and activity, while my higher vibration in the capsule felt peaceful and quiet. It was two "time zones"—time on the outside, and timelessness inside.

Then I got a distinct impression from my helpers: they wanted me to understand that this experience of being in two dimensions at once is no different than the soul's journey in the physical body. We have a timeless nature within ourselves; we are also directed by time in our physical world.

My journey through the earth was symbolic of the way in which our souls traverse earthly experience. Our soul matter actually zips across the stage of physical matter without leaving a trace—much as the elusive neutrino penetrates atomic matter as if it were so much mist. But what about our physical bodies and physical memories—our ashes scattered upon the earth? All these soon pass away, because they are only reflections of the real. My flight "through" matter had been quite an object lesson.

When I reached what appeared to be the center, or heart, of the earth, the energy was so different from that of the earth's outer crust that it almost shocked my system. I knew I had to keep moving, that I could not stand too much of the earth-core energy at one time.

At one particular point in the earth's center, tremendous energies were "pumping" through. It was as if I were literally in the "heart" of the earth. And I knew intuitively that this point led to another dimension completely different from that of the earth, but still connected to it. It was as if here, physical matter was transformed into antimatter and into another dimension! One break in the ocean floor, such as in the area of the Bermuda Triangle, could cause this same transformation to take place on the earth's outer surface. I had encountered a "black hole" phenomenon at the center of the earth, where matter is transformed and enters another dimension.

Next I realized we were rising through an ocean. When we left the ocean we kept right on going, until I could look back and see the earth getting smaller and smaller, like a tiny ball floating in space.

To have my energy body interface with Mother Earth's energy form had been an awesome experience, giving me a completely different perspective. Now I talk to Mother Earth as I would talk to a real, spiritual being—which she is.

7

I CAN PERCEIVE THAT WHICH IS GREATER

Now that my Invisible Helpers had given me an overview of the earth's energies, they said their next goal was to help me to perceive and experience a greater aspect of these energies. Or should I say they wanted me to experience some new dimensions of "her" personality? Thus we began our next session:

RAM: "Reel time: 22 minutes."

ROMC: "I am in my energy balloon. I am experiencing energy bodies all around me. They seem to be moving around me quite rapidly. I am in the middle, feeling very energized. All of a sudden I feel a sense of great joy, laughter, and freedom."

RAM: "Go with the flow to see what will happen."

ROMC: "My helpers are indicating to me that I am going to experience the consciousness of many levels of the earth's dimensions."

RAM: "So, how do you feel about this?"

ROMC: "I feel great joy over being at one with all."

RAM: "So what is happening now?"

ROMC: "I am very relaxed, and feel a sense of floating. I can see a frog in front of me. Now I am getting closer. Wow, I am going into the frog to experience the consciousness of being a frog."

RAM: "Are you in the frog yet?"

ROMC: "This is humorous. I can see out of the eyes of this frog. There's a bug. Oh, it's going to grab the bug in its mouth. Ick! But my helpers are indicating that I must learn to understand that the frog has to live on other forms of life."

RAM: "Are you still in the frog?"

ROMC: "Now I'm floating again. I really couldn't get that relaxed in the frog. My helpers are indicating to me that I must relax and let go if I am to experience universal consciousness."

RAM: "Where are you now?"

ROMC: "Goodness—there's a snake! Oh, they're going to send me into a snake. I have a fear of snakes. I don't know if I can handle this but I'll try to relax and go with it."

RAM: "Okay. Relax as best you can."

ROMC: "I am going inside the snake. Wow, it's better inside than out! I didn't take a good look at it to see what color it is. I think it might be black."

RAM: "So what is it like to be inside a snake?"

ROMC: "I am beginning to feel a sense of attunement with the earth. There is an earth energy inside this reptile because it is so close to the earth. I feel a great sense of peace and gentleness. I feel that I am supposed to talk for the reptile."

RAM: "Can you do that?"

ROMC: "I'll try: 'There is such joy in being a part of the grass and the earth. I never want to harm anyone. I believe in harmony. But I am forced to protect myself.

"'I can tell a lot about the human by the vibrations of the footsteps. Most of the time we know when to get out of the way to keep from being killed. Humans kill to kill. We kill to survive. I feel that it is very unfortunate that humans as a whole are not in attunement with our kingdom, because we work at the very base of the lifeforce in the universe. It is important for us all to work together.'"

RAM: "Thank you for sharing the views of the snake. Where are you now?"

ROMC: "I am moving into another area of consciousness. I can see a rose. Oh, how beautiful. It is shimmering in the sunlight. What a wonderful smell."

RAM: "Are you going into the rose?"

ROMC: "Yes. As I come into the rose I sense its consciousness communicating the following. 'We bring beauty to the earth. However, we are a reflection of the beauty that is within all humans. When they look upon us and experience the joy of beauty, they are experiencing their own true natures. Our very essence is a pure state of joy and beauty. Those who experience the essence of our nature experience the true essence of their own being. We find such joy in giving our pure beauty to humans. And we bring joy to so many on planet Earth.'"

RAM: "Thank you. What a beautiful statement."

ROMC: "I'm starting to leave the rose. I feel a great affinity for the rose since that is part of my name. It was such a good feeling being inside it that I would like to have just stayed there. But the message is that I can live in this rose-consciousness of pure beauty and joy anyway. I am this consciousness."

RAM: "Relax and go where you are to go next."

ROMC: "I'm floating again. Oh, I can see grass below me. What beautiful green. I'm going into it. What a good feeling! I'm sensing that levels of color in nature are so important. Color is all a part of the vibration of the consciousness level of everything."

RAM: "So, what does the grass say?"

ROMC: "Green is the color that brings balance into the universe. I am in the consciousness level of the grass, and I smell so good. I feel such a freshness, and a feeling of floating. There is a great feeling of freedom and strength that comes from the level of consciousness of a blade of grass. Strength and vitality are the basis of the grass-consciousness.

"I sense the grass saying, 'I am surrounding humans for a very specific purpose. They come into contact with us almost every day of their lives. We give strength and vitality to those who will accept it from us. Humans receive such great joy in running barefoot in our midst. Humans should never lose this vitality. We are always here; our basic purpose is to be walked upon. We do enjoy the appreciation of humans who share and delight in the very purpose of our existence.

"'Much natural strength is destroyed in cities that replace us with man-made substance. Where we are lacking, the whole consciousness of an area is changed. Humans who do not have ready access to us lose a great amount of energy that we help to generate. Children have a natural affinity for us because they are in tune with us and know our purpose for their lives.'"

RAM: "Where are you going next?"

ROMC: "I'm floating over some trees. I'm going into them. I'm in the trunk of a large pine tree."

RAM: "How does it feel?"

ROMC: "I'm at the base, heading toward the top. The tree says, 'What a great feeling of grandeur I have as I look out over my brother and sister trees. I feel such freedom, even though I am rooted in the ground. I give strength and inspiration to humans. I feel stability. I give off very strong energies that help lift the energies of humans.

"'Humans are attracted to certain types of trees, just as they are attracted to certain types of people. We each have our own energy levels. If humans would relate at least five minutes a day to their favorite tree by sitting under us, touching us, climbing us, they would become revitalized. We act as a battery for humans. We give special charge when needed. And we enjoy acting as fuel for those who need our special kind of warmth. Our purpose in life is to bring stability and regeneration.'"

RAM: "Thank you so much. Now I know why my trees have always been so important to me. Does the tree have more to say?"

ROMC: "I'm speaking as myself; and as the consciousness of this pine tree I have experienced a sense of infinity, an endless source of energy. The tree-consciousness represents infinity in that it is rooted in the earth but lifts into the heavens. It seems to reach into all levels and dimensions. The tree is there always to serve man and to share strength and vitality. And the levels of consciousness within trees change with the change in seasons. When humans get into contact with the consciousness levels of trees, they go into the heights and depths of their own universal attunement."

RAM: "Relax and see where your Invisible Helpers take you next."

ROMC: "I'm floating again. I'm looking down upon a great body of water. I'm starting to get the feeling of flow and movement."

RAM: "So go with the flow."

ROMC: "I feel that I am the consciousness of rain falling down through the atmosphere. Oh, what a great feeling of freedom, movement, joy, freshness! I'm coming down through the atmosphere as a raindrop. I am floating free. All of a sudden I splash on a human being. I feel that I am the life force of man. Without me humans would not exist for very long.

"As water-consciousness, I am never still. I am continual movement and an important part of everything on earth. I am important to the consciousness of man. I go through man's body, and come out and back to the earth. I go up through the trees and the grass. I go back into the atmosphere and am purified. I become clouds.

"I turn earth into mud—which brings joy to children who love to squish their toes through me, and pigs who love to lay in me. I can become part of a stream, which becomes a river—continually on the move. In my pure form I give strength and life to everything that I touch. I move from rivers to oceans, which, as one body, represent great, great strength. I am important to the life flow of man; when he comes into contact with me, I give life.

"I represent not only flow and movement, but also the higher consciousness of man. I represent that movement of energy into its higher levels. I am the higher mental level of consciousness. I represent the service aspect of the earth. I am joyful movement through every element on the earth. I feel great joy in service and giving."

RAM: "Well, thank you. I have a glass of water sitting here beside me and you have inspired me to take a drink of you now. Without you we couldn't live long. So, ROMC, where do you go next?"

ROMC: "I'm moving from the water into the earth itself. As the consciousness of earth, I am in the level that holds things together. I am the cementing aspect of the whole earth, the very basis on which man finds his physical being. I am not movement, like water. But like water, I am vitality and strength. I give nourishment.

"I am the substance that all other levels of life need in order to go through their stages of growth. I can feel throbbing energy as the consciousness of earth. I feel the experience of infinity, because as the earth's consciousness I am the glue that holds everything together. The water lies upon and goes through me.

"I'm the stable factor for other levels of consciousness, because I give nutrition to the body and soul, which is important to all levels of life. I feel great joy in giving myself to animals, vegetables, and minerals. I have magnetism and life force. I have all levels of energy within my being and continually revitalize. As all aspects of life come into communion with my consciousness, there is communion with the consciousness of their own levels."

RAM: "What is your main relationship to humans?"

ROMC: "It is important for humans to realize that all that exists is in movement—but there also is a stable level of consciousness. I help bring balance to those who know how to give and receive with joy and appreciation.

"Many humans are out of attunement because they are takers, not givers and receivers. When humans take from nature and fellow humans and do not appreciate that which was given, they cut themselves off from aspects of their own natures. They live a stagnant rather than a circular existence.

"When humans are a joyful part of the great symphony of life there is freedom and growth. But when humans take and trample that which is so freely given, they cut themselves off. This is where death begins. Death is that aspect of human consciousness that is not in movement and not in communion with the flow and vitality of all energy levels.

"Humans were put upon me to help raise my consciousness, as well as the consciousness of all forms of life. But this cannot be done without attunement. Within the consciousness of nature there is a great hierarchy of beings who work to bring attunement among all levels of life. As humans open to attunement with all other life forms, there is an opening up that goes beyond time and space. When this attunement takes place, it not only raises the human soul level, but also helps raise the consciousness of levels within me.

"As earth, I have all levels of consciousness, and humans and I must go through change as I work through the flow of my own existence. There are many imbalances in my system, just as there are in the physical level of many humans. Changes must take place for these imbalances to be corrected, which in turn brings greater growth and nourishment to all who need me.

"The consciousness of those who live upon me affects me in many ways. Strong areas of negativity become imbedded in my aura and penetrate my existence. Therefore, an energy healing must take place to release these negative, imbalanced energies. The breakdown of my elements leads to this healing. Humans, who contributed to this imbalance, must go with the flow of my existence—just as I must go with the flow of the existence of those who walk upon me and find nourishment from me.

"Man has helped bring the imbalance by taking from me without giving back to me. We must give to and receive from each other just as any loved ones would do, appreciating, respecting, and loving those qualities that we bring out in each other. However, many humans walk upon me as if I were nothing more than dirt, continually taking, and giving very little in return but negative energies.

"This can happen only so long, and then the breakdown begins to take place. Certain areas of high negative energies will be the first areas of cleansing. Humans are starting to sense this imbalance in their own natures, and in their relationships with all other life forms. Fears of insecurity are arising, and many are thinking selfishly of their own survival. But survival is something that goes far beyond the physical level.

"A soul living in the flow of its own existence will survive stagnant imbalance. As I change, those humans that are in balance within will continue as they are, whether in the physical or etheric existence. Those souls concerned only with survival are caught up in their own imbalances. Those souls concerned with attunement to all levels of life can give and receive joyfully and gracefully, and can help in the raising of all levels of my consciousness, without the painful breakdown of my elements.

"Breakdowns are energies trying to come back into their necessary balance. This shift will be a new beginning of a higher level of consciousness, because humans will also come into an awakening of their own stagnant energies.

"Such energy shifts come in waves. These waves have been taking place upon me from the beginning of my existence. I grow just as a child of human origin grows. Children lose an old set of teeth and gain a new set. They lose childish concepts and grow into maturity. I am yet a child in the cosmos and have much growing to do. My growth has a lot to do with the overall consciousness of all souls who are a part of my outer existence.

"I am going from puberty into adulthood, and within the next several years of earth time many growing pains will take place. The energies are going to be intense within and upon me; furthermore, the energies of my brother and sister planets are also intensifying. We work together, and they are very supportive of my growth. They help in my balancing process. My brother and sister planets also nurture me with special energies of the higher vibrations that come from experience and age.

"Just remember that what man conceives of as pain and disaster is only a changing concept in man's mind, and is not reality in the true sense. The outer manifestation is only a shadow existence of the real. Everything that happens is helping to bring all levels of consciousness back into their own higher existence."

RAM: "It is such a great privilege to hear from the consciousness of earth. We certainly do take you for granted. Thank you for reminding us why you are so important to us."

ROMC: "I feel so elated over this experience of communion with earth that I feel very light. I'm floating in the air. I'm the consciousness of air. What a free feeling! I feel almost as if I don't exist—as if I'm not even here.

"As the consciousness of air, I'm going out into infinity. As air-consciousness, it's as if I *am* infinity. There is no beginning and no end. I represent man's highest spiritual self. I am the life force that gives freedom to man. As air, I'm a basic kind of energy that is important to everything it touches. I am so basic that I feel I'm taken for granted.

"I give all, and go through everything. I am like the gold of the universe. I help to keep the universe in balance. I have so many different dimensions, many that humans can't even comprehend. I am the pulse of all levels of life and energy. I have no limits. Humans desire to fly through me to rise to my levels of consciousness.

"As humans rise to my level, they can become free. That great understanding that is a part of my nature is attunement, because I am a part of everything that is. Man seeks my nature, and he seeks what I represent. I give all to man, and as he comes into attunement with my nature he comes into attunement with his higher self.

"There are no limitations within my consciousness. A soul freed into its higher level has no limits. There are no limitations on the consciousness of humans, other than those they put on themselves.

"I am pure service because I nurture all that I come into contact with. Humans are also on earth to serve. Life is a giving and receiving, not just a taking. Humans have shifted more into a taking consciousness and have gotten everything out of balance. All is one, and one is all. Everything in the universe has an effect on everything else. Humans whose inner energies are in proper balance know well the give-and-take of existence and have great appreciation for all levels of consciousness."

RAM: "I give thanks to air for the breath of life. Without you, we wouldn't be here."

ROMC: "I'm dropping back down out of the air-consciousness. As I come close to the earth I see a light below me. I see flames and smell smoke. I'm dropping down into these flames. I meld with the fast-moving molecules of the fire, and I feel a great sense of strength and transformation as I take on the consciousness of fire. Just as the earth was the physical consciousness, the water the mental, and the air spiritual, I feel that fire is the emotional level of consciousness."

RAM: "What does fire have to say for itself?"

ROMC: "As fire, I am that balancing point in consciousness that creates friction, thus transformation. Nothing is destroyed. It is only transformed from one element to another. I am the factor that helps in the miracle of transformation. I carry great power and responsibility. I am the soul of the universe because I register all dimensions within my transforming nature. I experience great joy in being given this responsibility of transformation.

"I am symbolic of all aspects of consciousness. In the physical level I symbolize duality, or the burning out of the dross of the denser levels of consciousness. In the higher dimensions, I represent heat and light and the finer levels of vibration. I represent movement, change, and higher energies.

"I represent energy because I am energy. I am the fast-moving vibrations that keep all levels of consciousness in contact. Because I represent change, in the earth-consciousness I represent pain. At the same time I am the giver of warmth and life, and thus represent sustenance.

"I am change. I am heat. I am movement. And in the higher emotional level of consciousness, I am love."

RAM: "Thanks to fire for all its levels of service. Are you moving on now?"

ROMC: "I am moving out of the fire. What a warm and energizing experience that was.

"My Invisible Helpers are now sending some thoughts. They are saying how important earth, water, fire, and air are to the consciousness of man. These are the levels of consciousness of the earth. They are all tied into the levels of human consciousness. Everything is so interdependent. One could not function without the other. 'All is one, and one is all.' There is no separation in consciousness. Separation is perceived only by the stagnation of human consciousness; it means living in a state of unreality.

"Humans are stagnating, cutting themselves off from experiencing their own true natures. Unless humans get back into attunement with the self, and thus with all levels of consciousness, they will destroy the physical manifestation of their own existence.

"Thankfulness, joy, stability, movement, beauty, and love are all aspects of this great symphony that is called life. Those who are not in tune with the universal music cannot experience true life, only stagnation and death. Stagnation is death. Humans were put upon earth to help raise the consciousness levels of the earth. But humans must get into attunement with their own inner orchestras.

"Peace and blessings to all. In our service, we bring love and joy."

RAM: "Thank you again for sharing. This has certainly been an important lesson.

"ROMC, come back down into your level when you are ready. Take your time and count yourself back down."

ROMC: (pause) "Wow! What an experience. It's really hard to get back into time. I'll just relax here a little bit."

RAM: "Okay, take your time. I'll turn on some music for your listening pleasure, and to help you get back to the earth energies. Or maybe I should say, get out of the earth energies and back into *your* energies, even though they are pretty much the same, from what your helpers say."

ROMC: "Thanks, that sounds good. It might put me to sleep!"

RAM: "That's okay. Just take your time."

~8~

Nature's Hierarchy

Following the exploratory session reported in Chapter 7, Bob and I had another wonderful philosophical discussion at Ho Jo's. One thing we didn't understand was a statement made about a "hierarchy of beings who work to bring attunement among all levels of life." This concept was just sort of dropped in without explanation. We decided that the Invisible Helpers were hoping that we would question it. Of course, we did. And we found that, indeed, they had been laying the groundwork for further information on the true nature of our physical world. Thus our next session began:

ROMC: "I am in the center of a pure energy ball, floating around and getting energized. It is light in here. I feel light—I can float. There is a lot of energy. I am gently floating around inside. It is like being in the center of an egg—or the nucleus of an atom. I feel very relaxed. I feel energy inside and outside of myself. Part of myself is going to stay inside here and just float around and be energized; another aspect of my energy self is going to float out. Once I have gotten energized, I am going to float right on up to another level. I'll just let myself go, and see where I go."

RAM: "Okay. Follow the flow."

ROMC: "I am gently floating out into space. Suddenly I find myself on a type of platform. I see my Invisible Helpers sitting on each corner of the platform—with their legs crossed! They are warm, friendly, and loving beings—and they all have smiles on their faces.

"I sense that this platform is my taking-off place into various other dimensions or experiences. There is a great feeling that something exciting is going to happen. They are reaching out their hands to invite me to sit down and join them. Now the platform has turned into a circular shape. I am joining the circle, sitting between two of the helpers. It is a wonderful feeling. There is so much love, and I can feel this energy going through me. There is an anticipation of a special kind of experience that we are going to have together.

"Now we are sending love as we sit in each other's presence. I am just going to absorb it. I am going to sit here awhile and not say anything—and just absorb this special energy."

RAM: "Enjoy it as long as you like." (pause)

ROMC: "It is a strange experience. I realize that I am in the midst of a wonderful love energy. That is what love is—it is an energy. There is a very strong feeling that penetrates us. We are in direct contact with one another's energy bodies. This energy is fascinating to experience—and to observe."

RAM: "What is it like?"

ROMC: "It is like I am in the energy, but I am also observing it. And what I am observing is that I can feel it but I can also see it. It seems that the round circle that I was in has floated up. I'm looking out and watching this take place. There are two dimensions of myself. There is the self that is observing, talking, standing aside, and watching. And there is the self that is experiencing."

RAM: "Continue to enjoy and relax."

ROMC: "What I see coming up from this circle is energy that is moving in a spiral. There is a circular motion, going up in a cone shape. The energy doesn't disappear. It seems to go somewhere—going out as if it is endless. And this cone is building up around us."

RAM: "Go with it to see where it takes you."

ROMC: "A strong cone-type of spiral is building up over us. And I sense that we are going to travel into this spiral of energy. This will be our means of travel. Now I am in this spiral.

"There are very strong vibrations here. Looking straight up through the center, I can see the earth. This is a special kind of energy beam that we will be traveling on. There is a strong feeling of security and warmth. I am in the center now and am just riding through this energy."

RAM: "Fine. Continue to go with the energy."

ROMC: "I am coming to the top of the spiral, and I can see the earth. I am taking a different look at the earth. I can see the pulsating energy around the earth that I saw before. It seems imbalanced in some areas. There is very dull energy coming out of areas that are built up in large cities. The energies in some areas seem dull; the colors are not as bright. Now I am being taken around the earth, and my friends are pointing out aspects of the earth that can be seen from this great distance. The bright and intense areas of energy are where the earth is in its natural state—forests, mountains, and lakes—where our human creations have not interfered as much.

"I am being told that there are ways that we can create on the earth but still preserve this vibrant energy. We must work in cooperation and communion with the forces of nature. We must build on the energies that are there, and not destroy them in the process of creating man-made forms.

"In the areas where the energies are dull, we have not cooperated with the elements of nature. We have worked against our natural environment instead of working with it. This has a lot to do with the consciousness levels of the humans who are inhabiting the earth. Many are not in communion or in touch with their own energies, let alone levels of the earth's energies. Where there is a lack of energy, it almost looks like a disease—dark and blotched. There are diseased places upon the earth, where the earth's energies have been blocked. Here, we have broken the natural balance of the earth.

"There are still a lot of bright energies radiating out of the earth's surface. My friends are taking me to a strong-energy area of the earth to give me an idea of what it means to be in communion with the higher forces of nature."

RAM: "Great. See what they have to show you next."

ROMC: "Now I am feeling a real sense of excitement again. I am coming down into a very radiant forest area. There are wonderful energies coming from it. We are still using the strong spiral of energy that we built up. As I come down into this area, I can see that everything is alive with color and vibration."

RAM: "Describe what you are seeing."

ROMC: "I can see some beautiful mountain flowers. As I land, I sense such a marvelous presence. I realize that I am not alone. I am in another dimension of the earth's consciousness. The flower that I am looking at is alive. It is smiling at me. I sense the presence of many small beings—all the parts of nature that are vibrantly alive. I can see these beautiful little creatures. I don't know what to call them. There are different kinds of little creatures dancing around, and I hear many tones of beautiful music."

RAM: "Ask your helpers what to call these creatures."

ROMC: "They must be what are called 'fairies.' The music comes from the energy that is generated from their dancing. It is so light and radiant, and they smile right out of the flowers. It is the consciousness level of this aspect of nature. As they dance around, I hear 'sparkles' of music. They seem to be aware of my presence and are putting on a little show for me. They are very joyful creatures. They seem very happy in their work, and very proud to be a part of the consciousness of the flowers. There is a harmony and light that radiates from the flowers because these fairies are working with them."

RAM: "How does it feel to be there with them?"

ROMC: "There is such a wonderful feeling of communion here among us. I feel a great sense of reverence, and a oneness in being close to this part of nature. And I can experience the communion between the consciousness of a flower and this creature of another dimension. This fairy is a part of the flower, but exists in another dimension. It is very much a part of the consciousness of life. It seems to be joy itself dancing there on the flower."

RAM: "What is its purpose?"

ROMC: "It is dancing out its purpose. The purpose is the pure joy of being alive. This is a dance of thankfulness, for being not only a part of nature, but a part of this beautiful energy that is the God-consciousness of the universe. This little creature is in tune, and this is the message that it seems to be dancing and playing for me.

"The flower and this beautiful light creature both seem to be bowing to me and my friends, saying, 'Thank you for listening to our tune of joy.' And now they are playing the tune, and the message that, 'Man must come into the same attunement with all aspects of nature, because everything around is alive with many levels of consciousness, many levels of life.'

"And now we have all bowed to this beautiful presence and the consciousness of the flower. We have thanked them for sharing with us."

RAM: "Are you moving on?"

ROMC: "Yes. As we move on, I can hear giggles around us, as though many creatures are around. We are walking down a pathway."

RAM: "Where is the pathway taking you?"

ROMC: "It is taking us into a beautiful forest. There is a feeling of floating because it is so alive with life and the presence of love energy. There are such beautiful colors. We are walking through a mossy area. I can hear the giggles again. As I look ahead of me, I see a moss-covered rock, and there are some other creatures."

RAM: "Do they see you?"

ROMC: "They are aware of our presence. They look different from the fairies. They are a little bigger and have a little more form. There is a large group of them and they are very happy. Let's see what they are working on."

RAM: "Do that, and let me know."

ROMC: "They appear to be little gnomes. They are a part of the consciousness of the wood and the trees. I am told that within every aspect of life, every element has its consciousness. But there are also other consciousness levels that work with the elements. They work in communion with each other. These creatures are called 'woodchucks.' There is a tree that has fallen down, and it has some moss growing on it. Part of the tree is hollow. The woodchucks are dancing around on this log and are playing an interesting tune. Some of them are using the log as a drum, and they are speaking in their own language to describe to us what their purpose is."

RAM: "What is their purpose?"

ROMC: "They are a part of the elemental kingdom, and work with the elements of the earth. Every element has its own consciousness. This is the soul level of the elements. They are playing a beautiful tune—different from the one the fairies were playing. Their tune has a deeper tone and is on a lower scale. I can hear the drums as they thump on the tree. From the hollow part of the tree I can hear the music. This log has fallen, but it really isn't dead. It has very special kinds of vibrations. Moss is growing all over it—so even though it seems to be disconnected from its base, it's still very much alive. The woodchucks live inside. They spend time in all the different trees in the forest. This is one of the places in the forest where they like to come to make their very special music. Some of them are dancing and humming along, making beautiful little sounds and melodious tunes."

RAM: "What is their message?"

ROMC: "The message that they are sharing is very similar to that of the fairies. It is a message of cooperation. They help the trees and all the wood aspects of nature grow in their fulfillment. Sometimes when a tree gets injured, they help it to heal. The injuries heal more rapidly with the woodchucks' helpful, healing energies. They are joyous in their responsibilities, and are happy to have this job. They have a great sense of fulfillment about what they are doing. Their message is that we all have jobs on the earth. And if we are in tune with what we are doing—or are supposed to be doing—we will feel a complete sense of fulfillment and purpose in living.

"There is a special purpose in nature for every being, and that purpose is to live in the fullness of your own creativity.

As you are released into this fulfillment, you will know nothing but great joy and love. If every being does what it should be doing, working and sharing for the growth and good of all, it will live in the highest of its energy levels. If human beings get too caught up in their own selves and their own selfish fulfillments, they lose the sense of joy and accomplishment that comes with being in tune and in touch with all aspects of nature."

RAM: "We certainly need to hear this message to remind us to slow down and enjoy life."

ROMC: "I am told by my friends that the reason I am being shown the earth aura from a distance is that the earth energies can become blocked just as our own personal energies can. The little woodchucks are a demonstration of beings that are living in the highest levels of their fulfillment. There is such happiness and joy coming from them."

RAM: "What do the woodchucks look like?"

ROMC: "These little beings are of a more dense color, like the dense colors of the forest. There are beautiful shades of brown, orange, and green. They blend right in with nature. They are dancing and giggling because they are so happy in what they are doing.

"Now they are sitting down on the log and are clapping in unison. We are bowing to them and clapping for them and thanking them. We are reaching out to touch them, and they are reaching out to touch us. It is such a great experience with so much joy radiating in the atmosphere. Now we are waving good-bye."

RAM: "Where do you go next?"'

ROMC: "We are going to walk a little farther. We are coming into a clearing where the sunlight is coming down and hitting a whole group of flowers. There are purple and violet flowers, along with some other wildflowers that have beautiful red petals. You can see the sunbeams as they drop through the darker areas of the forest onto these flowers. It is as if the sunbeams are themselves a consciousness. Descending from the sunbeams and onto the flowers is another type of little being."

RAM: "What are they called?"

ROMC: "They are 'sunbeings' and there is laughter among them. There is a harp-type of music coming from them. The little woodchucks played the more base level of the forest orchestra. The sunbeings are in the higher octaves. These little sunbeings are coming in on the light beams and are sliding right down onto the flowers. The music changes its pitch when they slide down the sunbeams. The flowers do so appreciate these sunbeings, because they give them energy and sustenance. They are a part of the consciousness of the sun and are bringing light into the forest. They bring light and energy to all the elements. They come in at all parts of the forest, and this beautiful harplike music that plays as they come in helps to bring the special energy."

RAM: "What kind of energy is it?"

ROMC: "It is a strong love energy. I am getting a message from them as I watch them work and play. They are sliding down the beams and when they get to the flowers they merge into them, and into the leaves of the trees, and into the grass. As they do, they blend in and disappear for a while. And then some more come in. They are all different colors, like the colors of the rainbow. Their wings have rainbow colors. As their wings flutter, you can hear the music. They are dancing in joyful glee because they are doing what they should be doing."

RAM: "What should they be doing?"

ROMC: "They are the nourishment of the forest—the sun elements. They are a part of the deva-consciousness of the universe. They are the 'devas'—the architects that help to create energy forms. They are helping to bring nourishment and energy, the food of the plant kingdom, and they are much appreciated. The flowers and plants seem to enjoy it each time that these sunbeings blend into them. As the sunbeings slide off a sunbeam onto a flower, all the flowers radiate and vibrate with great joy. Wonderful, harmonious sounds come from this blending."

RAM: "I can almost hear the music as you describe it."

ROMC: "The message of the sunbeings is that everything in the universe is interrelated and each must help the rest. You can hear their harmonious music echo throughout the forest, just as harmonies of human beings that blend together in purpose and achievement can echo throughout the world.

"Every element is playing its melody in the harmonious orchestra of life, just as every soul has its own special tune to play in the universal orchestra. Everything is special. Nothing is wasted. Everything and everyone has purpose and meaning in the universe.

"Now we are bowing to these wonderful creatures and thanking them for their message of love and communion."

RAM: "Where are the helpers taking you now?"

ROMC: "We are starting to float up from this area. As I look down I can see the great colors and vibrations and hear the beautiful music coming from the very essence of all the forest life. I know I will have to return, for there is so much to see, learn, and experience."

RAM: "Perhaps you will."

ROMC: "I am floating back up into this spiral of energy. As I do, I can look back upon the earth. I am being told that man will destroy his very nature if he does not come into a better attunement with nature itself. Humans must learn to give as well as receive. The 'taking' consciousness brings imbalance into the universe. By taking and destroying, humans eventually destroy their own life energies."

RAM: "What must humans do to change?"

ROMC: "There has to be an interplay of giving and receiving in this universe. Humans must be conscious of greater appreciation for their own nature—their own being. As a result, they will respect and appreciate all levels of life. You have to have love energies in order to give love. Therefore, humans must begin by loving self so much that they share this love energy with everything they come into contact with. Our human bodies are miraculous vehicles—each a universe in and of itself—with every cell containing all knowledge and carrying a pattern of the whole. We stunt our individual growth and the growth of the universe around us when we get locked into our own negative and selfish energies. So the message is that we must learn to release, with love, our innate energies.

"There must be a continuous flow going into and out of us at all times—just as the sunbeings go into and out of all levels of life, including humans. We should allow the joy of the sunbeings to enrich our lives as we receive nourishment from the sun's energies. We should be continually appreciative and thankful. Thankfulness creates a very special circular energy in our lives—a creative flow of giving and receiving. Those who continually take without being thankful create a stagnation in their energy systems because they do not have the circular flow.

"The darker, diseased areas of the earth's energies can be revitalized as humans clean up their personal states of consciousness—change the way they think, creating flow instead of stagnation."

RAM: "How can this be done?"

ROMC: "The earth has to be cleaned up from inside out. We are what we think. The earth becomes that which humans are, because the energies are so interrelated. Where there are polluted thoughts, there are polluted areas upon the earth's surface—dark, gray, diseased spots in the earth's aura.

"Now we are coming back up through the spiral. It has been a great experience. But I sense sadness among my Invisible Helpers because of the imbalanced energies in the earth. We are coming back up to the platform.

"There is such great compassion among my helpers. They want no credit for what they are doing, because their purpose is not only to help me, but to help others to come into attunement with themselves and their higher energies.

"Great joy, love, and attunement radiates from them. This is part of the lesson they are teaching me. I have a long way to go in my own attunement in order to get in touch with my own higher and more clarified energies. I sense no criticism on their part—only a feeling of loving acceptance for my being just as I am, but with room to grow. When I am in their presence, I sense that I need to get much, much, much more in tune with myself, so that I can get in tune with all levels of consciousness.

"I feel good about myself when I am in their presence, and I forget that there is time on our plane. I would like to stay in their timeless love energies. It is a beautiful feeling of oneness and love. I feel that I live in the highest levels of my consciousness when I am in their presence. That is a sign of greatness—when you are in the presence of someone who makes you feel so good about yourself. It is almost that another's high level brings you into the experience of your own highest level."

RAM: "Thank your helpers as they prepare to leave."

ROMC: "I am relaxing, and they are withdrawing. I am thanking them. I am waving to them and thanking them for the wonderful experience we had together. I am relaxing on my platform, and the energies are withdrawing. It is getting dark—except around me. I must go back down to blend in with the other dimensions of myself. A ball of energy is floating up to me and I am to step into it. It is a beautiful energy ball. I would love to stay here, but I can't. They are encouraging me to get into the energy ball."

RAM: "Do what they suggest."

ROMC: "Okay, I will. Now I am in—and I am beginning to get blended back into myself. I must float back down into my physical body."

RAM: "Come back down slowly. Take your time."

*Therefore, I Deeply Desire to
Expand, to Experience, to Know,
to Understand, to Control . . .*

~9~

EXPAND:
TO THE MOON
AND A SPACESHIP

If this were flight school, I would have been ready to receive my wings. I was going so deep in my exploratory sessions with Bob that I no longer had conscious memories of them when I came out. I was expanding, my Invisible Helpers informed us, and I was now ready to move beyond the earth level and into the far reaches of the universe. My journey in our next session amazed me. Come with me to the moon . . . and beyond!

ROMC: "It's very dark up here—wherever I am. I get the impression that I am to go on a 'sound trip' before I'll be able to see things. I'm going to be taken through different levels of sound."

RAM: "Okay. Go with the flow."

ROMC: "I can hear the sound of drums all around me. It seems as if the molecules within me are speeding up with the vibration from the different sound rhythms. I feel myself starting to float.

"It's as though I'm floating on the sound waves. The sound is underneath me and not around me. I'm gently bouncing on the sound waves. There are drums beating—different drums with various rhythms. I feel different vibrations and rhythms in various parts of my body. I'm floating on the rhythms of my own existence. It's a great and energizing feeling.

"Now I hear the sound of flutes—different flute tones. I'm starting to float on the flute vibrations. The flutes have very haunting sounds; and the sounds are penetrating different parts of my body—the parts that need their vibrations.

"I'm getting a strong G. The key of G is penetrating every part of my body, causing all my cells to vibrate. The sound is penetrating the center of my brain. It's as if I'm on an endless sea of melody.

"Now the key of D is working on my hands! The beautiful sound of the flute is playing right into the cells of my fingers. It makes my fingers feel light and airy. It's like being on a music cloud. The sounds are going into my toes. And now all the sounds are playing all at once in different parts of my body.

"Now I feel something in my forehead. It's like a funny pain. The music is penetrating my 'third eye.' Several flutes are playing different tones. The key-of-C vibrations are coming right into my eyes, helping them to relax—and to "C" better! It's as if I'm going to open my eyes and be able to see into other dimensions.

"Now I can hear piano music—and a harpsichord. It's as if many stringed instruments are playing. Music from a harp is blending with the harpsichord and piano, and there's also a guitar—and another type of instrument I don't recognize. I'm floating on the music, but it is also penetrating me. Particular harp notes are tapping into certain parts of my body. When C is plucked it seems to strike right in the middle of my head. It's moving to higher keys—and it's going up and down my entire body. The piano is still playing in the background.

"Now the piano music is bringing energy from my toes through my legs, and on through all the energy levels of my body, right up to my head. I feel so light. And the harp is working on my 'fine' energy points—the more intricate energy of my nervous system. It's a tiny harp with high pitches. It's releasing special kinds of energy that are helping me relax. I can feel it all through my spine, lifting the energies in my spinal *chord* as each note is played. The energy is moving higher and higher.

"The piano and harp are working together to bring the energy up through my spine. It's at my heart level now. Now it's in my neck. It's floating through my head, in a circular motion. All the instruments are working together, and I feel my energies going higher and higher. I'm just floating right on out.

"I'm beginning to see colors coming from the music. I see fantastic shades of blue coming from the sounds, and I'm floating gently on them. The color is swirling around me—and it feels so good! Now the music is moving into a different key, and the colors change with the key. I see shades of red, orange, and yellow.

"I'm now very much in the yellow and am very relaxed. The music is slowing down, and beautiful shades of yellow and gold, with shots of red and orange, are coming like waves. It feels so good to float on the sound waves and experience the color shooting up around me—and into me as well, shooting all through my body. I'm bathing in the colors!

"It's as if my head, or mind, is a great concert hall, and I'm experiencing the music to the fullest. This is a part of the universe of the soul. The music and colors are alive! They penetrate every fiber of my body and soul. I'm rolling over and over.

"The music is beginning to get fainter, and I'm floating up and up.

"Now I'm lying on my platform again. I'm so relaxed; that was such a good experience. My Invisible Helpers are with me now. I can perceive from their thoughts that we are going to do something different. They are taking me by the hand, and I'm going to start using my body now. I'm supposed to stretch my body on my own, without the music. We're going to take great strides into other dimensions. They will show me how to take these steps.

"It seems that each time I stretch my legs, I go a long distance, like having seven-league boots. Every time I put a leg out, I seem to span a universe! They're showing me how to completely span universes.

"They're holding onto my hands. This is fun; it's like a game. As we go long distances it's as though I'm exercising my ability to step into other dimensions. I have to stretch. I have to let my mind stretch—realizing that there are no limits. I'm using all aspects of myself, my body and my mind. Whatever my mind thinks, my body does.

"Now we're standing still, and we are all holding hands. They want me to think about where I want to go. I'm thinking now that I would like to go to the moon.

"Okay. Now we're all holding hands, and we're thinking of the moon. (pause) All of a sudden we're standing on the moon! It happened in a split second of thought. It's just like pictures I've seen of the moon. It's sort of dusty. I'm going to jump around. This is fun. I can bound all over the moon. When I hit, the dust flares up. I can see craters. It's so desolate. But there seems to be an energy force here—an eerie energy.

"I want to explore a crater. Now we're in a crater. It's very, very dark down here. And the deeper we go, the stronger the vibrations. It's as if an energy force is pushing us back. The gravity is very strange, but we are pushing on. It's so dark.

"Now we're on the other side of the gravity force—and I have a strange feeling. It's a hollow, empty feeling. But there is also a very strong presence here. A different level of consciousness is around us, but I'm not yet able to identify it.

"I get the feeling that I'm just supposed to experience the vibrations—to feel and to hear. But I don't want to stay here very long; I feel we aren't quite welcome. It's as if we're out of the area of our own vibratory level.

"We're going to hold hands again and go someplace else. I'd like to go back to my platform, which was warm and secure. And we're back—with my very thought of wanting to be back! Now we're brushing each other off to get rid of the foreign vibrations.

"They're going to give me one more chance to go somewhere. We're holding hands. I would like to go onto a spaceship. (pause) Wow, where am I?

"We're standing in a room with some strange people. I think they're aware of our presence, but they're poring over some kind of maps. I'm walking over to them. It's a long, plain room, with nothing but a window that looks like a television screen.

"I'm looking over their shoulders, and it appears they're looking at a map of the universe. I think they're aware of our presence, but they haven't made any indication that they are.

"There's something like a table in the middle of the room. There is indirect lighting. And there are more rooms.

"It seems very warm here—but I think that's because I'm of a different vibration. My Invisible Helpers are beckoning me to follow them. We're going down into another part of the ship, but it doesn't seem that there's much there.

"Now, we're in the room that runs the ship—though I don't see any motors, as we know them. There's something like a small generator that is filled with a gaseous substance. It's operated by light energies. It seems that the light energy contrasts with other types of energies, and when they come together a friction is created that causes the ship to move. It's as if when light strikes, two contrasting kinds of energies come together, causing it to change colors, and creating movement.

There is no sound at all. They're using the same types of energies we see and work with all the time, but they know how to channel these energies. Our fuels are on a much lower energy level. They are working with light and sound energies and a type of fluid. I think the fluid is mercury. It's a very clean energy. It's a matter of pushing these buttons, creating the friction, which creates rapid movement. It's something we can use. We can tap into this energy.

"They're aware of our presence and seem to be showing us around. The beings on this ship are of a very high level of consciousness, and very, very high intelligence. I feel an extreme energy flow just from being around them. They don't use words—just thoughts. Everything is done through mental communication. In fact, they can even push the buttons with thought.

These are beings with high love energy. And they're extremely task-oriented, with specific goals. They are indicating that they are in touch with the earth level through thought-waves. They're on a very high vibration and can tap into any earth thought-wave, at any time. They can do this with their minds, but there is also a machine here that they can use. They're telling me through thought that this machine can register any thought-wave in the universe. They turn it to the necessary wavelengths and pick up the thought patterns.

"This machine is not bound by time. They can tune to the thought-waves of living persons, or any thought-waves of the past or the future! So, they're capable of tuning into anything that ever happens on the earth level. They can pick up in minute detail any thought-waves from the earth.

"They're not only able to use thoughts to communicate with each other, but they are also so highly evolved that they can communicate by thought with humans on earth.

"This machine runs constantly, and through it they are keeping in touch with all levels of the earth-consciousness. They see the combinations of thoughts that create overall patterns. They look at the overall patterns of different countries and know what the countries are going to do in relation to each other. I can see a panel with colors where you can push a button, put two countries together, and get the thought patterns of both countries—and their relationship to each other. They can do this with individuals as well as with group thought patterns.

"This has been going on from the time earth came into physical being. They work with the earth as a part of an overall plan. They are working methodically on thought and energy levels.

"Monitoring the energy vibrations of the earth is very important, because negative energy patterns can affect energy systems throughout the universe. They're not able to make the conscious physical contact with the earth that they would like to have, until our overall thought patterns become less conflicting. If they can find any level on the earth, or can find any individual, where there isn't great mental conflict, they are able to make direct contact. The contrast in thoughts, the friction created by the negative versus the positive poles of energy of the earth-consciousness, creates vibrations that affect them. Energy patterns in all physical universes affect everything else either directly or indirectly. It's an amazing kind of interaction of energies.

"So, if on the earth there is one individual, or one group of people, who really concentrates on positive levels of communication without conflicting thoughts—which include such emotions as fear, anger, anxiety, and jealousy—these space beings are able to beam down. In other words, open levels of communication allow contact with them to take place. They are constantly looking for areas on the earth where they can beam down with direct contact and communication. They have many ways of keeping a 'consciousness gauge' on the earth's constantly changing vibrations.

"They have a major concern for us because we are all part of the same energy patterns. But they don't feel they should interfere in our growth process. They do work to influence our growth in indirect ways. They have been in contact with more highly evolved individuals and have taken numerous people onto their ships over the centuries to monitor them, but conflicting energies are a constant concern.

"As I look at this box, I can see different waves coming out of the earth, different colors coming up. The vibrations and colors are especially mixed over the populated city areas. There are dark waves that come in like static in those areas with many levels of human vibrations.

"They're trying to get through to certain groups and certain levels of consciousness. They want to help raise the consciousness of the earth because it's all part of their task and their goal. It is also a great challenge to them. Vibrations from the earth go out into all levels of the universe; everything in the universe relates to everything else. If we destroy ourselves, this will affect them directly.

"The earth also has its counterpart in another level of the universe—a positive counterpart. The earth is of the slower, negative vibrations. Its counterpart is of the higher-vibratory level, which helps to keep us in balance. Extreme negativity can throw the whole universe off balance, and not just in our galaxy. It reverberates through all galaxies. So, besides our positive earth counterpart, there are other energy systems helping to keep us in balance.

"I can see through the box that some of those from other planets who make contact with the earth are not as highly evolved as the space beings I am with now. The beings I am with keep track of those from other planets of lower energy levels—who in turn are on a higher rate of vibration than the earth. But those alien intruders don't have the same concern for our welfare as the beings I'm with. Our negative energy patterns often attract negative forces from outer space. It's the like-attracts-like principle. This concerns our alien friends, but they don't feel they should intervene unless it's absolutely necessary to do so.

"Those I am with have been conducting something like research on earth for a long time. They have been observing us closely, just as parents would oversee the development of a child, trying to let it grow naturally on its own but intervening when mature guidance and help are needed.

"They are quite a distance from us—actually, in another galaxy. They have special platforms where they keep their mother ships. They don't need to be too close to the earth. They are also studying planets in other galaxies.

"It works almost the way we study minute life forms through a microscope. We are much more advanced than these lower biological forms (or so we think), but the fact that no conscious communication takes place between us doesn't mean that either one does not exist. We are more advanced than such microscopic creatures, and we study their life forms and energy systems even though we do not consider them consciously evolved enough to be aware of our existence. So they go their merry way, do their own thing, and are seemingly not aware of us—just as we are not consciously aware of our concerned and interested brethren in outer space.

"These 'space brothers' will not interfere with our growth patterns unless we reach the point of suicide or self-destruction. Then they would have to intervene, since from experience they know that when other planets have destroyed themselves, the destruction set up reverberating patterns of destructive energies throughout the galaxies.

"The energy forms from the planets that destroy themselves seek similar energy forms on other planets, and this disturbs the energy patterns of these planets—just like an earthbound spirit that attaches itself to a physical home. When these stray energies implant themselves in other energy forms, they create many types of problems.

"Another problem is that when death comes rapidly and traumatically to a planet, the inhabitants are frequently unaware that their physical forms have been destroyed. They are now in their etheric-substance energies, but they experience this as they would their previous physical energy bodies. Thus, many energy forms from a destroyed planet can get caught in a time warp, thinking they still exist in their physical forms. It's as if, for example, the world is destroyed by an atomic war, but the deceased earth residents go on living as if nothing has happened. This sets up even stranger and stronger energy-reality patterns, and it takes longer for evolutionary growth to take place.

"It is like a rescue case on the earth plane. Someone has died and doesn't realize it. The person gets locked into a time warp, and it takes a higher consciousness breakthrough to help release him or her from these emotionally charged energy cells. Thus it's like a 'ghost' in our earth system, a strong emotional energy form that keeps playing out its final scenario. When you have a planetary ghost floating through the physical galaxies replaying its scenario on a different vibration, it poses a problem to all concerned."

RAM: "Ask them if they can make contact with our group."

ROMC: "They are making contact—right now! There can be direct contact, but many conflicts have to be cleared up first. Our group will have to work on blending and purifying our energies for more direct communication.

"You are in a good physical location because it is not heavily populated. The less populated, the fewer the conflicting energies. If your group would work more on blending energies, there would be a greater possibility for more direct contact. Cleansing your thoughts and energies is very important. Also, the energies have to be blended and raised with higher thought-forms and levels of love. Everything is energy; how this energy is utilized makes the difference."

RAM: "Can you see what happens to the earth in the future through the box?"

ROMC: "I can see a twenty-year span. There is a friction, or shifting, in the raising of the consciousness of the earth. I can see the earth a little bit out of shape. There is a pulling from the sister planets. Other planets have gotten off balance, too. It is like a chain reaction.

"1988 seems to be a turning point. There is a shift—but it is not physical. There is going to be a breakdown in various countries, like some very drastic changes within these countries. Some of the countries that are quiet now are going to be coming into their own. There are some uprisings.

"There are going to be many frictions among people of the earth because of the energy imbalance of the earth. There will be extremes of wet and dry spells. And there will be earthquakes, but not all at once. They will come in cycles—like waves."

RAM: "When do they start?"

ROMC: "They have been taking place steadily, but will intensify in the late '80s. As the consciousness of the earth rises, individuals and groups will be in more direct contact with higher energy sources, such as the space beings. In other words, we have to get into the right energy levels to get into the mental contact. It is just impossible for them to penetrate the lower thought-forms by themselves. So when humans are really open to communication with them, it will take place.

"As I said, contact has already taken place with certain individuals in human history. Some of their energy has gone into human form to aid in this communication process. These are the individuals through whom most of the communication has taken place. However, the majority of those on our planet consider such a thing impossible—weird or insane."

RAM: "Is this spaceship a physical spaceship? And do the beings have physical bodies?"

ROMC: "Yes, they are physical, but on a higher physical vibration than we are on. Because they are on a higher level of vibration, they can vibrate into and out of our system if they desire. That's why some people can see them and some can't. Those who are on a high level of vibration can perceive the higher energies. Those on the lower vibrations can't. They don't often come into our system physically, but they have on various occasions."

RAM: "Is it possible for us to understand some of the technology that operates the spaceships?"

ROMC: "Yes. If a highly evolved human would really center on the desire to know, these beings could send through the thought. They are very willing to help. They are guardians of the earth in the sense that they have been studying and protecting us since our birth as a planet."

RAM: "It sounds as if the major problem of those of us on earth is some sort of mind-vibration pollution."

ROMC: "That's a good way to put it. We have to clean up all levels of pollution on planet Earth, including our thoughts. Actually, it begins there. It is back to the cause-and-effect principle. The outer manifestation is a representation of the inner energies. If the thoughts are polluted, so is the physical earth.

"Once we get in control of our thought patterns, we get in better control of the physical realm, and thus we affect the energies around us positively.

"I feel that it's time to return to earth. My friends are signaling that my time is up. We're going to think ourselves back to earth. We're holding hands. (pause) Okay, we're back."

RAM: "Very good. Come out slowly. You have been on quite an extensive journey."

ROMC: (pause) "I think I'm completely back now."

RAM: "How do you feel?"

ROMC: "Really spaced out. Wow! It will take a little bit to get my energies reintegrated. I'll just lie here and relax until I'm completely together."

RAM: "Take your time."

On Bob's first "birthday" in the spirit world—March 17, 1996—I saw something fascinating on a television program called *Sightings*. It was a special segment on UFOs. On the show, two expert UFO researchers who were interviewed reported that they are members of groups in Chilca, Peru, that have worked for more than 21 years using meditation and relaxation techniques to make mental contact with extraterrestrial visitors. One of the researchers said the extraterrestrials have explained that the vibrations emanating from the groups are what makes it possible for them to come here and interact with us, as I learned in the session just described.

The researchers agreed that in every case the ETs have been extremely friendly, with positive intentions. One group member described them as having the attitude of an older brother, trying to make us aware that our planet is beautiful, and that we must preserve it for the future.

On January 31, 1987, a light appeared while one of the groups was meditating, and its leader—a major researcher—was taken onto a spacecraft. The program concluded by stating that a series of U.S. government reports confirms numerous UFO sightings off the coast of Peru—and that sightings have been reported there for many centuries.

~10~

EXPERIENCE: THE AFTERLIFE AND THE ANIMAL DIMENSION

When I was thirteen, my mother gave birth to twins—Larry and Linda. It was like having two live doll babies in the house when they came home from the hospital. It was fun to play with them, feed them, bathe them. I was very close to them.

On Thanksgiving Day of the year David and I moved to Virginia, Larry was killed. It was a tragic automobile accident. Larry and his new bride of six months, Lynda, were coming to spend Thanksgiving with me and David. Leaving their home in Syracuse, Indiana, they first stopped in Dayton, Ohio, to visit Mom and Dad. As they prepared to leave Dayton early Thanksgiving morning, Larry told Mom and Dad in a very special way how much he loved them. An early snowstorm had hit West Virginia and Virginia. But Larry was a drivers' education instructor at the school where he taught, and he had a job interview scheduled in Richmond the following Monday. So they came ahead.

I had prepared a big Thanksgiving dinner—baking Cornish hen for the first time. We expected Larry and Lynda, and their toy poodle Frenchie, by noon. When they didn't arrive by one o'clock, or call us, we became worried. We waited anxiously until the phone rang at five o'clock. It was Lynda, calling from Martinsburg, West Virginia. Her first words, in a stunned voice, were: "Larry's dead." She was in the hospital under heavy sedation. When I hung up the phone, I lay down with a terrible, sick feeling in my stomach. No matter what we believe about life after death, it seems the sting of death itself can never be lessened.

David and I drove to Martinsburg as soon as possible and learned the details of the accident. They had skidded into the back of a tractor-trailer that was parked under an overpass on Interstate 81 outside of Martinsburg. When the state patrolman arrived and opened the car door, Frenchie jumped out and ran away. Larry was unconscious from a head injury and soon died.

Two weeks later two miracles happened. Frenchie was found in Martinsburg. And Lynda discovered she was about two weeks pregnant. Becky Jo Buck was born in mid-August of the next year. This is the background of another incredible journey at the Monroe laboratory.

ROMC: "I think I'm probably in Focus 10. I am very, very aware of the presence of my younger brother, Larry. I'm being told to follow a point of light. It's as if he was alive. Of course, he is alive! He is so vibrant and full of life, and so young—which he was when he passed over.

"I'm to follow this point of light. It seems that I am to go somewhere with him. I have an impression there is some special project we are going to do together."

RAM: "Very good."

ROMC: "I'm traveling on a light beam. I'm coming into an area where I can see Larry—and two dogs. Wow! There's Cookie, our little poodle who died of cancer, and Frenchie, Larry's poodle who died recently. They are so alive and happy. They're with Larry. How exciting to be with the three of them! The surroundings are so beautiful. We're following a pathway, and I'm not sure where it's going to take us. Larry is telling me that he has been learning so much. There is no time here, and he has been working on different energy levels. When he was on earth, he coached young people in wrestling and other athletics. He is saying that he has stepped into a type of energy different from physical energy. He has been having some training. He says he has been present and observing what is going on in my sessions here—but hasn't made himself known, because it is part of his training.

"Now he's going to show me a few of the things he's been doing. It's so exciting, and such a great feeling to be with him!

"I am receiving that we were very much alike on the earth level; and there is a tie between dimensions because we are on the same energy levels. We were so close while he was living on the earth. There is a very important love tie between us.

"Let's see where I'm going to be taken now. It's different here. Matter on the earth level is so much more dense. The atmosphere is so unusual; there is something energizing in the air. You don't breathe here the way we breathe on earth. On the earth level we breathe in and out to become energized and to stay alive. Here, it seems as if there is something in the atmosphere that energizes you without breathing.

"Larry is demonstrating that the mind is pure energy—and that what you think is brought instantly into reality. There are no hidden thoughts. On earth, when you think, 'I want to go someplace,' then you walk, or get in your car and go. But here, when you think of going someplace, you are there instantly. In this dimension the thought is the action. The souls that are here are honest, free—and are hiding nothing.

"On the earth plane we live under an illusion, because we see and experience thought and energy as a dimension beyond self. Here, thought and energy are the reality. They *are* the self. We are in the habit of separating thought and action—as if it were a two-step process. But thoughts are things. Thoughts are reality.

"Larry is showing me that he can be with anyone he wants in any dimension, inside and outside of time. He has been working with his little daughter, Becky Jo, who was born after he passed over. He is very close to her. When he thinks of being with her, he is right there. It's not a matter of thinking and then doing.

"And we can do the same thing from the earth dimension. I can think about being with Larry, and I'm with him! Thought is the reality. He is telling me that this is the basis of his training. He is learning many different uses of this process. And we can do the same kind of training here on earth.

"Often on the earth plane we are confused about the nature of reality. We discount our inner experiences as being somehow not real. But the awareness I am having now, these teachings, and the experience of being with Larry in this time-less dimension are more real than most experiences on the earth plane.

"We must learn to use pure thought-forms on the earth plane. In healing, we can learn to release negative energy from our bodies and allow pure energy to come in. Everything is live energy.

"Some people wonder whether our pets live on after they leave the earth plane. They exist on the same energy princi-ple. They are live energy forms; and these little beings are just as alive—even more alive—after they leave the earth plane. When an animal dies, it is attracted by love energy. If it has a close tie to an owner, it will usually be with that person no matter where that person is. If the owner is on the earth level, the little soul will often stay with the owner—even though it is not usually perceived. Sometimes, the animal will reincar-nate as soon as possible to be with its old owner. If the owner dies first, then the pet will be with him or her upon release from its physical body.

"As for animals that don't have a loving master, they stay in a group animal soul—that is, a group of animals that are on the same energy level.

"Animals that are put to sleep or die through abuse come into a special area where they are loved and nurtured.

"There is a purity of dedication in our pets that is helpful in the growth process of human beings. They are on the emo-tional level of human energies. They don't naturally carry the same types of fears and problems that humans do—unless they pick them up from their masters, or from some other aspect of the earth experience. Some animals take on the conditions of their masters as an act of love and a way of relieving them from the full burden of certain problems. Animals are not affected by rejection in the way humans are. Animals evolve as a result of the love they receive from the human level. Some animals stay with their masters both here and beyond until they are ready to evolve into a higher group soul. Like attracts like.

"Larry is showing me something. He is pointing out that Frenchie and Cookie can read each other's minds. Larry and the two poodles are such good friends, working together on some special missions. I'm being taken to a place where there are many animals that have experienced rejection on the earth plane. All of these animals had gone to the earth level to evolve with the help of human beings but were never accepted by humans. Now they are staying with their soul group until they're ready to reincarnate again to experience the love-growth process.

"Each time humans reject or harm an animal, they are actually delaying their own growth process. By rejecting animals, by treating them badly, humans create negative energies around themselves that they get locked into, and that are sometimes difficult to work out of.

"But all of these rejected animals appear radiant, even though they have been mistreated on the earth plane. They are beautiful, pure little animals. There are beings that are in charge of them. It is like a large animal shelter, and they are all well taken care of. Frenchie and Cookie are going over to communicate with some of them. They don't talk in words, of course. They relate on the pure energy level. It's as if they *experience* one another—which is what they do on the earth plane as well. Each knows directly what the other is feeling and experiencing.

"Larry is pointing out that throughout the universe—in every dimension—nothing is destroyed. Even though the bodies of these animals died or were put to sleep, they are still very much alive.

"In many cases, animals go to the earth plane to help teach human beings lessons that they might not learn otherwise. Animals can often teach better because of the pureness of their dedication and their love. Some humans can relate easier to animals than to other human beings. And animals want to help wherever they can."

RAM: "Are there any of what we call wild animals there?"

ROMC: "There aren't any wild animals in this area. I'll see if Larry can show me some.

"Now I'm with some wild animals—it happened just as fast as I wanted to be with them. Larry was aware of your question as soon as you thought it, and we're suddenly in a beautiful kind of a jungle. It's extremely colorful. It seems like a replica of an earth jungle, but it's more beautiful. I don't have the fear that I would have in an earth jungle—being afraid of snakes, or of something wild jumping out. Fear isn't even present in this dimension.

"I'm perceiving from Larry that the animals we call wild are in more complete attunement in this state of consciousness. On earth they have to come into attunement with the forces around them—the natural forces—to find balance in relation to them. Then, having evolved on earth, they continue their evolution in the next dimension.

"There is absolutely no fear here. Such animals do not have to fight and struggle for food or survival. They don't have to eat food, of course, as they did on earth. There is something in this atmosphere that brings nourishment and regeneration.

"Larry is walking over to pet a tiger—and it's licking him and wagging its tail. Even on the earth level, when the fear is removed, you can relate to these animals. If humans show fear, the animals respond to this fear. This tiger is putting on a little show. It is actually laughing, to show that it is happy!

"Now an alligator is coming up out of what seems like water. This whole atmosphere is so different. Everything is in attunement. And now Frenchie and Cookie are going over to the alligator. They're wagging their tails and are communicating with it. Now the alligator is turning over on its back, and the dogs are licking its belly. There is great affection between them.

"Here again, these animals have come through the earth-consciousness, and are learning to rise above some of the denser energies that surrounded them there. They also have group-soul relationships. When the group soul evolves to a certain level, then a choice can be made. If an individual animal wants to evolve into another type of animal, or species, to learn a certain type of lesson, it can.

"It seems that the energies of every soul go through all of the elements. The energies of a stone or rock evolve into vegetation—flowers and trees. Then these energies evolve into movable forms from the immovable—they can begin to have a type of mobility that is not as dense. There is thus an evolution through the mineral, vegetable, and animal kingdoms. In the animal kingdom, wild animals can evolve into more domesticated ones. And then, at a certain point, a group soul of animals can evolve into a human consciousness.

"This is a very difficult concept to explain and understand. It's not that a human being was once a rock, a tree, a dog, or a cat. It's that we have all the levels of consciousness within us that exist in all aspects of the earth-consciousness, and we must experience these aspects of our being before we can evolve into our higher natures. We are all these levels of consciousness because all energies are one. We experience these consciousness levels in order to be in attunement with all life. There are many dimensions of energies within the mineral, vegetable, and animal kingdoms. To describe this would take a book in itself."

RAM: "So, how does this evolution take place?"

ROMC: "Again there are many different levels and ways that it can take place. It has to do with choice—and the needs of the soul. There are many levels that souls on the earth plane have not experienced. The earth plane is just one very small drop in the ocean of the levels and types of consciousness that exist in the universe. Those souls that are attracted to the earth level are on a certain rate of vibration. So there are many types of evolution; life force and souls go through certain types of substance for special kinds of evolvement."

RAM: "Is there any evolvement in the earth plane beyond what we know as human?"

ROMC: "I can see that on the earth plane there is another dimension. It's like looking into a mirror. Everything has its own reflection. For every flower, every tree, every person, there's a reflection or a dimension that's a part of it—which is more speeded up, or not as dense, as the earth level. It's as if everything has both a dense and a pure state, connected, working on a consciousness level together.

"There are group souls that every human being is a part of on another level. They are called teachers, angels, helpers, or guides. Whatever they're called, every soul on the earth has a reflection of its highest self, which it can tune into at any time for help, guidance, and support.

"It's the same for everything that's alive—and everything in the universe is alive. There's a consciousness level that oversees it and is a part of it. There's no aloneness in the universe other than that which a soul creates itself. Everything in the universe works in an interrelationship. 'All is one, and one is all.' In the world of nature there are devas, nature spirits, elementals, or whatever you choose to call them, that are the soul forces of nature. Everything is alive. And there are consciousness levels that work in relationship to all aspects of nature.

"The earth level is simply the reflection of the higher levels. There is always movement and balancing taking place, with the higher nature bringing itself into a balancing point of perfection. The earth level is merely the reflection of the true reality."

RAM: "Can you perceive a basic reason for such a pattern of evolution?"

ROMC: "It's that same pattern that's perceived in the great religions' patterns throughout earth history—the concept of the negative and positive, the yin and yang. There are energy poles. For every positive, there is a negative. There are attractions that keep working in relation to each other to keep balance in the universe. Everything works in patterns of rhythm. The life and death pattern is an example of this rhythm. It is part of a flow. It's the vibration of every soul.

"This is the same pattern through which souls reincarnate into the earth level. We put concepts of 'good' and 'bad,' 'right' and 'wrong' on patterns of evolution that are at work. But everything has its pure state; the polar energies are continually at work bringing all things back to the pure nature of perfection.

"Therefore, in its perfect state, nothing on the earth level is real as perceived—because it also exists in a different energy dimension. There is continual movement and transformation of energy, working in rhythmic beauty toward the universal consciousness of Oneness."

RAM: "How and why did all of this begin?"

ROMC: "There is no beginning and no end of what is real. There has been a beginning of the more dense earth and its levels. But 'beginning' is only a term used in human consciousness—in the time zone. The reason there is no beginning and no end is because in reality, there is no time. The 'beginning' is the consciousness level of time.

"There are pure energy groups that began to experiment with their own natures. All was, and is, the pure mind of God. All levels were originally operating in absolute balance. Aspects of the creative nature split from its pure energy forces—the pure soul, the pure thought. This is what is meant by God creating the earth. God, or what man terms the highest energy force, allowed part of itself, or its reflection, to come into a more dense nature, which was the physical universe. This is how it is perceived from the point of view of time.

"There are many, many levels of souls, in all aspects of forms, in various parts of a massive universe. The soul of man evolved through many levels of consciousness, and is working back toward its own purity through these levels and experiences. Time came into existence when man put limitations upon himself. The denser body was created around the pure energy forms.

"Then the male and female were created as a symbol of the illusion of separation. The male and female are symbolic of the need of the soul to come back into the balance and oneness of its higher reality. These are two parts of one whole. This is all a part of the rhythm of the universe.

"Actually, the earth level is the shadow of what man really is. Therefore, it is all one and the same, and part of the only reality—which is called 'God' in earth terms. So, the soul works back into its timeless nature. Just as the sun shining upon man changes the nature of the shadow, so time and rhythm on the earth level change aspects of life. There is always movement in the universe of the earth level, because it is the unreal existence working back into its true state."

RAM: "Why did man make such a decision to enter the unreal?"

ROMC: "This results from the complete and absolute freedom that exists in the universe. We are a beautiful rhythm of God's creation. Souls that began to exist outside the pure Source started to experience loneliness and fear and the human aspects of what is termed 'evil,'—which is the state of being cut off from the true Source. Dualism exists outside of the God-nature. Oneness exists inside the God-nature. Therefore, life is a journey back to our true Source. When we return to the oneness, we leave dualism, or the shadow existence.

"But this oneness can be experienced in the earth body, when the soul comes into the realization of its Source and turns its energies into the channels of purity and perfection, which is oneness."

RAM: "Very good. Is Larry still with you?"

ROMC: "Yes. He is over with the animals. Someone else has been talking through me; or maybe it is my higher soul source."

RAM: "Ask the other person and Larry if they have any other messages for us."

ROMC: "They say that there is great rejoicing over the property you have purchased for your new center. The vibrations there are very high. And the nature spirits are happy because they know they will be treated well. All aspects of nature at that property know they will be respected. The animals are happy, because they know they will be as happy there as over here. There is much happiness here. When everybody is doing what they should be doing, there is happiness."

RAM: "Ask Larry if he will visit us on the 'New Land,' where the center will be."

ROMC: "Larry says that he actually visited it the day I went over there for the first time. He sees much light around the whole area and a lot of activity there. He says that everything must be built with a good attitude from the ground up—so that even the buildings will have the right vibrations. Everything must be constructed with the attitude of love. He sees a beautiful flow of love and energy on the property."

RAM: "We will certainly do everything we can to make it so. Ask Larry if we can join him again sometime."

ROMC: "Larry says that I will be with him many times. And he has been with me often—and would be happy to show me other dimensions and other things that he is working with. He is a very beautiful soul."

RAM: "I'm sure you'll look forward to that. I certainly will. Begin your return. Tell them all you will see them again."

ROMC: "Okay."

In a session in April 1979 I was taken to visit Larry again. This time I was delighted to visit with my father, who had died the year before:

RAM: "ROMC has moved out of Focus 10 and up to 12."

ROMC: "I'm up on my platform now—which is an extension of myself in a higher dimension. Space and time are different in this level. I feel wholeness and a strong sense of being.

"I hear a voice saying very clearly, 'Come with me, Rosalind.' I'll follow to see where I go. I feel I'm moving rapidly through the universe . . . through space. I can see points of light in all directions. I don't know where I'm going; I'm following the energy that asked me to follow. Now I'm going through a spiral—a kind of a tunnel. (pause)

"I can hear a voice saying, 'Rosalind, now that you are separated from your body, where would you like to go? When you get to this state you can go wherever you desire. Is there anything special you would like to do?'

"I'm thinking that my father and brother are both in another dimension. I'd like to visit them and see what they are doing.

"I still feel as if I'm moving. I see a point of light ahead of me. I'm keeping my eye on this point of light—and I'm being drawn to it. I don't see anything yet, but I have a very strong feeling of a personality. (pause) It's my brother Larry. I can see him in the distance. He's laughing, and is so happy to see me—and is motioning for me to join him. And my father . . . I can't see him yet, but I can sense his presence.

"Now the light is expanding. I see a field of green—beautiful green. Wow! It's magnificent here. The colors are magnified a thousand times compared to the colors of earth. I'm running through the field. It's a different feeling. There is such lightness about it—and such great light.

"In a distance I can see some people. I'm running. There is great excitement. I'm getting closer. It's such a beautiful area. I'm coming to a group. There's Larry. He's grabbing and hugging me. He seems so young! He's so full of life; there is a glow about him. He's so happy to see me.

"There's my father! We're hugging and laughing. I can read his mind. He's telling me that he didn't believe in the afterlife while on earth, but Larry met him when he died. Larry was right there to meet him, and Dad knew immediately that he'd been wrong. He's laughing about it. He's saying, 'We all make mistakes.' He seems so happy that he was wrong.

"He's in a place now where he can travel freely. He loved to travel while he was on earth. He and Larry have been taking all kinds of trips. Things are different here—similar in some ways, but different. You travel by thought.

"Dad was very creative on earth, and loved to build. Now he tells me that he builds with his mind. He has created a place to live—created it with his mind. Larry showed him how to do it. It's not necessary to have a place to live, but if one wants to create a thought-form, it's possible to do so. This is a creative pastime.

"Dad made his transition in his sleep, so it took him a while to get acclimated. He says he has a place for Mom when she comes over. But it's going to be a while yet before Mom comes over to join him.

"I have an aunt who just went over—Dad's sister. She's not with them, but I'm picking up that she is fine. You don't have to converse. You just think. Aunt Eleanor is adjusting quite well to the new energies. My Grandpa and Grandmother Buck, her parents, were there to meet her. They were tied into the same energies on earth. Because of similar energies, loved ones usually meet loved ones over here.

"There is a change of energies between the earth dimension and this dimension, and it takes some people quite a bit of 'time' to get oriented. However, there is actually no time in this dimension. Aunt Eleanor is adjusting well and seems very happy.

"Larry has been active in many kinds of interesting projects. He's doing some special work with children since I visited him here before. He's working with children who have come over without parents. He greets them when there are no relatives here to meet them. Larry has such a wonderful personality and sense of humor.

"I'm perceiving that children become adjusted to this side very rapidly. There is no fear. And, since there is no time in this dimension, you can choose to be of any age. If you want to be a child, you can stay a child until you want to change. I see a community of children, and all the beautiful beings who are working with them. Larry is really enjoying this.

"He works a lot with his own daughter, whom he left behind on earth. Becky Jo was born a few months after he died, but he has a close tie with her. There's no separation in time and space. With the thought of being there, one is instantly with a loved one. So Larry is with Becky Jo often. Everyone must realize that there is no separation. When people on earth think about a loved one, they are in instant contact with them. Thought is energy, and transmits instantly.

"Larry has chosen to work with children because that keeps him in close contact with the child-consciousness of the earth.

"Dad is a very social person, and he has enjoyed visiting here with many people he knew in his lifetime. He has branched out and met others, too. He's learning many things—exciting things. He always had an inquisitive mind. But learning is different here. It seems that you experience concepts. He has been enjoying the creative process. You think of what you want to create—and it's right in front of you!

"It's the same for movement. You think where you want to be, and you're there instantly. In this dimension, like-minded people are together just as on the earth. There are many different dimensions, and many different kinds of people. He's enjoyed exploring this new territory of existence.

"Now I must say good-bye. I can return here at any time. There's really no separation of this dimension and the earth dimension. I can just think about being with my loved ones, and I'm with them.

"There are many dimensions and levels beyond the level I just visited—going into higher areas of light-consciousness. And from each level there are higher light beings working with those on slower vibrations."

Just moments after I completed this chapter, a remarkable thing happened. There was a knock on my door, and the postman handed me a package. I quickly opened it and there in front of me were the words *Hello from Heaven!* What an incredible confirmation.

My good friends Bill Guggenheim and his ex-wife Judy had completed the book they had researched for eight years. They interviewed approximately 2,000 people throughout the United States and Canada who've had after-death communication (ADC) experiences. Their ADC project, now in book form, included personal experiences of people who had confirmation from beyond that their loved ones were fully alive and happily existing in another dimension. Sensing a presence, hearing a voice, seeing full appearances, and going out-of-body to visit loved ones are all included in the 23 chapters of *Hello from Heaven!*

The book is now in paperback (Bantam Books) and is already in print in several countries. It's exciting to have research corroborating the results of my exploratory sessions with Robert Monroe.

Know:
The Importance of
Knowing

When we're young we often think that we know everything. As we get older we begin to realize that there is so much we don't know—until finally, like Socrates, we suspect that we don't know anything! According to the information brought through by my Invisible Helpers, however, the knowledge of everything is within us. If that's true, then in a real sense, we know everything!

So when the youthful think they know everything, they're onto something. But when it's our inflated egos that believe this, we usually aren't interested in learning anything new—including learning the reason we really do know everything. So, if you feel that you don't know everything, and would like to learn why you actually do know everything, travel with me to the *knowing* level and learn about what you already know . . .

ROMC: "I am on my platform and am very relaxed. It's a different type of atmosphere. I looked in one direction and saw a large cluster of stars, like a cloud. As I looked at it I heard the words, 'The cloud of the unknowing.' And then I heard, 'The cloud of the knowing.'

"I could see myself standing on the platform in a beautiful, flowing Grecian-type robe. When I looked down at the earth it was as if I was looking into all dimensions—into timelessness and all the levels of knowing and unknowing.

"Then I got a picture of life on this planet. It's as if I'm going to be taken into different aspects of a timeless element of existence on this planet. I'll see what's going to happen."

RAM: "Go with the flow."

ROMC: "I'll describe things as they're happening, instead of watching them first and then telling you about them.

"I'm being taken back in time—but also into timelessness. The very nature of the soul, the higher self, is timeless. The soul exists and works out aspects of its nature within time. The 'unknowing' is the time-nature of self, and the 'knowing' is its timeless nature. So I'm going to be shown the knowing and unknowing aspects of the self or soul.

"As I look down on the earth, it's a beautiful ball turning slowly. As it rotates, I can hear some voices and somehow see individuals at different points on earth. I'm told that these people are actually different aspects of myself. In the timeless dimension, I exist in all of these natures. There is no separation. But in the time zone, I experience other people as separate existences.

"It's fascinating to observe myself and the earth in both time and timelessness. The balancing of my energies is related to my earth existence. We come into the time zone of earth at certain levels for special lessons in balance. Our souls choose these time-zone lessons, and we go to specific areas where the energies are right for our personal growth.

"I'm now zoning in on a certain energy point of earth time. I can hear a strong Scottish accent. I see and hear a lady complaining that life is very difficult for her. As the earth turns, I can see myself in a Germanic country. There's a heaviness about this existence. As the earth continues to rotate, I can see Greece—and I feel lighter and happier.

"These are three of my past-life incarnations. The first two had a heavier feeling and were in a northern, colder climate. My life in the Germanic country was during a time of the roaming tribes called the Huns. It was a very tough period—but good for growth. The difficult lifetimes were important in burning out some heavy stuff within my soul aspects—of my lower energies.

"Because of the intensity of the Scottish and Germanic lifetimes, I shifted next to a light climate, into the Golden Age of Greece. I moved from base earth energies into higher emotional levels. The energies are so different, and I feel lighter just observing the difference.

"Soul growth takes place through achieving balance. Everything in the universe is rhythm and balance. We incarnate into the earth-time level in that same pattern of rhythm and balance. It's a beautiful feeling of rhythm. I can sense and see the rhythms and patterns of my overall existence before me in one beautiful picture. When things get really hard, it's all for a very important reason—spiritual growth.

"In seeing the overall picture of my soul growth, I'm told that this is the 'knowing' aspect of the self. 'Unknowing' is when we are in specific situations in the time zone of earth, and do not know and remember the other aspects of our life and growth—that is, unless the knowing part of us brings them consciously to our attention. In reality, we always know. It's a matter of knowing that we know.

"The earth also goes through a process of growth. When I was going through a trying period in a lifetime, the consciousness of the whole country I lived in was going through similar growth stages. And, of course, this continues.

"During the Golden Age of Greece, the earth was at a very high level of energy. During these lighter periods of history, the soul grows in the finer, sensitive points. Many souls come in at the same moment in time for similar growth patterns. Like attracts like.

"There was both outer and inner peace during this creative Greek period. Naturally, I feel better about a place where I had good experiences, and I feel good about my lifetimes in Greece. I did have one trying lifetime there, but I grew a lot—and am still working out some of those energies.

"I'm aware of being back on my platform. The earth continues to rotate. Again, I see fluctuation points in the earth's energies. Now I see some very, very high energy levels. And I hear the words 'Mu' and 'Atlantis.' People who came in at these times were living at very high energy levels within their own being.

"Each soul has its higher and lower points of energy. As the soul develops, it vibrates at faster rates. Souls whose vibration rates are on slower or denser levels will continue to come back to the earth in situations in which the energies of the earth are more dense and on a slower vibration. The denser situation creates a friction that has a way of speeding up the soul level of growth.

"Souls can come back only into the level to which they have developed. A soul would not come in at the energy levels of a Mu or Atlantis if it had not been vibrating at higher energies within. After a high experience, the soul might come back into an earth area of its lowest-vibrating energies in order to bring all parts of itself into higher energies.

"It works in rhythmic patterns. A soul can fluctuate back and forth from its lowest to its highest energy levels. And it would come into those points of earth time where the needed energy levels exist. The soul of the earth goes through similar patterns of growth. And every soul that lives on the earth affects the energy patterns of the earth.

"There are times when souls come into the earth-time zone for teaching and sharing purposes. In this case a higher-vibratory soul comes into the lower earth vibration in order to teach and share from its higher energy patterns. This is also part of the rhythm of the universe. 'All is one, and one is all.'

"Everything in the universe works in relation to all other energy patterns. Everything that a soul ever does or thinks affects all dimensions of time and timelessness. Thus, souls that have evolved into higher energy patterns work with souls of lower vibration, as well as in lower-vibratory periods in the earth-time zone.

"There is continual movement in the universe. Nothing evolves to a higher-energy level and then ceases functioning.

The higher the vibratory level, the greater the responsibility. This is a universal principle. There are always teachers, and there are always students. And the teachers also need to be students—and the students need to be teachers. 'All is one, and one is all.' There is no real separation in the universe. Separation is experienced by individual souls when they have cut themselves off from the innate Source . . . the level of knowing.

"The souls that come back more for service than growth must release the truth and knowledge that is a part of them, or they will cease to grow. That is another universal law. Souls cannot progress unless they help others on the road to enlightenment. In other words, they must continually give, put their energies out to the earth levels of existence, in order to experience continual growth. Give—and you shall receive. Souls that continually take get locked into very heavy levels of their existence.

"Therefore, the soul that is living in its highest freedom has a continual energy flow coming in and out of its existence. These are the higher love energies, the energies that are reaching out into all levels of the universe, helping lift other souls into their knowing levels of existence.

"Now, I'm looking again at the very highly evolved cultures called Mu and Atlantis. Atlantis seems to be tied in with the Golden Age of Greece. And I can also see highly evolved cultures in Central and South America.

"All these cultures collapsed because of the misuse of energy, and also because they were imbalanced in relation to the rest of the world around them. When a culture evolves to a very high level but does nothing to raise the vibrations of surrounding cultures, there will be internal collapse. It is the same giving-and-receiving principle.

"Thus, cultures that are highly evolved, but do nothing for their fellow nations, get locked into themselves—and actually destroy themselves in the earth plane. Everything that is learned must be released into the universe. Nothing in the universe can be possessed. No person can possess another person without negative energies creating internal destruction.

"Flow and release is the secret of growth. It is unnecessary to hold onto anything in the physical universe. Nothing is real in this physical realm, and it will all pass away. The holding-on nature of consciousness just delays the growth of a soul. Greedy and selfish souls will continue to come back into energy situations where they will lose everything that is meaningful to them. This will happen again and again until the soul learns the meaning of release.

"Everything that is given comes back in many forms. The souls that have learned the lesson of release and flow will have plenty. And they will find their greatest satisfaction on the unseen levels of existence—the levels of knowing.

"The earth is an entity in itself. The patterns of soul growth and earth growth are very similar. The earth has many unseen dimensions, just as each soul has many unseen dimensions.

"Now I am tuning into the combination of all of the souls who have ever lived on planet Earth. There is no time in the universe. All that was, is. It is all there to be seen and experienced in timelessness.

"Now I'm seeing the American Indian cultures. I see myself in an Indian nation in Central America. Again, this was an intense and heavy learning situation. This was a point of friction that was also a point of growth.

"At this time in North America there were different energies than in Central America. There was attunement. The highest level of energies in our continent's history was when the Native American Indian culture was at it height. Many of the souls that came in at this time were vibrating on an extremely high level. The Native American culture understood the nature of inner attunement and harmony with all of nature. This was an intense period in earth's growth, with very high energies on the etheric level around the earth. The aura of the earth was so beautiful at this time.

"Again, I'm watching the earth turn slowly, and I sense the overall presence of all the souls who have ever lived on earth. There is no time, and thus all souls actually exist in all levels at once. I can see the whole soul-energy community working together from the beginning to the end until the last souls are able to rise into the highest levels of their natures.

"My Invisible Helpers are telling me that there is no beginning and no end in the timeless levels of knowing. 'Beginning' and 'end' are time terms; there is no such thing as a beginning and an end, because there is no such thing as time.

"The highest energy is love energy—a basic concept that Jesus came to show the earth. We are our brother's keepers. We must allow ourselves to come into attunement; as a result, we can help bring others into attunement as well.

"Jesus, a very evolved teacher and light being, came into the earth to show others the secrets of rising into their higher selves. When he moved into the timeless zone, Jesus left the commission that greater things would we do than he. He is from the most highly evolved level, the godhead, and he came to help raise souls into the higher levels of their own existence.

"The Christ-consciousness is the earth's soul—its spiritual energy. Besides Jesus the Christ, great teachers and masters of high vibration such as Abraham, Buddha, Mohammed, and others throughout the ages have come on special rays of this light energy into human form to awaken various aspects of spirituality in the slumbering souls of humankind.

"Since there is no time, I can see into the future of the planet. The next 100 years is an intense energy period in the growth of the planet. The highest- and lowest-vibratory souls will be back on the earth at the same time. There will be a great concentration of friction points because of the contrasts between energy soul levels, and there will be great growth.

"There will be changes in the physical earth structure that will represent shifts in the consciousness of the earth level. The earth is moving into a higher level from more gross energies. It will be shaking off many lower energies. Therefore, there will be shifts in its physical structure as it moves into a higher energy. Areas where there has been the strongest negative/positive concentration of energies will disappear, and new continents will appear upon the earth's surface.

"Many souls who choose to remain, or who come during or after this growth spurt of the earth's consciousness, will be on high energy levels. The whole earth will work with the higher energies. Countries cannot ignore each other at times of such need and will therefore work together. If they do ignore each other, the Golden Age of Higher Energies will not come to pass.

"And at this time, many types of energy beings from other dimensions and universes will be coming into the earth's atmosphere. Again, like attracts like. When the earth reaches its higher-energy level, it is ready to receive evolved energy beings from more highly developed areas. Many highly evolved souls have come into the earth energies, but not in such great numbers as I am seeing in the future.

"There will eventually be a complete change in the nature of physical man. We become what we think. When we begin using our higher energies, our physical bodies will change. They will become less dense. We will use the energies of our minds in different ways. And therefore the whole earth-consciousness will change.

"Again, the turning point will be in how we share what we have learned. If our inner motives are for the good of all, then there will be evolvement in the earth-time zone. If the energies become selfish and get locked in, then there will be periods of breakdown until we learn our lessons."

RAM: "Are any of your friends around you?"

ROMC: "Yes, they have been showing me all of this. But they haven't been dictating. They say that I've been picking the information up on the knowing level. Each soul has this ability.

"In some ways I was alone—but not alone. This is how we often feel in our earth bodies. By the very nature of our unknowing consciousness, we feel a sense of isolation. But when we tune into our inmost knowing levels, we know that we are not alone.

"It's awe-inspiring, because many universes and levels of understanding and living open up to us on the knowing level.

"We only need to tune into ourselves and know who we are, to know that we are not alone in the universe. Unknowing is when we close ourselves off from the true knowledge that is there to be tapped. When the soul is truly in touch with itself, there are no levels of unknowing, because unknowing is on a time level and therefore doesn't exist."

RAM: "And how does a soul get in touch with this knowing level?"

ROMC: "It's important for souls to turn within. This is the very essence of prayer and meditation. Prayer is talking to God—or giving. And meditation is listening to God—or receiving. We need this circular balance in order to come into wholeness.

"Also, we must become much more sensitive to what is happening to ourselves. We need to work continually to allow the higher self, rather than the lower, to take control of our lives.

"Our dreams are important in keeping us in touch with our emotional state. Be very interested in what your higher self is telling you through the dream state. We continually work out problem situations through our dreams. We also receive many insights into ourselves. Dreams keep our daily emotional 'temperature.' Look at the thermometer of the soul to see where you are each day.

"Be aware of what you think of others. If you see a negative aspect of another person and are critical, it is often an aspect of yourself that seems to glare out from the other being. Each time you are critical of another person, turn within yourself to see what it is within that triggers this reaction. It is usually because you are seeing a mirror reflection of something you don't like about yourself. Look into this mirror continually and release these negative emotions when you discover them to be your own.

"So the greatest stumbling block of human nature is the ego of the lower self. This is the self that sees only itself and believes that only what is connected to it is important. Anything outside of its own world is to be judged and condemned, just because it isn't part of this lower ego-consciousness. That is, the ego doesn't perceive itself to be connected with anything that it considers undesirable. The ego is strongly embedded in the earth-consciousness of duality. It thinks that there is always something working in opposition to it.

"Know that by the very nature of your earth-time existence you are learning lessons daily. Life is how you perceive it. Live each day on the tiptoes of excitement. And know that everything in the universe is good, even the hardest experiences, and everything is working toward your evolvement. Go with the flow of life, and do not resist your lessons. Give everything away that you receive. You will find that what you receive in return is a greater understanding of your oneness with all. All is one, and one is all. Know this from the knowing level.

"My friends are telling me that I'm now ready to come back from my platform. I'll work my way back."

RAM: "Good. Just relax. (pause) How do you feel now?"

ROMC: "A little tired—but energized. What an intense experience. I'm going to move rapidly back into myself."

~12~

UNDERSTAND: THE GOLDEN LEVEL OF LOVE

One day a television crew from Canada arrived to do a special report on the Monroe Institute laboratory—a 20-minute segment for a prime-time special. Bob chose me as the Explorer to be filmed.

The situation presented some unique challenges. One problem was that the CHEC Units were completely enclosed cubicles just eight by ten feet, with little room for anything except the Explorer's water bed. On my right, jammed in one corner, was a cameraman. On my left was a man with a large boxlike instrument designed to register the change in my electromagnetic field as I went out-of-body. They asked me to put my left hand in the box. Then, since the CHEC Units are normally completely dark, I was blindfolded so that the cameraman's light wouldn't bother me. So the atmosphere of the session was quite different from usual.

After the session—which went well in spite of the distractions—a female interviewer was clearly hoping I had had a sexual experience in the out-of-body state—along the lines of what Bob described in his book *Journeys Out of the Body*. In the out-of-body state, it appears, when two energy bodies merge there can be a tremendous energy charge that goes far beyond the energizing that occurs in physical orgasm. The interviewer thought that a story of out-of-body sex would be quite a hit with the television audience. As it turned out, I didn't have that kind of experience to report to her, though I did participate in a circle of love that was exhilarating.

When I saw a video of the television special I was fascinated to see what had happened to the energy they were measuring in my hand: the colors changed dramatically, and the glow around my fingers expanded considerably as I relaxed into the Focus 10 and 12 states. To illustrate me going out-of-body on the film, they used nude bodies floating into the air—the only suggestion of something sexual, and somewhat comical to see.

Now, come with me to the *love dimension* . . .

RAM: "ROMC is now in Focus 12 after building her energy balloon."

ROMC: "I've built the balloon and I'm floating up . . . I have the energy around me—and I feel as if I'm going to be taken through various parts of my own body.

"Wow, I'm in my own stomach! I'm rolling and floating around, and going up and down the sides of my stomach. I'm building a special energy in my stomach.

"Now I'm in my mouth, doing the same thing. What a big cave! I'm so small in here. My teeth look like big boulders.

"Now I'm in my ear. It's dark and hollow, with all kinds of fuzzy little hairs. I'm slipping and sliding around, and working to energize my ears.

"Now, I'm in my brain. I'm going to be building energy bubbles in different parts of my brain. I'm floating around in a brain cell in the right side of my brain. And now I am going to shift to the left side. I'm building up an energy circle inside some of the brain cells. Every area gets light and energized when I do.

"Now I'm in my heart. I can hear it beating. I'm floating around inside a large artery. The rhythm is really neat . . . *thump, thump, thump.*

"I'm going to go with the blood flow to different parts of my body—first, down the artery in my arm. I'm just floating along as though I'm on a river. I feel light and bouncy. As I travel, everything I touch is being energized. It's really great—like going from room to room in a fun house.

"Now I'm on my way down to my intestines. I'm winding through my intestines, energizing them as I go. I'm going down through both legs. Now I'm going through the center of my bones. I'm in the bone marrow. Gee—I have good, strong bones. It's like going down a slow elevator. I'm dropping down . . . down. I'm in my kneecap. I'm going to swirl around a bit to get it extra energized. I'm heading on down to my toes.

"Now my energy elevator is starting up. I feel very light—and clear and energized inside. Everything is glowing with a special energy. This is a very important method of reenergizing the whole body and cleaning out any physical blockages. But it cleanses and energizes more than the physical energy body—it also works on the energies of all the dimensions of the self.

"I'm starting to float out of my body. I feel light, energized, and very relaxed. I can turn around and bounce on this energized air. It's such a good feeling. Now I see my body from a distance. It's glowing, and I can see right through it. Everything is dark all around except my body, which is glowing in every cell. It's as if a light has been lit inside of me.

"I'm floating up to my platform. Now I'm landing on it. All of a sudden something is changing. I'm aware of the presence of my four Invisible Helpers. I'm shifting into a new phase of this experience.

"Someone is coming up behind me and putting a shimmering type of outfit on me. It's like a space suit. Now they're putting some kind of helmet over my head. I don't know what they're going to do with me. I'm starting to float again. The material in this suit is so very fine that I can't even feel it. It's so light that it makes me feel as if I'm disappearing. It's a different texture from anything I've ever felt.

"The suit has buttons on the front. The instructions indicate that these buttons are going to help me control what I'll be doing. I'm going to be escorted on another special journey.

This outfit will help take me into another dimension. It's a multidimensional suit. My helpers each have a suit on, also. They're standing on each corner of the platform.

"One is giving me instructions. I'm supposed to get very relaxed and push the first button on the suit. I'm going to be traveling faster than the speed of light. I'm to relax, go with the flow, and not worry how I get there.

"I'm supposed to push the top button, which is a golden-yellow button. Now I'm traveling somewhere. I feel enclosed in energy—and I'm speeding up. Now I'm arriving. Everything seems different: very bright and radiant, and shimmering gold. My four helpers no longer have their travel suits on. They've become very radiant. Perhaps this is the dimension they are from. I feel so good about myself just being around them. They have big smiles on their faces. I get the feeling that this is the golden level of love and happiness. I feel so confident in their presence.

"We're standing on a mountaintop. I'm to relax, explore, and enjoy a very special journey. This is a totally different dimension, a place where there are no cares or worries. It's completely beyond the earth. I'm supposed to walk with them as we explore together. They're going to show me around. There's a kind of road leading down from this mountain. Everyone and everything has a golden hue, even the road. It also vibrates, like living energy.

"A beautiful little animal is coming from the side of the road. It's very friendly—and has a glow of happiness just like the faces of my four helpers. It's sort of furry, like a little golden lion. It has such a beautiful smile on its face. It's not afraid, and I'm not afraid of it.

"It's licking my hand. Each time it licks I get a surge of energy through me, a special charge. It's letting me pet it. It's so full of warmth and love.

"So much warmth and love radiate from the atmosphere here—and there's a complete absence of fear. Now my friends have walked ahead and I must keep going. I'm picking up the little animal, since it seems to want me to carry it. Its love and warmth seem to radiate into my own body, and feels so nice.

"Now we're rounding a corner on our way down the mountain. What a breathtaking view. It's as if you can see forever into a timeless dimension. Everything is pulsating in a valley below, radiating different rays of color. This is so different from the earth. On earth we experience the feeling of complete love and relaxation sometimes; here it is constant.

"I hear sounds. They're coming from the colors as they pulsate—like visual sounds. I'm walking over to a tree to experience this more directly. The tree is green but is changing colors to gold, red—and now blue. Beautiful music is accompanying the changing colors. It's as if everything has its own music. The sounds go off into the atmosphere. They seem eternal and timeless, and go on and on . . . never dying. The tree has a consciousness that I feel and can communicate with. It's like everything else here, in that I experience warmth, joy, and love coming from it.

"My Invisible Helpers want me to get completely absorbed in this atmosphere. It's a strange feeling, because it seems as if there is no time here. With everything I experience, I just want to stay for eternity and not move. I feel I could just get lost in this atmosphere and never, ever have any needs. I feel completely absorbed in everything I'm doing. As I related to the tree, I felt I had become the tree and could feel each change that was taking place in it. I could feel the music and the life of the tree.

"My friends are telling me that this is what they want me to do—to get completely immersed in the consciousness of other levels here. They want me to become so fully involved that I can understand and know and experience other living consciousness as if it were my own. They're pointing out that it is the same as my consciousness.

"Even the road I'm walking on—it's so alive I want to sit down and become one with it. I can feel it pulsating. It's so welcoming! I just want to sit down by the tree and hold this little animal for eternity. This feels like eternity.

"Now I'm going to pick up some of the dust on the road to get the feel of it. It's very, very fine, and as I pick it up it goes through my fingers and sort of floats out into the atmosphere. It's like fine gold dust—not like earth dust. This has a vibrancy and energy that I can feel just holding it.

"The little animal in my arms is lapping up some of the dust with his tongue. I get the feeling that I should do this to let it go through my body so I can experience it inside. Wow! It's so energizing. I can feel it—and almost see it going through my body. It's as if I'm becoming part of the dust. It makes me feel light and shimmery. It's like tasting pure energy. I am becoming part of it, and it's becoming part of me—a feeling of absolute communion. I have become part of the road, and the road is part of me. But 'road' isn't the right word for it. It's too alive and vibrant.

"My friends are telling me that there is no hurry— that we are here for a purpose. They're teaching me to get completely attuned to life around me, that this is an important part of existence. They are radiating such patience and compassion. There's no feeling of having to go anywhere or do anything—since there's no time. I'm living in the here and now. The now is the only important part of existence, because there isn't anything else.

"Now we're sitting down in what looks like a type of grass. Gosh, it's soft and bouncy—and very fine. It's so hard to find words to describe this dimension because it goes beyond anything I've experienced on earth. It is also so alive, with its own consciousness. How refreshing it feels. And fun! I'm letting my little animal go because it wants to bounce around on the grass, too. Now I'm lying down and rolling. It's so energizing.

"Now my friends are sitting in a circle and I'm getting the message that we will sit in absolute silence and allow ourselves to be absorbed in the experience of being—and of being together. I'm already getting absorbed into their presence and consciousness. And we can read each other's thoughts.

"The energy is moving rapidly around the circle. My friends are such loving beings. It's hard to tell whether they are male or female. But it doesn't seem to matter. They seem to be a combination of both. They are integrated beings, on a level higher than we humans.

"I'm picking up various feelings from them. We're radiating joy around the circle—pure joy. It's the joy of just being . . . the joy of existence . . . the joy of being in the presence of love—the joy of *being love*. The joy of being in timelessness.

"Now I'm feeling pure relaxation, and I'm getting the feeling of being completely myself—like being so much myself that I feel I'm everything and everyone. This is an experience of being. They are helping me turn in to see myself. Being in their presence I feel complete acceptance of myself and absolute joy for being.

"I'm feeling a timeless joy of self-acceptance. I feel a reverence for this self that is a part of all consciousness. Everyone and everything is a part of me, and I am a part of them. It's the consciousness of pure love. And this helps me to see myself more completely. There is absolutely no fear and no doubt.

"One of my friends is sending a thought to me—that before a person can really do anything, he or she must know and experience the absolute importance of his or her own existence. One must have total and complete love for self before one can know and experience love for another. Love is energy. We must experience the miracle of living, loving, being, and becoming. We must see and accept this within ourselves.

"This is the very basis of the training they are putting me through. This love, with no fear and no criticism, starts from within and radiates out into levels of others' consciousness. Whenever I feel a need to be in this level of consciousness, I am to push my golden love button right at my heart level. Whenever I feel doubt, hate, or fear creeping in, I'm to push this golden button, and it will immediately shift me into the level of consciousness where negative emotions are transformed into a higher energy. In turn it will reach out to others with whom I come in contact.

"They are telling me that once I've experienced this level of love, I can always go back to it instantly when I want to. Anyone who comes in contact with this concept can absorb it, release it, and tune into it again whenever needed. They're saying that there is no time, even on the earth level. We perceive time, but actually there is no time, so we can be outside of time in this pure golden level of love at any 'time' we perceive it to be so.

"My lessons have been learned for the day. They took me through the experience to learn in every cell of my body. What an experience it has been!

"Now I must say good-bye to my friends for the time being. But they say that there is no such thing as good-bye, since we are always together in this level of consciousness. I must go back into the time zone. They are all reaching out and touching me. It feels so good. It's like a wonderful hug. Now my little animal friend is giving me a lick on the hand.

"Suddenly I have my travel suit on again. I'm starting to float. They told me to push the next button, which returns me to my regular state of consciousness. I feel myself coming back, swirling through space, and shifting consciousness.

"I'm back on my platform. (pause) I'm ready to come back."

RAM: "How do you feel?"

ROMC: "Very good, and relaxed. My feet are tingling."

~13~

CONTROL: THE FOODS YOU EAT

It never occurred to me that my Invisible Helpers would reprimand me or Bob. They always worked with us so patiently, taking time to work with any situations—often physical—that might stand in the way of our having productive sessions.

Perhaps they followed us up Afton Mountain for our Howard Johnson specials after our sessions! If so, we were in trouble. I could blame our good friend, George Durrette, for the many goodies he would ask us to sample from the kitchen. But Bob succeeded in convincing George to work full-time with him as his farm manager shortly after we started our Explorer sessions. So I can't blame George.

When Bob moved his operation from Whistlefield Farm to the 600 acres of New Land, George took on more extensive duties. In fact, George should be called Bob's "dream manager," since he was the main factor that helped Bob's dreams in his new location become a reality. Bob would have an idea, such as building a fence in a certain spot, and George would manifest it. But sometimes George would have to unmanifest it until Bob decided for sure what he wanted. In fact George was so patient with Bob's somewhat flexible energies that he should really be called Saint George.

George has been with Bob longer than any other associate, and still remains at the Institute helping to keep the physical realities of the New Land intact. I've always felt that George was the cement that has held the Institute together all these years. He is somewhat like my Invisible Helpers: always there, but not seeking recognition for his many accomplishments. Bob, of course, recognized George's commitment to his work—and one day threw a very special surprise thank-you party to express appreciation for his invaluable contribution to the Institute's success. I want to thank George, too. If not for Saint George, our sessions wouldn't have run nearly as smoothly. George was even there to help recharge our car batteries when we parked too close to CHEC Unit 2 during a high-energy session. Thanks, George!

The day Bob and I were reprimanded by our Invisible Friends came two weeks after the beginning of the year. Maybe they waited two weeks after New Year's Day, hoping we might eventually make some resolutions! But we didn't—and with this result:

ROMC: "I'm lying here trying to figure out what is going on. The new sound that you have, Bob, I think is affecting me differently. I feel nothing happening. However, I heard a voice that said, 'Unless you are really willing to work with us on some serious disciplines, we are going to have to withdraw from working with you."

RAM: "Ask them what they mean."

ROMC: "I hear the words, 'We are trying to get across the point that you must get into the right balance within your systems. With the right energy balance, you can be in contact with other dimensions at any time. There are many dimensions around and within; it is a matter of being in the right state of consciousness to come into the proper communication with them. The goal should be to keep the channels open at all times, to be in constant communication. Certain things cut off communication. One is cutting off the vital energies that help produce the right state of consciousness.

"'The message that we want to get across to both of you is that, if you take this work seriously, you should be willing to work carefully with your own vehicles and your own energy systems by following disciplines. You must follow the disciplines that you know within yourselves are the important ones to help accomplish the work that is to be done. It is important to set an example to yourselves, as much as to anyone else. It is not important to be concerned about what others think; it is important to be in control of, and to be respectful of, your own decision-making process.'"

RAM: "Yes, we have been remiss in not understanding this. We will certainly attempt to change the pattern."

ROMC: "'It can be done in a slow process. You will find that the body has its habits as well. The body is a separate being in and of itself. It gets used to certain habits and types of food, which makes change difficult. When you give up things that you have taken into your system for many years, cravings will occur. To switch habits creates a withdrawal that is not easy for your bodies.

"'It is important to take on one main discipline at a time, and to stick to it. Do not take on more disciplines than you can achieve. You will overload your system in trying to put too many changes upon it at once.'"

RAM: "Is there one critical food that is most detrimental to our systems?"

ROMC: "'The problem is with the amount of food that is taken in. Also, the important foods to eat are the natural foods—foods that have not been tampered with by humans. Artificial ingredients that enhance a food's taste and appearance are detrimental to the energy system.

"'Many of the diseases that are a part of the modern life on the earth come through the foods that have artificial, man-made ingredients. What happens is that the energy balance in the food is thrown off, and important vitamins are often destroyed. The artificial ingredients, in turn, throw the energy balance off within the body. Many people in societies such as yours, where there is plenty, are victims of vitamin deprivation and starvation, even though there is plenty to eat. The body becomes starved for its natural sources of energy; if it is not satisfied, disease sets in. Disease occurs when the body gets out of balance. The mind and emotions also have a great deal to do with the energy imbalance and disease.

"'An important rule to follow is to seek the natural flow of energies—natural foods, your own natural flow of energies, your own natural thoughts. Stay away from the artificial—that which is not in tune with your energies—food-wise and thought-wise. This also includes humans. Do not let artificial humans have control over your life. Anything that is artificial is not in touch with its own energies.'"

RAM: "What foods are especially good for the system?"

ROMC: "'Fresh juices are excellent for the system. It is good to cleanse the system with fresh juices. Citrus juices are especially helpful to the body. The body can receive natural sugar through all types of fruits.

"'In your society, dyes and sprays are put on the fruits; therefore, it is important to cleanse carefully everything that you eat. It is preferable to eat foods that have not been dyed or sprayed. If this is not possible, careful cleansing is important.

"'Back to the amount of food taken into the system: Those who tend to eat from an emotional level often take foods into the body to overcompensate for emotional deprivation. This is detrimental to the body. One must eat from a mental level, having control over the food that is taken in. When the emotions are in control, then the body is often abused.

"'The body will crave the kinds of foods it is used to. When it is cleansed of the wrong food vibrations, it craves only the live foods. This is why it is important to put the body through cleansing periods called fasting, so that the body can get in touch with its own energies.

"'We stress fruits and vegetables because they have most of what the body needs for proper energy. It is important to get in tune with the foods that you eat, as well as foods being in tune with you. When you eat the natural foods, you are eating live foods. Live foods are foods that have the vital life energy source still in them. The live elements in each cell in the body crave the live elements in natural foods. It is the like-attracts-like principle. When the consciousness levels of the self become stagnant or dead, so to speak, they attract *dead* foods. When the self is vibrantly alive, it attracts the *alive* foods. When humans are really in tune with themselves, they will get the most mileage out of their systems.'"

RAM: "Other than citrus fruits, is there any other food that can cleanse us with some rapidity?"

ROMC: "'Eating green, leafy vegetables is another good form of cleansing. Also, the yellow vegetables are good for cleansing. You will find that all live vegetables have a purifying effect upon the body; the more of the live vegetables and fruits that you eat, the better.

"'However, do know that there are combinations of these live foods that can create an imbalance. One rule is not to mix fruits and vegetables at the same period of eating. It is important not to overload the system with large amounts of meat products. Some systems cannot handle meat products. And some systems do not need meat products. But there is no system that should have a large amount of meat products, for they can affect the digestive system in an adverse manner.

"'Meat products are heavier in vibration and put a great load on the digestive system. People who overload the system with meats will have more energy problems, because the body is spending most of its energy digesting these products. Meat energies take away from the bodily energies. But the live foods, being lighter in vibration, do not put a great strain on the digestive system—therefore giving the body more energy for external functioning.'"

RAM: "Would you say, then, that it is important to raise as many of your own foods as you can, so that you know exactly what goes into them?"

ROMC: "'Yes. Remember that everything has vibrations. Everyone that handles a product leaves a vibration on it. Therefore, you are getting mixed vibrations into your system when you eat foods that go through many human processes. Even the seeds you purchase for raising your own foods are usually touched by human hands, so you need to cleanse and bless them with loving thoughts.

"'So you see why the emphasis is on what is natural. The many mixed vibrations, including unnatural ingredients, can have an adverse effect on your physical, mental, and emotional energies.

"'I do want to say that the meats also have a variety of different vibrations. Animals of the lower earth vibrations, directly connected to the earth, would have the slower-vibratory levels. Those humans of the lower earth vibrations are strongly attracted to the flesh of the earth-associated animals. Again, this is the like-attracts-like principle. Those who load their systems heavily with red meat, pork, and other meat of earth-associated animals, those whose feet directly connect to the earth, are vibrating very strongly in the lower levels of their earth-consciousness.

"'The vibrations of fish and fowl are of a higher source of energy. Those who are attracted to the higher-vibratory animals are functioning on a different energy rate within their systems.'"

RAM: "You say that one is attracted to the certain types of meat products because of the consciousness level on which they are functioning internally. Could a person change his or her vibrations by dropping the red meats and eating only the higher-vibratory foods?"

ROMC: "'Yes, that is certainly possible. If you keep the lower-vibratory animal foods within you, which are also heavily laden with the emotional levels of these animals, it will be more difficult for your energy levels to shift into the finer vibratory levels. If one purposely drops the earth meats and goes to the higher-vibratory levels of fish and fowl, this helps in the facilitation of energy changes within the system. There are those who prefer to drop meats altogether. When they get into the absolute flow of their own systems, they are able to lose the dependence on outside sources of meat products. In following the flow of their own systems, they follow their inner guidance on the proper foods for the proper internal balance of energies.

"'Remember that the life force within the foods you eat responds to the life force within you. If your system is locked into itself with a dead response to its own energy balance, you will be attracted to dead foods, which are made up of artificial energies. If you are alive to the rhythm of your own existence and want to live more fully in the flow from within, you will be attracted to the live foods. It is possible to change your energy vibrations by consciously working on filling the system with live foods of a higher vibration.

"'You can build an interrelationship with the flow of energies in the plants you raise. This is what must take place as we shift into the new levels of consciousness. Many souls are becoming aware of this.'"

RAM: "Thank you very much. Is there any method that we can employ to remove such destructive vibrations that are in things like clothes?"

ROMC: "'Yes, with everything that you receive, put a blessing of thanks upon it. Be thankful for every bit of food that you put into your mouth. The live elements within foods are in touch with the consciousness of thanksgiving. Do everything with appreciation and thanksgiving. This puts a new level of vibration upon everything that you take onto yourself. This attitude of praise and thanksgiving has a cleansing element about it. This attitude will also help everything that you take onto yourself have a stronger return in value.

"'This same thought of cleansing and thanksgiving should take place with the clothes that you put on your body. Bless everything that you put on your body and ask that any negative vibrations be removed that might have been put there before they came into your possession. Also bless all the hands that were responsible for supplying you with bounty. These good vibrations will in turn flow back to the source from which the bounty came, and souls are always appreciative of blessings.'"

RAM: "Well, we certainly thank you for sharing these important thoughts on the foods that we eat. Thank you very much for coming."

ROMC: "'It is always our privilege.'"

*To Use Such Greater Energies
and Energy Systems . . .*

14

GREATER ENERGIES AND ENERGY SYSTEMS

ROMC: "I felt as if I was going into a dream state. A lot was going through my mind. Then all of a sudden I saw the face of a man very clearly—with a beam coming from the center of his forehead toward me. I think it means that it's time to receive the thoughts."

RAM: "Very good."

ROMC: "I'll see what comes next. I'm getting a picture of everything that's going to be discussed. It's coming into my mind. I must say what I'm getting because the voice I'm hearing builds up energy as I talk. It helps the energy flow of the vibrations that are sent.

"They say that the vibrations are sent in forms of energy, and I pick up these energy forms as they enter into my own mental system. Then the forms are transposed into my own level of communication and thought. It's at this point that the communication can be misconstrued as it comes into the earth level.

"The incoming information goes through various energy systems. When the channels are clear, the energy is stronger and the communication comes through in a purer form; however, there is never a completely pure form of communication.

"We spoke before of the energy systems within the human body: physical, etheric-substance, emotional, mental, and spiritual. There are many dimensions of these five systems. Within each system are many levels and dimensions. It's difficult to describe these in earth terms.

"Now we want to point out that within the earth itself, similar energy systems are in operation.

"There is a balancing point between time and timelessness right in the middle of the five levels. The first two and a half levels are those that can be experienced through the physical, and the other two and a half are those that go beyond the five senses.

"Now within each energy system there are many energies at work. Those humans who function in the higher levels can experience the higher levels of the earth energy systems. They can tune into the nature forces and many levels of light beings that work with the earth dimensions.

"The fourth dimension is a vibration that is more highly evolved. This system is in tune with all the energies beyond the physical universe.

"The fifth dimension is the highest vibration in the earth system. There are few on the earth plane who are released into this state within their own being.

"However, because of the makeup of the human system, there are many beings who can have brief experiences of the various energy levels and dimensions. They come as intuitive flashes of understanding.

"Now we want to step into an inner dimension and describe the interrelationship of this dimension with certain energy levels beyond the earth plane.

"We want to discuss the relationship to what are called 'unidentified objects' in the earth terms. These can be perceived by beings on the earth plane on different levels of perception.

"Some of these energy systems from beyond the earth come into the earth plane on the first and second dimensions of energy. Most humans perceive them, because they are within the vibration of the five senses.

"But the outer energy systems come into the earth plane from all dimensions or vibrations. When they come in from the higher half of the third emotional level or beyond, many in human form cannot perceive them because they are outside the physical realm of vibration.

"The highly evolved energy forms from beyond are capable of changing their frequency. They can be seen at the first or second levels, and then change their vibrations to higher levels and become invisible to the human perception.

"There are some in human form who have experienced being taken on board and do not remember, because their memory banks have been erased from the conscious level. When this takes place, the alien vessel is functioning on the earth level of vibration. Otherwise, the human body could not be taken into the higher-vibratory energies, because it is not interrelated with the earth-body vibration.

"The higher energy forms' reason for vibrating into the earth dimension is to get a closer look and better understanding of the levels on which the human consciousness is operating. They are learning a great deal about the energies of humans on planet Earth. Their main purpose is to learn how they will be able to work on a conscious level with beings of planet Earth's consciousness.

"They work in many ways with the earth-consciousness. They send out mental vibration thought-forms to humans on the earth plane who are highly enough evolved to pick up the communication. There are many in the earth plane who are receiving these communications. Many do not understand what is happening, and many do. There are many who just disregard the communication. A small percentage of beings are picking up the communication and are aware of its purpose. Continuous waves are sent out toward the earth. Those who are ready to pick up the communication will do so.

"Understanding is the second important step. Once humans begin to pick up this wavelength from other energy systems, and have a higher understanding of the purpose, they will be able to work on a more conscious physical level with the earth plane. In other words, when the consciousness of the earth level is at a higher vibration, it will be ready for direct contact with this higher communication.

"This type of communication has been taking place since the conception of planet Earth. Planet Earth is now coming into a new level of energies. When enough humans are in the higher consciousness, the conscious communication with the higher energy forms will take place.

"On the first two and a half levels of consciousness, where the earth is functioning now, there is so much fear that direct communication would not be possible. The first two and a half levels are in the time/earth consciousness where fear is very prevalent. The higher levels are the opening-up, love-acceptance stages. The earth-consciousness is just beginning to come into this level. It is not there yet.

"Many higher-vibration souls from other dimensions are inhabiting human bodies in the earth plane to help in the opening up of the consciousness of the earth level. It will be observed that many youth around planet Earth will possess higher energy levels than the norm.

"Just as you have to lead a small child through levels of knowledge as it grows, so it is with the earth level, which is still in its puberty state. It has not been ready for the higher knowledge, but it is being prepared. If direct communication took place, there would be so much fear and panic that more harm than good would occur, because planet Earth is not ready. The groundwork has to be laid very carefully.

"Much energy is being directed to the earth from all dimensions of higher-energy levels, preparing it for its shift into higher consciousness. This will be a turning point in the growth of planet Earth."

RAM: "Why is this turning point to take place?"

ROMC: "This is part of the evolution of earth. Just as a baby grows physically, mentally, and emotionally through its stages of life, the earth also goes through these stages. All who are on the earth plane at different levels of the earth growth are there for specific reasons of growth. There are no mistakes in the universe. Everything happens for a reason. It is happening as part of the natural growth process of consciousness. The earth is merely a child in the large cosmos of energies."

RAM: "How can we help souls move into this third dimension, this third level of energy?"

ROMC: "There are many ways. But the first, most important step is that each soul must function more fully from its own inner space. This brings greater balance within the system of growth. The energies become more integrated and less influenced by outer energies. As the energy polar systems within the self come into greater balance, they begin to shift into higher levels of vibration. When the systems are not balanced, they are constantly working against themselves.

"The work you are doing is helping souls get into a deeper understanding of their own existence. This is very important.

"We say that it is important to follow your highest inner self, which is guiding you. As you do, you are given the tools that lead you into higher-vibratory living. All beings have within them the same basic system of knowledge and the same basic system of energy.

"However, all beings are different because of the combinations of the flow of these energies. So it is important that each being follow its own force-field. You follow that within, which is that which you are. As you get into the flow of your own being, you grow into levels of higher consciousness."

RAM: "In terms of these levels of communication and levels of energy, at what level is this communication taking place right now?"

ROMC: "This communication is taking place between the lower and higher third level, which is the balancing point of the five levels or dimensions. The lower energies are still in touch with the earth energies, and the higher energies are moving into the finer vibratory energies. It is necessary to start at this balancing point of energy, for communication with the earth plane.

"Once the balancing of the initial communication takes place, then we can move into the higher energies of this being. We cannot send through higher energies or use higher energies than this system is able to accept. We cannot overload the circuit or we would blow it out. Every system has its built-in circuit breakers.

"As the channels are opened up, we are able to work in the higher energies. With this system, now we are able to work freely in levels three and four, because the energy channels have been cleared and the vibrations are more speeded up. This is why we do cleansing and raising of the vibrations before most sessions. We come to the center—the two and a half level—of the five dimensions, and as the energies speed up, we work in the higher dimensions. When we get into higher levels of dimension four, there is usually no conscious remembrance on the part of the energy channel.

"Now many are probably wondering how it is possible for this entity to communicate when she is functioning at these higher levels. We have said that the voice vibrations are important in keeping the energy flowing. Therefore, the vocal communication is contributing a great deal in the whole process. It is helping to generate and facilitate the flow into the higher vibrations. The vocal cords and the lower mind can function freely while the higher mental energies are at work in other dimensions. The human system is quite astounding, and many levels are always at work at once."

RAM: "Yes, indeed. I appreciate very much the care and concern that you have. Are we able to understand the source of where you are before you make this transposition at the balancing point? What dimension are you on as a source?"

ROMC: "We are working from the nonphysical dimension of time. We are outside the earth vibration, and therefore would be invisible, in the sense of being in a higher vibratory rate. At the same time, we are a dimension of the higher level of this being."

RAM: "Do you exist at level three, four, or five—or beyond that?"

ROMC: "As we have said before, the levels from one to five are a part of the earth-consciousness. There are many levels beyond that, of which we cannot speak, because they are outside the energy perception of the human system.

"We are able to work in the energies of the human system because we are on a higher vibration and can slow our vibrations to get into these lower energies. We exist beyond level five of the earth-consciousness. We are a level of energy, and we are a system. We are connected with the consciousness of earth for various reasons. But we are not of these dimensions.

"When a being of the earth-consciousness is released from its physical form, which means that it no longer exists in—or will no longer be tied into—earth energies, then it moves into a different energy dimension that goes beyond levels one to five. We are not of human consciousness, and we are released into those dimensions that go beyond. We are working to help raise the consciousness of planet Earth and its inhabitants."

RAM: "Is it possible for any of us in this physical reality to temporarily visit your dimension?"

ROMC: "This is always possible when the soul is able to work in levels outside of time. The first two and a half levels are in time, and the second two and a half reach into the timeless dimension.

"When the energies are balanced within, much work takes place—especially in the sleep state. If the body is imbalanced, most energy is used in just balancing the internal aspects of the consciousness. When the bodily energies become balanced, and use less time during the sleep state to readjust the balance or the internal energy structures, then the person is able to work in the higher energies.

"Many are aware of these experiences when they awaken in the morning. Some of the experiences are so intense that they are beyond the conscious memory. These experiences help to raise the consciousness of the individual.

"There is a regeneration level of all energy systems that helps to keep balance in the body. This regeneration takes place mostly during the sleep state. The energy balance which takes place during the sleeping state helps the individual find more balance during the waking state. The majority of souls on the earth level go into their higher energy system during this period of regeneration.

"As we have said, they usually cannot recollect these experiences in the memory system because they are not understood or recorded in the earth plane. However, when the individual begins to recollect these experiences, then the soul is rising into a higher balance within its own system of perception.

"Therefore, the sleep state is very important in the earth-consciousness because it is then that the body, mind, emotions, and spirit go through a regeneration. It is like a generator recharging the energy system.

"All energy dimensions of the human self are working their way into balance during the sleep state. This includes the physical, etheric, emotional, mental, and spiritual. Those individuals who are living more in the energy levels of the first two and a half dimensions are more closely connected to the earth/time dimension, and their dreams will be much more on a functional level.

"When their lower energies are balanced temporarily, they can go into the higher levels, but rarely remember them. They mainly remember the dreams that are more earth-oriented, which is a working out of emotional and mental blocks or a balancing of energies in these lower-vibratory levels.

"Those individuals who function on a higher-energy level will have higher-energy dreams, which the individual would interpret as more real than the conscious state. You call this 'lucid' dreaming. It is more real because it is the reality levels of the higher consciousness. Most individuals will have an experience of this type of dream when all systems are balanced and they are freed to go into their higher, timeless dimensions. Individuals who exist in the higher levels of their consciousness will have many dreams of this nature.

"Let us say that children in the earth plane will have dreams related to the earth-consciousness. Infant babies sleep and dream a great deal in the first months of their earth existence to get their energies integrated and balanced into the earth-consciousness. Many of their dreams are of animals and earth objects.

"As their consciousness is opening up in the earth level, they are working their way through their own inner levels of consciousness and are mainly in the lower two earth/time dimensions in the early stages of their existence. This is just a working-out of the earth-level energies through their systems."

RAM: "Then, it is possible for one—with practice—to move temporarily to your level while still connected to the physical body?"

ROMC: "When the soul begins to travel into the timeless dimension, it is possible to come into the dimensions from whence this communication is taking place."

RAM: "Thank you so much for this. It is very interesting and very stimulating—and of course poses more questions that need answers."

ROMC: "This is certainly understandable. That is why we like to reveal this knowledge that all beings know. It is a matter of opening it out. The questions that come from within your own system are important, and as they arise they will be answered in one way or another. 'Ask and you shall receive.'

"As the question comes into your consciousness, it is opening up a level where the answer will be known and understood. Either it will come from within, which is the best way, or you will receive the answer from another source.

"Once the thought is out, the energy is there and the answer will come. It is important for the individual to be patient and not put his or her own expectations on how and when the answer will come. Following the flow is the most important thing. This will lead one into the answer."

RAM: "You spoke earlier of humans being taken onto ships from other dimensions and having their memories erased. Has this happened to any in our group?"

ROMC: "This has not happened to any of your group."

RAM: "Thank you. That clarifies a point for us."

ROMC: "There are physical necessities now, and we must step out of this communication process and turn it off."

RAM: "Thank you so much for coming."

ROMC: "It is a privilege to send through the energy, and to help open out new levels and dimensions of thought on the earth plane."

RAM: "Thank you for your love and concern for us."

15

OUT-OF-BODY ENERGIES

When I was in my mid-twenties, one night as I was just going off to sleep I had a strong feeling that someone was standing over me and watching me. I quickly opened my eyes and there in front of me, beside the bed, was the beautiful form of a lady in a shimmering blue, flowing gown. I noticed as we looked at each other that she had a wonderful glow about her. Then she gently floated away and disappeared.

I was so startled by this experience that I couldn't go back to sleep. I lay there thinking and wondering, recalling the beautiful woman in my mind. As I reflected on the incident, I could come up with only one thought: I was somehow looking at myself. When I awoke the next morning my mother came into my room. I told her about the experience as she listened intently. I concluded by saying, "Mom, I have a feeling that I was looking at myself—and that a part of myself was looking at me."

However, I couldn't figure out how this could be, since I had no understanding of the higher, unseen dimensions of life. I suppose my Invisible Helpers would say that I was in an "unknowing" stage at the time.

Recently, after reviewing the following session, I began to understand how I could have been looking at myself. I feel that my nonphysical body was simply moving out of my physical body. As it did, it woke me—and we looked at each other! My nonphysical self was absolutely beautiful, and I now realize how magnificent we all are in our real selves. When I recall the incident, I still have a warm and wonderful feeling.

Let me share now what my Invisible Helpers taught me and Bob one day about this out-of-body capability of our several selves.

ROMC: "I am receiving guidance that you are to ask questions again today."

RAM: "Okay. Thank you. I would like to ask about the death process. Can they tell us more about the meaning of death?"

ROMC: "There is great joy in this dimension when a new soul is born. It is very similar to the birth process on the earth level. When the soul graduates into this dimension, having come through the more dense level of the earth, there is great rejoicing and celebration. Now the soul is released into the highest level of vibration it was in when it dropped its physical form.

"The grief process on the earth plane of those who experience the loss of their loved one is an important stage to go through, because it is a way of releasing the emotional energies that are tied in with the energies of the soul who has made the transition. These ties are so strong that they often can affect the soul who has passed into its finer energy forms. Such strong thoughts from the earth level often slow down the transition process. When the grief process has passed, the soul in transition is more free to continue its journey into new levels of its own being.

"Souls are in different states when they pass into their new energy forms. When a soul passes through rapidly, or has had an extended period of illness in which all of the energy levels have been depleted, it sometimes takes longer for the energies to become adjusted in the higher vibratory rate in this dimension.

"In the earth level you think of death in terms of time. But from the timeless dimension, death is merely a change in the rate of vibration in its movement into a new existence. For many who come over temporarily, and experience a movement through a tunnel and see the light at the other end, this is merely a change in the rate of vibration within the self. It is experienced as movement through space, but it is really movement through the vibrations of the inner self into higher vibrations, and therefore higher light-levels of energy.

"When there is a shift from the physical realm into the more etheric levels of existence, the vibrations change within the soul-self, and begin to function on the highest level of existence previously experienced by that soul. Souls who have lived freely in the flow of their own existence are not hindered by emotional or mental thought-forms that can confine or hold them down in the more dense earth-level vibrations. The heavy earth vibrations are often experienced as great darkness and isolation, mixed with various negative emotions—which can include pain, hatred, fear, and selfishness.

"The change in vibration gives the soul the feeling of movement. However, in the timeless dimension there is no time or space; thus, there is no actual movement, as in the time level. When an individual soul has the experience of going out of the body, it is felt as movement through space. But a true out-of-body experience is not movement through space; it is a change in the vibration from the denser physical self to the higher-vibratory levels of the etheric self. I think that you can understand this process. Is this not so?"

RAM: "Yes, I understand. I have discovered this of my own accord. Indeed, it is a change of vibration."

ROMC: "It is good for you to make this clear to those who think in terms of traveling out-of-body. It is important to understand that at any time in the earth existence they can go into dimensions of their own being without dropping the physical body. The experience of the soul is that of movement, and can be described as 'going through a tunnel'—as this entity has experienced. But it is movement of the molecules of the level of consciousness of the being experiencing it.

"During the process of transition from the physical world into the level of higher energies, there is a period during the first part of the experience that relates to the earth/time reality. However, the soul is merely allowing its vibrations to adjust in the new dimension. Therefore, from the earth level it would seem that this takes a period of time. But it is a matter of each soul adjusting to its own level and rate of vibration. As indicated, once the body is dropped, a soul will be on the highest level on which it was functioning in the earth existence.

"During the periods of living in the physical body there is a spectrum within the consciousness on which the soul functions. It is like a spotlight shining upon one area. That area is illuminated and experienced—but this does not mean that other areas around it do not exist. In fact, the areas around and beyond the spotlight have limitless possibilities and dimensions. The spotlight can be adjusted to light up more and more areas. And it can move around to pick up different perspectives.

"This relates to the concept of different lifetimes in the earth dimension. One simply experiences different aspects of one's own being from new perspectives. These are all aspects that exist on a timeless level but are experienced in different ways, for different reasons. The spotlight can change color as it moves around. Different aspects of the self are experienced in the time dimension for different types of growth But the whole spectrum is always there; different parts are merely spotlighted and perceived on the consciousness level in various time slots.

"This means that all souls are living in all lifetimes in the timeless dimension, but are experiencing them from the time perspective as if they were happening one at a time. The whole spectrum of the self exists in the timeless dimension, while various aspects of the energy levels are experienced in the time dimension for reasons of growth and perception. Multiple personalities can surface simultaneously during an earth-life experience when undue stress is put upon an individual. This is how some souls cope with the earth experience. They send in their 'navy.' But it does create inner conflict and controversy as to who is running the ship. Much confusion can arise, and help is often needed to refocus and thus reintegrate the personality.

"Do you have any questions at this point?"

RAM: "Many people have had out-of-body experiences, as I have. But there is still much we don't understand about what is happening. Can you give us more detail about the out-of-body experience?"

ROMC: "As you know, we have spoken of the five bodies of the human self—physical, etheric-substance, emotional, mental, and spiritual. People go out-of-body at different dimensions of these five bodies.

"When the soul has the out-of-body experience where it can look down or back and view its physical body and then explore in the physical or astral realms of consciousness, it is functioning from the second dimension of self, called etheric substance. When the soul functions on this level, there is usually strong sexual energy flowing. It often works to facilitate the separation of the etheric-substance body and all dimensions of self above it into a flow or pattern whereby the self experiences itself separated from self.

"Even though the self experiences itself to be in movement or out-of-body, it is actually functioning in higher-vibratory levels within the physical body. I say 'within,' because in reality there is only within. In fact, life is not spatial, but dimensional. In reality there is neither time nor space. All that is perceived to be 'without' is not of the real universe. But I will use terms indicating movement because this is how souls in the physical realm experience and can conceive of this energy pattern.

"From this base, most of the soul's exploration is in the astral level. Often it will encounter strong energies of a lower vibration. In many cases these are aspects of the self. In some cases they are encounters with beings locked into the etheric-substance or astral level, which is a lower vibration of earth-consciousness and closely associated with the energies of the earth.

"In this second dimension of self, the experiences are more vivid and real from the standpoint of being more closely tied to the earth energies, and therefore more related to the consciousness of the soul having the experience.

"Often this dimensional state is associated with exploration of the physical level on the earth plane itself. Many souls will be attracted to loved ones, or to places where they have existed in past lives, just to get reenergized—to 'check in,' so to speak. In this dimension of travel, the soul is often recognized when it is out prowling around. The physical beings that recognize these souls perceive them as ghosts or apparitions.

"The next level of separation is the third dimension *of self*, which is the emotional level. Souls that separate at this level leave both their physical and etheric bodies behind. Therefore they are a finer substance, and usually are traveling on emotional thought-forms. In this dimension physical experiences are not as vivid, but the emotional levels are stimulated.

"Thus when a person has had a strong third-dimensional experience, the emotions of the experiences are often much more prevalent than the visual images. Here, the soul will come into contact with many with whom it has been strongly tied through many energy levels of lifetimes. Such souls will also experience direct confrontations or meetings with loved ones.

"In this emotional level, one often has powerful experiences of reliving strong energies from a past lifetime upon the earth—that is, from a thought-form embedded in this emotional body. These experiences will be so vivid in the emotional level that the soul knows that it has been there, wherever 'there' might be. However, 'there' is usually outside the time-bounds of the earth level.

"Remember that when the soul separates from self at the third level it takes with it all the selves beyond that, leaving the physical and etheric bodies in quiet relaxation. The energy tie is always there, but the first two dimensions of the self are not actively functioning.

"Let me say here that there is always the fear that a wandering soul will take over the physical body when the higher aspects of the self are wandering through other levels. The greatest possibility of this is when the soul goes out from dimension two and leaves the physical body in isolation. There are no other levels than the physical there to provide protection, and the body is more susceptible to invasion. Thus, for those aware of this type of second-dimensional travel, it is important to call in all known energies for protection. This could be an affirmation of protection, or the calling in of soul or spirit guides to watch over the body.

"It is also possible to put strong energy barriers around the body to keep out foreign energy levels. There are many souls that are 'dead,' so to speak, that are still attached to the lower physical realm and seek shelter in any pattern that has any type of opening for entry. There is more protection when the soul travels out at dimension three because its etheric body is left behind with the physical. This automatically leaves a stronger energy force in the energy systems that are isolated from the other levels of the self.

"When the soul separates at level four—the mental level, or the fourth dimension of self—it is separating at a higher level of its vibration, leaving the emotional, etheric, and physical in isolation with the self. Traveling at the mental level is an experience of complete separation from the physical self. At this level, the self experiences many energy systems beyond itself. It travels in timeless dimensions, because it is based in the higher levels of the timeless self. There are no barriers.

"I might say that in dimension two of the strong physical and etheric levels, there is often much fear involved, mainly because fear is characteristic of these levels of vibration. It is often difficult for souls to get beyond this fear barrier—which usually folds back into its bodily dimension.

"But on the emotional and the mental levels, there is no lasting fear. Fear is sometimes felt when the soul begins the experience, because it is traveling through some of the fear levels of the emotional self. Once these are overcome, the self is free to explore many areas of timeless reality. Often the experiences do not seem as vivid, but rather more distant. They feel distant and less distinct because they come from higher levels of the self, levels that are not often encountered in everyday existence.

"Usually it is difficult to bring these experiences back into everyday reality, and sometimes they fade away just as a dream would when the consciousness level of the soul changes. However, the individual who travels frequently in its fourth dimension of mental perception can practice techniques for remembering. It is important for one to program the self to bring these experiences back into normal consciousness whenever desired.

"In this level, there is very little possibility of invasion by lower energy forces, because three of the energy bodies are integrated and left behind. Therefore, there is much more protection in this state of consciousness. But it is still important to use an affirmation, or energy protection.

"Those adept at this level of travel are functioning more fully in the timeless dimensions. It is not to say that they can't have the two- and three-dimensional experiences. They can if they choose. But they find more freedom in this state. It is like leaving some of the unneeded baggage behind for a less burdensome trip.

"Travel in the fifth dimension of self, or the spiritual dimension, is rare from the earth perspective because of the physical ties of the self to the earth level. This level gives the explanation for bi-location, or being seen at two places at once. The self has control of all the bodily dimensions below the fifth level, and can be in more than one place at once.

"Very highly evolved souls have worked freely in this dimension. And as I said earlier, they can take their physical bodies in and out of the physical realm of existence if they so desire. The laws of the higher vibrations override the lower physical laws. The fifth level is the highest level of vibration from earth standards.

"This is how Jesus, the Christ, the highest vibratory being who lived on earth, could appear and disappear at will before and even after he was crucified. His body disappeared from the tomb because his fifth-dimensional self was in control. He functioned from his highest vibratory level.

"I want to say here that the five dimensions of the self that we refer to are dimensions of the self related to the earth-consciousness. There are other levels that we will not go into because they are not related to the earth-consciousness and would not be understood in earth terms. To be able to comprehend and conceive of what has already been shared will be enough to stretch the minds of the souls of the many who will come into contact with the vibrations of this information."

RAM: "We here at the Institute believe that most people have out-of-body experiences while they sleep. Earlier, you seemed to indicate that this is true. Could you elaborate on that?"

ROMC: "The dream process is an energy-cleansing process and goes through all five bodies during each major period of sleep. When the first two and a half levels have been processed in the time dimension, the second two and a half levels, being higher energy systems, are processed in another way, for they exist in the timeless level. Souls wander around in all dimensions in this state, visiting loved ones and doing whatever is necessary to survive the earth trauma.

"When souls reach the two-and-a-half dimension point, they experience themselves as flying, because at this point they are moving into the timeless dimension and are released from the magnetism of the earth energy. Most souls can remember the flying dreams because they are still connected to the earth-consciousness level; they often wake up feeling refreshed and ready to tackle the world. Unless one is an advanced soul who lives somewhat consciously in its higher energy state of two and a half and beyond, he or she will not remember out-of-body experiences.

"The service souls—those more spiritually advanced and living in the miracle levels of fifth-dimensional energy—do some very conscious work in the higher energy states during their dreaming period. Their work from this higher-energy level is to gather their helpers to go into the lower energies to help release souls and answer prayers for help. They are 'angels,' and can often appear in human form to help in different areas of the world. They are in control of their energies and can be at more than one place at a time. The service souls of angelic substance work in the dream state, and also in a consciously awake state, at all times."

RAM: "This has been quite interesting and revealing. From what you have said, it would be more appropriate for my book title to be *Journeys Into the Body* instead of *Journeys Out of the Body*."

ROMC: "Indeed it would. But most humans do not understand the concept that there is no time or space, and that all that is exists within. So, we will let them continue in their illusion until they discover the truth for themselves.

"It is time now for us to leave—even though we don't exist in time! It is very difficult to have discussions on the earth plane without referring to time."

RAM: "We did have a good time."

ROMC: "Yes, and as you would say, 'We've had the time of our lives.' So, we will say good-bye until next time."

RAM: (Bob chuckles) "Yes, it is time to go. Thanks again. ROMC, bring yourself on out—and take your time coming back."

ROMC: "Thanks. I'll take my time!"

~16~

ALIEN ENERGY SYSTEMS

After many sessions of intense cleansing and preparation, my Invisible Helpers were ready to take me back onto an alien spacecraft. I must have been working at a very deep energy level during the spacecraft experiences that followed, because I could not remember any details after each of these sessions.

Bob was eager to get back in contact with the aliens so that he could get more information. He was particularly fascinated with the technology involved in getting me onto the spacecraft. The Invisible Helpers would put me on some kind of a beam and actually "beam me up" *Star Trek*-style!

ROMC: "I'm in a state that seems so clear. I can hear the words, 'You are going to be in a crystal-clear energy field and will feel very alert. We are going to take you through a special experience today.'"

RAM: "Okay. Follow the flow as usual."

ROMC: "I am going down a road. I can see trees around me, and a car in front of me. I'm traveling at a fast rate of speed. All of a sudden everything is changing. The road under me is like a reflection and is getting farther and farther away. I'm taking off from the planet . . .

"Now I'm being put into a special kind of chamber—a clear energy ball. I'm traveling in it, and it seems that I am being cleansed. My mind, energy body, and all aspects of me are being cleansed to prepare me for this experience. The thought just went through my mind, again, that everything seems so clear. Then I heard the words, 'You must have a crystal-clear perception. That is what we are trying to create.'

"I'm traveling rapidly on a light wave, and in a very direct channel toward an object. It looks like what would be considered an unidentified flying object. I can hear the words: 'We are taking you to do some work here and to continue teaching you from this standpoint.'

"As I'm coming closer, it appears to be a very large type of spacecraft, like a mother ship. I get the impression that my friends are going to take me through it and describe to me what's there. I've come in on a beam to the very center of this spacecraft. The ship is oblong, and I'm being taken into the top area. Now I'm in a beautiful dome that sticks up on the top. From here we can look out and see the rest of the ship. It's very long, and I can see the glow from all kinds of windows along the side. I can see in all directions. We're suspended in space. It seems to be dark outside. I can look straight out to stars and planets.

"There are some people—or whatever you would call them—who seem to be working. Two of them are sitting at some instruments and appear to be talking. I can hear strange sounds, like a loud gibberish. They're working over the instruments. I'll go closer.

"Wow. On the instrument panel are all types of glowing, vibrating colors. And there's a steady hum in this room. The room is circular, and there is something in the center—a beam that comes right up into this dome. The beam is pulsating and changing colors some way in relation to the lights along the sides of the ship. And the lights seem to change. It's a special type of energy. I get the impression that this is the control room that runs the ship.

"Let me describe the two beings. They are proportioned differently from us. Overall they are more triangular-shaped. Their chests are higher and bigger than ours, and they have larger heads. In fact, they have very large heads. Their shoulders are fairly broad, but their arms aren't very long. Then they come down into a narrow waist; their legs aren't long either. They both seem to have something around their heads—I think to use in running the ship.

"And their faces are . . . well, it doesn't look as if they have any ears. And I can see little—what must be eyes, but they aren't very big and are extremely smooth. They don't seem to have noses. Their mouths seem to be little more than slits—with different volumes of sounds coming from them.

"Now my Invisible Helpers are letting me know that they are going to take me through this ship. There's a group of the extraterrestrial beings I'm to talk with. These beings have a plan and a purpose, which we are going to discuss. But this will take several sessions; this is only the introduction. They tell me that I have to go back, now, to planet Earth. They are going to send me back on the energy beam. But I will return later."

Bob was so excited as we began working with the extraterrestrials that he encouraged me to have extra sessions beyond our regularly scheduled ones. These meetings took place in December 1976, and January 1977. At that time not much was being said or published about UFOs, to my knowledge.

Interestingly, in late 1995 a news broadcast special stated that with the breakup of the USSR, the Soviet government's UFO files had become public record. These records indicated some major UFO sightings in 1977 in parts of the Soviet Union.

In one incident a spacecraft hovered over a major atomic-energy center, setting off an alarm that could have triggered atomic missiles. The alarm was quickly shut off, and no action was taken. Was a spacecraft checking to see how the extraterrestrials could prevent an atomic war? I was fascinated by this news special, since it was reporting on the time period when I was being taken onto the mother ship in our lab sessions.

ROMC: "I hear a very high tone. I get the impression that it's associated with the energy wave I'm traveling on. Now I'm going through the cleansing process again. It's very energizing. I see a circle at the end of the energy beam. The circle is the crystal-clear energy ball I traveled in before. (pause) Now I'm traveling very rapidly; suddenly my body is in an expanded state of awareness.

"We are approaching what seems like the same spacecraft as before. But the beam that's carrying me appears to be coming in at the bottom of the craft this time. I didn't realize it had a type of control center—like an inverted dome—extending out at the bottom of the ship. I am going in.

"I don't feel quite all together yet. The tone that I heard has changed to a lower pitch; it has a special energy. The sound is elusive and hard to describe, almost like a silent sound, or something you're not really hearing with your ears. It seems to have to do with traveling. It also seems like an energy that is being generated to tune into my energy—and to change it?

"Now I've come into a large, circular room. In the center is the inverted dome I saw from the outside. Looking down through it I can see stars, just as I did looking through the dome on top, before.

"I feel that I need to get my bearings. It's as if part of me is here, and part of me is somewhere else. My energies are divided. But now they are going to rebalance me. I am standing on a little platform. The energy is going to come in and balance me and bring me all together. A new sound is being sent through me now. It sounds higher. It's that strange, silent sound that seems to blend in with my own energy. Now, I am getting everything together—and my mind feels extremely clear.

"I don't see anyone in this room. There are sounds, and lights flashing, and something is happening. Now the inverted dome is opening up and it looks as if a saucer-type object is coming in, just floating right in. But I don't see anyone around doing anything. Everything seems to be operating, but without anyone to operate it. The room is so large. It is almost as if it has expanded.

"Now the saucer has come into this ship and is moving over to the side of the room. When I first came in I didn't realize how big this room is! Now, the circular ship—which is fairly large itself—has set down. It's as if it has a spot it moves into, similar to an airplane hangar. But no other saucers are in here.

"Now the dome has closed up; the color has changed. It had been gold and yellow, with some blue. All of a sudden it turned to a reddish-orange, when the saucer came in. It's so quiet in here—except for the tone that's around me. It's the tone that brought me here, and it's staying with me. It has changed again—it's lower. This seems to be my own tone. If there were any beings in that little saucer, they must have gotten out another way, because I still haven't seen anyone.

"Wow, it's so very quiet . . . strangely quiet. I want to do some exploring and see what's around here. The floor has an odd, metallic quality—a different material from anything I've ever experienced. It seems to be almost alive with energy. When I step on it, I can see right through my feet. A mysterious energy seems to make me transparent. And now I am stepping around on the floor, which is a very smooth, light substance. Everything seems to be aglow in this room.

"There are more 'hangar' spaces for other saucers. The saucer that is parked is about two times my height, and probably twelve feet in diameter. It looks like two domes put together, with little windowlike openings all the way around.

"It is very quiet in here. I don't know what's going on. There are lights all around the room, and maybe a dozen places for vehicles to park. The other saucers must be out on business! Now the colors are starting to change again. Something's happening. I want to get out of this area. Though I don't see anyone around, I feel as if someone is watching me, or is aware that I'm here.

"There's a light flashing. I'm going to follow it to see where it goes. (pause) It's taking me up to a little platform, but I don't see any way to get out. Now, I'm at the light, but there's no door. Or is there? Wow! The wall is pure energy, and I can go right through.

"There's a different feeling in this area. I had a very 'hollow' feeling in that other area, as if I was in a vacuum. Or maybe it's like being depressurized after you've been in deep water in a diving suit. I feel as though I had to be demagnetized to be able to come into this main area.

"Here's some kind of hallway. Everything is very strange, especially the sense of space. It seems like a hall, or a long room; on the other hand, it seems to expand as I move. It is as if the walls are an energy force-field, not solid walls as we know them. In that first area I came into, the space at first felt small, but after the vehicle came in, I experienced the space as being huge and very expanded.

"I'm going to keep moving. I still don't see anyone, but I continue to sense that there are beings around. I have a feeling that they can make themselves invisible to me with their ability to control energy. If they want to, they allow themselves to be seen; if not, I don't see them. It's eerie. Maybe it's some kind of hypnosis, where they can control my mind so that I see only what they want me to see.

"Now I'm in another type of hallway, with soft-energy walls that have a nice glow that seems to change as I walk. I say 'walk'—but I'm practically floating. My feet don't seem to touch the floor. The color now is a silver-gold. I feel someone guiding me around, telling me where to go. So I'll just follow whatever it is that's leading me.

"I'm coming to another hall. I just heard a voice say, 'Rosalind, we are with you.' It's my Invisible Helpers! I was so caught up in seeing what was around, I wasn't even aware of them. Maybe they are the ones I felt were invisibly present.

"Now I'm being taken somewhere. Wow. I'm in the room I was in on my previous visit to this ship. It's so different than the other areas. It's like going from the belly of a ship up to the captain's quarters. The colors are much brighter, and it has a warm, comfortable feeling. The colors are always changing, but they're relaxing.

"And there are the two beings I saw when I first entered. This room appears to be circular, and they're sitting up by some type of panels. I hear those strange sounds around them.

"They don't act as if they're aware that I'm in the room—but I'm sure they must be. This room has a beam coming right up from the center of it, with circular lights all around the base of the dome. The beam seems to come up through the floor. It must be their energy system. Then, there are beams that come from all around the base of the dome. The lights keep changing to different colors, and it's beautiful.

"I'm going to move closer to these creatures and see what else I can observe. Maybe they're the navigators of this ship. The sounds that seem to be coming from them are getting louder. Is it their voices? It's like a tape recording played on fast speed! And the speed changes.

"I'm going to see what's going on. As I'm standing behind them, I realize the sounds aren't coming from them at all, but from the panels, the instruments. And I see that they don't need to communicate with words. They're using thought-forms to communicate. They don't have ears because they don't need ears. I can perceive their thoughts because I'm in a different energy body. They're certainly intent on what they are doing. Now I've received the thought: 'As to your question about what is going on: Yes, this is our energy system.'

"I can see the entire panel now. It's amazing. Lines are moving on displays, and lights are flashing. Now, I'm receiving the thought that this is their system for communicating with the other spaceships that are out. It's their radar system. Some dots are moving and some are standing still. And when a dot moves, there's a unique kind of sound. That's why I heard the different kinds of sounds with different pitches; each ship has its own sound. Also, each one has a different color code. It's like a big game board that's alive with color and sound. How fantastic to see!

"Now I think they're going to communicate with one of the spaceships. These are their exploring ships. They go to investigate in different regions, including planet Earth. The dots move so rapidly.

"I'm being told that the color has to do with the frequency on which a ship is operating. When they move at high rates of speed, they shift their frequency and the color changes. They're pointing out that the ships that are in a traveling phase are gold in color. They seem to be going as fast as the speed of light. The ones we observe from planet Earth are more of a red-orange color, and they are slowed down quite a bit.

"This mother ship keeps in constant communication with all of her ships, no matter how far away in the universe they are. When a ship is reporting, the sound comes in. The mother ship is in touch at all times with everything that's going on. There is an immediate transmission and recording of information, done with light and sound energy.

"Now, they're directing my attention to something overhead. They're showing me that there's another way of keeping track of where the ships are. The mother ship must be moving continuously. What I thought was a dome through which I could look at the stars is more like a living planetarium. The lights on the dome's surface change continually—producing a continuously up-to-date record of what is happening in the universe. It's an updating map.

"The other panel keeps record of their smaller ships. But this larger dome keeps track of other mother ships, planets, stars, and so forth. If they are in the galaxy where planet Earth exists, this dome shows everything going on there. And as this mother ship moves, everything in the dome changes in perspective. I can't conceive of the space that these panels are keeping track of. My mind can't even comprehend it.

"They tell me that you're going to be able to ask questions, but not at this moment. I have to get adjusted to this first. It's such a completely different concept than anything I'm used to.

"They are willing to talk more. But they say that before you begin, my energies have to interrelate better with theirs. I still don't have myself together. Therefore I can't understand very clearly. I will have to make several visits just to get oriented. I'm really not all here—as if part of me were in a different energy, or time zone. They are willing to deal with many questions, but my energies have to be right. So the question period will have to wait.

"It's so hard to conceive of the magnitude of what they are showing me. Later, I'll be able to understand more about who they are and where they are located—and will be able to relate through their energy system.

"The two beings I'm with seem to be the same two I described before. They look alike to me. I can sense a kind of chuckle coming from them—they're thinking that we humans look alike to them! They have fairly large heads. One of them is standing beside me, and he isn't quite as tall as I am. (I'm five-foot-four.)

"And now I get the question, 'Why do you think *he*?' I don't know. I don't know if they even have different sexes. I'm being told that there are actually three genders and also a fourth state of being. They have the equivalent of the male and the female. But they also have 'neutral' beings—like drones in a beehive. Then they have highly evolved beings, who combine the male and female principle—or have gone beyond it.

"This is why they laughed. I'm perceiving from an earthly point of view—which is the duality principle. They are on a completely different dimension, a more highly evolved energy level. Therefore, there are some in their group who are an integration of the masculine and feminine principles. Their leaders are the more highly evolved beings, who are integrated and do most of the thinking.

"The rest do the work. The two I am with are workers. I'll see if they'll tell me whether they are male or female—or neither. I can see there is a bit of humor taking place. I'm trying to figure out how to determine whether they are male or female and they are both standing up and slowly turning around for me to observe. I'm trying to see if there's anything different about either of them.

"They have no ears. But there are little holes there. They have very small eyes. And they seem to have little holes where we have noses. Their bodies really look exactly alike to me. They are wearing a similar outfit, which has a smooth, metallic appearance.

"I would say they are of the same gender. And I don't know why, but I think they are males. I guess when I meet someone else I can compare them with these two. They tell me that I will know the difference when I meet others—and that's why they want me to take a good look. They obviously have a good sense of humor, and definite personalities. They're not just robots.

"Now, they tell me that they're going to have to keep track of what is going on, even though everything is monitored mechanically. They must keep in communication with every one of the spaceships.

"A door seems to be opening on the other side of the room. There's a light, and it's getting brighter. Someone is walking in—but I don't see anyone there. Now, I can sense laughter over my trying to figure out what's going on. All of a sudden I feel a presence—a very intense presence. Something is starting to materialize. A glowing being that is quite a bit taller than the others is appearing.

"Now I realize that this being was already there; I just wasn't able to perceive its presence until now. It's a leader—the male/female combination. Instead of tight metallic clothing, it's wearing a type of robe. I've just received the thought, 'Follow me.'

"I guess I will follow this . . . I don't know who 'this' is, but I'll follow. I want to say good-bye to my other friends. They are busy, and I get a 'we'll-be-seeing-you-around' kind of impression from them. So, I'll follow the leader!

"What a beautiful robe this individual has on. And its body is different from my previous friends' bodies. The head is wider and taller, though not as big in proportion to the rest of the body. This being is over six feet tall.

"Now I'm going down a hallway, and a door is opening. It seems that I'm being taken into that little saucer that docked earlier. The leader is going to show me around in the saucer, so that I'll understand its purpose. It's very plain inside this saucer—almost a duplicate of the room I came into downstairs, but smaller. There's a platform, or table, in the center, and a large, eyelike object over the table.

"The leader has pushed a button and tells me to lie on the table. Now 'he's' bringing the eyelike thing down over me and is turning the table around so I can see what's behind me—which is a large screen. Now, the eye comes down over me, and I can see pictures of me when I was a little girl! I can see whole experiences, both pleasant and unpleasant. The beings are taking pictures out of my brain and displaying them on the screen.

This instrument records the complete consciousness of the individual. There are different colors for the emotional, physical, mental, etheric, and spiritual levels of consciousness. If fear is there, it's recorded as a certain color. Now he's showing me my mental self. Next he's recording the emotional self—and the color is changing. And this technology can show other lifetimes of a person—including the future. This instrument is going deeply into my whole history and is throwing it right up there on the screen. Nothing is hidden.

"He's sending me the thought that when these beings come into a planetary area, they can take the mental and emotional 'temperatures' of the planet by putting different individuals on this scanning apparatus. Then they keep a type of computer tracking of where individuals are, and the growth they have had. This machine can also erase a person's memories of this scanning experience. So when they have finished, the person normally has no memory of having been on the saucer.

"But I get the impression that this device doesn't just measure brain waves. It can tap into any bodily system. It knows exactly what is in the body—every cell, every molecule, every physical problem. Thus it can diagnose illness. But it is also able to create the conditions for healing. And it can even alter our thought-forms.

"The leader is communicating that they can also open up areas in the brain where knowledge is stored, for the individual's benefit. They can't do this for everyone. But when they take a person on for a scan, if the person is evolved and balanced enough physically, they enable him or her to access new areas of the brain. The person then has a great deal of knowledge available that he or she was not conscious of before.

"Now I'm going to be given an overview of what they do here. They are not going to go into the reasons as to why it is being done, yet. They have been doing this for some time with many different people. They will be able to share more with us on planet Earth after our consciousness has been raised. They're keeping in continual touch to determine when we will be able to handle the knowledge they have to share. Some day they will be able to work openly with people on planet Earth.

"They want to put me through a complete scan—but that will have to be another session. This will be an important session, because I need to understand not only what they are doing, but why they are doing it.

"Now I am told that I'm to go out the other door of the saucer into a demagnetizing chamber to get prepared to come back into my body at the lab. I am to have several sessions. They have much to share. They don't want to overtax my energy.

"They've put me back on a little platform. It's as if I'm going to be sent back into myself. I'm going to receive an infusion of energy. I hear that sound again; it starts low and is getting higher. It seems to be my own frequency getting attunement from outside myself.

"Now I'm going to be put on an energy beam to be beamed back down. The sound is intensifying. Everything is starting to get dark and hazy, and it seems as if I'm moving. But I feel as if I'm standing completely still at the same time. (long pause) I feel as if I'm back in myself now!"

Can you think of a more unique way to begin the New Year than with a good cleansing on a spaceship? That's how 1977 began for me . . .

ROMC: "As I came through what I call the 'thick stage' I saw all kinds of interesting faces—some of them in groups. The faces were unusual. They seemed to have very large heads and strange noses. They weren't looking at me; I was just observing them. They were certainly not human faces. I don't know what, or who, they were. But perhaps I'll find out.

"These beings were doing something with energy. I was told to hold my hands with palms up—which I did—and I felt a great surge of energy. And I could hear a discussion on energy. I'm going to be told how my energies can be recharged.

"They are saying that I'll be working with a new level of energy. I'm told that the whole earth is rising into a new energy level. Those who are balanced, and are able to receive and accept this new energy, will use it constructively for higher purposes. And some will use it for the most construc-tive purposes. New energies will be coming into the earth level from all dimensions. The many sensitive people on the earth level are going to be experiencing this higher intensity of energy."

RAM: "Very good. Just go with the flow."

ROMC: "Okay. They are working to get me into that spe-cial vibration so that I can continue learning about the mother ship where I was before. It will take a little time to get me prepared. Again I'll travel on a type of light beam. I'm a little out of balance, so they are building up the vibrations around me. They are going to cleanse my vibrations.

"I'm beginning to pick up that silent sound again. The vibration is speeding up. I feel as though I am moving rapidly. I'm getting into the right vibration.

"I seem to be coming into the lower entrance of the mother ship. The light ray is coming out of the bottom, and I'm coming into the domelike area. Now I'm moving into the room that is the decomposition chamber—or a cleansing chamber. As I described before, the walls are made of a type of light energy. When I first enter, the room seems very small, because my consciousness can only penetrate the level right around me. As I begin to get demagnetized and reenergized into this different state of consciousness, the walls seem to open up.

"Again, as before, my energy body seems to be split from my consciousness. I feel a little bit off center. Now I'm being guided to step onto a platform where I'm going to get re-centered into the vibration where I'll be working. It's a small platform with a beam coming down onto it. I'm supposed to stand on it.

"I feel almost as though I'm being stretched or pulled. It's as if I am a funnel and am being stretched out until I'm very tall. It's a strange sensation. But it isn't my body that's being stretched—it's an aspect of my consciousness. The ray is coming through the top of my head down to my feet. All around me very small lights of different colors are shooting into me from all directions, going right up my body.

"I'm beginning to feel energized throughout my body. The energies are swirling around me. This is a cleansing and balancing process, to get me into a more perceptive level of consciousness. Now the vibrations are slowing down. I'm going to step down from this platform.

"The room still seems very small, and I don't perceive much around me. I'm going to stand very quietly to tune into what to do next.

"I see a large flashing light overhead, with letters that spell out 'l-i-s-t-e-n.' I'll listen. Everything seems to be moving. I feel as if I were in one of those fun houses, where the floor is tilted and you feel unstable. I feel strangely dizzy, and I don't know what is happening.

"I must listen. I'm being told that it is possible to listen at a much deeper level than human ears can perceive. What they want me to do is to begin to listen at this deeper level, which goes beyond the physical ears.

"It's important for human beings to learn to listen at a level beyond what words can describe. Through inner listening, we can perceive the many dimensions that are within. Humans have trouble listening because so many physical distractions are considered to be the 'real' level of existence. The physical level of the five senses is not the real level.

"At the real level of existence, we can perceive the truth of human existence through inner attunement. This is something we must work on. In moments of inner silence, if we practice extending consciousness antennas, we can perceive the roots of our own being. It's important not to live in the vibrations of others for our guidance. We must learn to live fully in our own realities—in our own vibrations. By tuning into ourselves we receive the guidance we need to become real persons.

"As we start into this new energy phase in the earth cycle, we are being reminded that the most important aspect of living is to get into attunement with our own personal vibrations. When we listen and tune in, there is no end to the energy levels that we will tap into.

"They have gotten across their main message, and I perceive that it's time to get back to my earth-consciousness—to get 'beamed down.'"

RAM: "Thank them for their help and assistance."

ROMC: "Okay. I can hear my silent sound, and I must come back to my own working level."

ROMC: "I want to report on what I've been perceiving. I feel a very clear state of consciousness. I feel very alert. It seems my auditory perception has intensified; I can hear a beat I haven't been aware of before. I think it's my heartbeat. Or it could be the sound of blood going through my veins. But it's so loud that it sounds like a tom-tom beating!

"So I was doing some experimenting with it—I was doing deep breathing along with the beat. I would breathe in, hold my breath—and the beat would speed up. When I would let my breath out, the beat would slow down again. It seemed that every sound was so intensified.

"At one point I was aware of people standing around. They were dressed in different kinds of costumes and were doing some kind of work with energy. I perceived that a pyramid was being put down over me. Energy started coming directly down from the top of the pyramid into me. I don't know exactly what was happening. But I was observing this and was still highly aware of the beat of my own inner rhythm.

"I want to see what I'm to do next. At one point, I heard a voice that told me to turn the palms of my hands up, and they sent energy right into my hands. This is what's happening now. They have been talking about intensifying the energy level in order to intensify my perceptions. My higher perception is to become more sensitive and alert. This is an assignment that I must work on at all times. I'm to be constantly perceptive of all levels and dimensions and must try to pick up my own inner guidance for everyday living.

"Let me see what's next."

RAM: "Fine. Simply go with the flow."

ROMC: "I see a pyramid with many, many steps. It's glowing at the top. I'm going to go up the pyramid. I'm taking one step at a time up the pyramid. It's like going up in vibrations. I'm going to receive energy slowly as I go up these steps. They are very short steps—but it's a large pyramid. I can see a bright light at the top. I'm going to continue going up slowly, until I get to the bright light.

"With each step there's a beat. I'm stepping to the beat of my own energy levels as I go up. I can hear the music of balance in my consciousness. With each step, I can hear a flood of music. It's like going right up the musical scale.

"I'm almost at the top. Suddenly, my feet feel very cold; I don't know why. The top of the pyramid is pure energy. I'm to walk into the middle of it. As I stand in the pure energy, my feet are starting to get warm. Now I feel cool again, but this time all over my body. But the energy is really penetrating through me. I feel that this energy is penetrating all levels of my seen and unseen dimensions. Now I feel a vibration throughout my body.

"I'm being told to breathe very slowly and deeply—to breathe in this energy. Then, I'm to let it out. The energy is coming right up through the pyramid to the top. I feel I'm swirling around rapidly. I feel invisible—I've become the energy itself.

"Now a strange thing is happening. I'm standing still. The energy of the pyramid is spinning around me. And I'm starting to lift off. An energy vacuum has been created, and I'm going right up with the energy that is coming out of the top of the pyramid. Now I'm moving very rapidly through a golden tunnel.

"I'm looking at myself. It's as if I'm looking at many different people! I can see my physical body—but also several other bodies. At one point it seemed that they were all in a circle, but separate.

"I feel I'm in a very special energy area. I want to explore to see where I am. I'm in a room with a dome. I can hear the words, 'Follow me.' I don't see who said this, but there must be someone. I hear 'Step up on the platform.' There's a type of runway up to a platform. Something seems to be opening up.

"I'm going through an opening and am in a hallway. I don't see anyone—but I feel that there are many people around somewhere. Now someone is coming into my field of vision—someone I've met before. It's a tall, stately gentleman—and I just realized that he was one of the faces I saw earlier.

"I say 'gentleman,' but this person isn't really a male. Anyway, this tall being is coming down a pathway of light and is wearing a brilliant robe. It's embroidered with light forms of different kinds. 'His' head is oblong, with a very high forehead. He doesn't seem to have much hair. There's something around his head; I'm not sure what it is. It's not a cap but is some type of instrument.

"Now, he's coming up to me. Without words, I can perceive that he is saying, 'Welcome back. We have much work to do together. I appreciate your trust, and the fact that you follow instructions carefully.'

"He is turning, and indicating, 'Follow me.' Now we're walking down the lighted way together. I shouldn't say 'walking,' because we seem to be floating. Everything is in movement, including the robe he has on. I can see live vibrations in everything. In fact, the colors in his robe change; there are different patterns as they change. Now the color of the instrument on his head is changing. It was plain, when I first noticed it—without color. But as he sends thoughts, colors seem to flash from the instrument.

"Now we've come to a different area, one I haven't been in before. It's so plain, almost silver-gray in color, and there doesn't seem to be much in it. He has walked over to a type of desk and is starting to look through a large book. He has his back to me, and I perceive that he is saying, 'Make yourself comfortable.' So I'm looking around, trying to see what's here.

"There's a large eyelike device that I've seen before. It's not turned on. As I walk around I see a row of circular windows all the way around the room. This is a dome—but very plain. In the center is a table for lying or sitting. There is also a box, with sound coming out of it—a *beep, beep, beep* sound. Each time I hear the sound, a light on the box changes color.

"I just received the thought that I'm to call my companion Zomar. I don't know what Zomar is doing with the book. He's looking through it very rapidly, as if he's searching for something. Now he's stopped at a page and is going down it with his finger.

"I sense that this is a book of all the galaxies. He's looking up something that has to do with planet Earth. I call it a book, but it's more like a glowing energy. He's trying to find some formula that relates to planet Earth. Now he has gotten up and gone over to a kind of energy box. He's waving his hand over it with certain motions, as if giving a combination.

"The eyelike instrument on the wall is now turned on. A purple beam is coming out of it. He's coming toward me, and I sense that he's saying, 'Now we can proceed in this investigation.' He has indicated that I can sit on the table. I feel very light on it.

"I'm being turned around with the violet beam. The eye is coming to the back of my head and I'm being given instructions to look at the screen. It's a strange feeling, as if I'm watching this—standing aside and observing everything—while another part of me is sitting here. It's almost as if I'm split into two parts, one participating and the other observing.

"Zomar is grinning because I am just now realizing the different dimensions that are a part of my existence. I'm aware that I'm more than one. He's telling me to relax and enjoy this experience—that it will be an experience of my lifetimes!

"The color from the eyelike instrument has turned to blue. Zomar's robe, and the whole room, have turned blue. My head is feeling very large. There's such intensity in my head that I think I could get a headache. Something is penetrating right to the center of my brain. Now he wants me to put my head back and describe what I see taking place on the screen in front of me.

"The screen shows what I was doing today in earth time. Everything is backing up in time. It's like a movie going backwards. I can see myself driving to the Institute. I can also see another dimension transposed over me. I'm rapidly going into another dimension and am shifting backwards in time. I can see all this happening on the screen.

"This machine seems to tap into my brain waves. As Zomar moves his hands over the box, everything goes backwards. Every once in a while, he stops. He's stopping at a time when I was 12, at Whippoorwill Hills, my Girl Scout camp, when I almost drowned in the swimming pool. He has stopped here for me to look at this experience. I'm struggling to get my breath. I hadn't thought of that incident for a long time. He is taking me back to points in my life at which I almost died. I'm having trouble breathing, because now he has taken me back to the moment of my birth.

"I'm just coming out of the womb, struggling to get my breath. Oh—I feel the doctor's cold hands around me. He's taking my head and shoulders now, and his hands are cold. I can hear and see my Aunt Nellie asking, 'What is it?' The doctor says, 'It's another Buck (my maiden name). It's a girl.'

"It's cold. I see my father standing there. Now they're finally putting me into a pan of warm water. That feels better.

"We're in a little bedroom at home. I can see my mother lying there, breathing heavily. The doctor walks over to my mother and says, 'Well, this is your fifth child. You're pretty experienced by now.'

"I recognize my Aunt Nellie. I am such a little thing. I see myself standing outside of my body observing this. I can see two parts of myself. I haven't even come fully into the body.

I'm in my body, but also observing—just as I was doing earlier. Now, I'm observing myself observing.

"Now this is starting to fade. Everything is very dark on the screen. I think I'm in the womb. It's very dark—but nice and warm in here. I'm floating around, and it feels good, so comfortable.

"Now I'm going back further. I'm in a big hall, a special kind of place. But it's not like anything on earth. I'm getting instructions that it's time to go again. I see a description of the father and mother that I am going to be with. There is a description that comes out of a kind of computer. But there's something more important. I'm getting a specialized lesson.

"Now, I see myself with a special group of people. We're in a circle and are discussing the fact that I have some important emotional growth to go through. I have to go back into a situation with a lot of people, a lot of brothers and sisters—to learn patience. It's important for me to learn patience, with myself and with other people. That is the main lesson I must learn on planet Earth.

"I can see my emotional self and my tendency to be hurt by what others say and think about me. I must learn not to be overly critical of others and myself. I need to learn the lesson of greater acceptance—soul acceptance, so to speak. It seems that my impatience comes out in the form of over-criticism.

"I basically must learn love and have to start by loving myself. I'm being put into a situation of four brothers and three sisters to learn that there is plenty of love to go around. I'm agreeing that I'll be happy to go, if this is the situation as the soul group sees it. This is my earth-life council meeting, made up of very perceptive and understanding souls. They say that there are several other possibilities, but this one seems to be the best.

"I'm at the point just before coming into the womb. They are showing me the experience of what it's like to come back into the earth. I feel very light. Everything around me is very light. There's a beam coming down on me, and they're showing me what it's like for the soul to come into the womb.

"I perceive that I don't have to stay in the womb all the time. I can go in and out, even while the embryo is being formed. I can go into the fetus and out, at will—trying it on for size as it develops. The body can form and operate without my spirit being there. In fact, I am being shown that I can do this all through life! I'm free to roam wherever I like. It's my body, and I am in complete charge and can come and go as I like.

"They're showing me two distinct parts of myself— the part that is experiencing, and the part that is observing. Then there is a third part that's observing the other two parts. Wow! I see several dimensions of myself. There is a moment when I can decide whether I want to stay or go.

"I have to decide if I want to take the responsibility of this lifetime. The soul has a two-month period to make a final decision. I stayed in on this one—even though I almost exited because my sister, Patsy, who was two years old when I was born, didn't like my being there, and beat me on the head with a stick until my mother was able to stop her. I was about a month old at the time. I guess I wanted to be where the action was, even though it was directed at me!

"Now what's happening? This seems to be a lesson on dimensions of reality and areas of perception. We are continually working on several levels at one time, even at the point of conception, coming into the physical body. We can always exist and operate in more than one dimension at one time. But humans often get caught in just one dimension, and stay there.

"Something is happening. I suddenly feel extremely hot. I'm not sure where I am. Everything has speeded up so rapidly. Zomar is indicating that we will do some more of this, that there is much to learn about the many dimensions of reality. They're going to take me back into past situations very, very rapidly. I feel as if I'm burning up! I don't understand what's happening.

"He tells me that I am working at an extremely rapid rate of vibration and am very energized. This machine that taps into brain waves also energizes. My molecules are so speeded up that I experience it as heat. The eyelike machine not only shows me pictures of my consciousness levels, but also reenergizes the brain. I feel a lot of mental energy—and will still receive many mental images after I have gotten off the machine, Zomar says.

"He's giving me instructions that when I receive mental images of the past, I should flow with the experiences and release them. This release is an important part of the process. He says that if they are good experiences, I should re-experience and absorb them. But if the experiences create emotional blockages, I am to release them. We are going to do this several more times. I'll be sorting out some of the emotional blockages that are still in the body, and I'm going to receive a higher sense perception through the release of these energy blockages.

"Now the device on his head has turned a bright red. He's picking up a message. He indicates that it's time for me to leave, and that they're preparing the exit chamber. Everything is opening out, and I'm stepping back into this room.

"I thank Zomar for helping me. He is a highly intelligent, loving, and accepting being. I get a sense that he looks right through me and knows all about me, but is not judging me. He's helping me to experience and work through some different levels of my 'personality-consciousness,' as he calls it. He indicates that after we work through this, we are going to get into some other levels.

"Now I'm back in this exit chamber, standing on the platform to be beamed down. I'm still warm, but I'm starting to cool down. A light that is rapidly moving around me is cooling me off. I felt as if I couldn't breathe for a while, just as I did earlier, during the regression period.

"I'm going down the light beam and am coming back into the pyramid. I'm getting ready for reentry into my body. I'm to stand in the pyramid for a few seconds. Now I hear the words, 'You can descend.'

"Whew! I feel much cooler. I'll count myself down from Focus 12."

RAM: "Come back slowly and easily from 12 to 10, and then back on down."

~17~

THE UNIVERSE OF HIGHER ENERGIES

ROMC: "I am told to build an energy ball that will take me to another level. I will be given instructions.

"The speaker tells me that the purpose is to lift my energy body out of my physical body so that I can work in the pure energy state. I am to begin.

"Breathing is important. It is going to help build the energy ball—to generate the proper kind of energy around me. I am told to breathe slowly: to breathe in and hold my breath to the count of five, and to breathe out and hold to the count of five. I will do this several times.

"I'm being told that I am now working with the white light. As I breathe in this white light, energy works through my body. As I breathe out, it is going to be generated around my body, coming out at various energy points on my body. I am working on this.

"Next, I'm to work with yellow light. I have to breathe in the same manner. It's turning to a bright orange, and I'm to breathe this energy color into my body through the energy points. It seems to go all through my body from the energy ball that's surrounding me. Now the color is starting to shift to red energy.

"I feel my body getting lighter. I'm shifting into the lighter energy colors: blue . . . green . . . violet. These are the lightening colors. The other colors were the energizing colors.

"I'm to continue breathing in the same manner. These colors are coming all through my body, and up and down my spine. They're coming into my body from my feet and head. I can see my body. I am told that the breathing process is very important.

"I'm feeling lighter and lighter and am starting to float. The ball around me is a protection around my energy body. It will also be propelling energy that will help carry me into different areas.

"I'm floating up and can observe my physical body. But I can also see my energy body floating. I am able to observe two levels of energy and two dimensions of the body.

"Now I've gotten up to my Focus 12 platform. It appears to be very, very dark around me. First, I'm told to stay in a reclining position. Now I am told to stand up. I'm going to stretch.

"The helpers who work with me during these experiences are very close. They have told me that I am to go with them. I have my protection, and I am to float right out with them to wherever they are taking me. I will follow instructions and go wherever they go. I get a warm feeling from their presence. It is the experience of being with close friends that you can relate to on a deep level. I have confidence when I am in their presence.

"I am moving rapidly through a tunnel, and I can see a point of light at the other end, which is getting larger and larger. It's as if I'm on a light beam that is helping to propel me.

"I'm starting to come out into the light. I'm slowing down all of a sudden and have come into a different dimension. I'm at the opening of the point of light, and I am coming through gently—and everything is green!

"It's a beautiful, bright green, and almost blinding as I come out of the tunnel. There is a different feeling about this atmosphere. In the tunnel I felt as if I was being propelled; now I feel a strong energy pressing against me. I'm at a new energy level. It's so bright that it's taking me a minute to adjust. Everything is shades of green, and the atmosphere seems to be throbbing. It's alive with green energy.

"I'm being taken to different places in this atmosphere. At first I absorbed the air. Now I'm being shown and told to observe the kinds of vegetation. It seems velvety. I'm to stand in the middle of the green leaves to absorb the energy.

"I will step out on the ground, which is like a thick, mossy carpet. I'm told to lie down and roll around. I'm doing this—and it feels good.

"I can see a lake at the bottom of the hill I am on. I'm told to go down and step in. (pause) I'm putting my feet in. It's an unusual feeling, a different kind of element. I'm getting completely immersed in the water, which is a soft blue-green. Oh, it's a strange feeling! I'm floating around in it and picking up a special kind of energy. I'm supposed to be absorbing the different kinds of elements. It's different than our water because it feels so light. I don't sink, but float without trying. The water seems to be throbbing, and giving off a special life energy.

"Now I'm rising straight up out of the water in a horizontal position and am beginning to float in the air. What a strange green atmosphere. The air is a different kind of green than I've ever experienced before.

"Green is a strong emotional ray, and I feel it penetrating my brain. The high mental energies are on the blue ray; the green is blending the emotional and mental rays, preparing me for a more intense experience on the higher mental plane of light energy. I'm bathing in the green atmosphere to keep me grounded as I go into these more intensified energies. It's also a cleansing of my lower emotional energies.

"I'm floating up over the water and am turning over gently. I could stay here forever. I feel so light, and the atmosphere around me is so light. Now I'm floating high enough that I can see down. I see a forest, a beautiful green forest.

"The green atmosphere is starting to fade, and I'm coming into other color levels. Now I'm moving through a blue atmosphere. I'm seeing something in a distance that looks like . . . it's hard to describe. It looks like something built out of light. It's radiating a different color. It's gold, and like pure light. I think I see something like buildings, but they are all pure light. They vary in intensity. Everything is so alive and vibrant—pulsating. I feel that I'm in the rhythm of whatever this universe is.

"There are many different colors, and they are so intense. I see light forms around one building of light. I'm floating over toward them. Now my friends are putting something over my eyes to protect them, because this light is so intense. They're putting strange goggles on me. The light is so powerful that I can feel it all through my energy body. I especially feel it in my solar plexus area. There is excitement in coming into these very strong energy fields.

"I'm being guided by my friends. Now I'm looking straight down into an energy form, and I feel light-headed. I'm on a high level, like a mountaintop. I'm starting to descend into this strong light.

"I'm in a type of courtyard surrounded by walls that are pulsating energy. I can see some energy beings walking around. No one seems to notice I am here. I'll try to describe what they look like.

"They are more or less human in form. But they are very tall and are pure energy, with shimmering color. They seem to be pulsating, just as the rest of the atmosphere is. I can look right through these forms. They are very beautiful beings of light.

"There is something taking place in this courtyard. I can hear some vibrations, like music. The beings seem to be working on something. They are building an energy form. They're around a big ball. They seem to be building it but not touching it.

"I can see funny bursts of light leaving their heads toward each other, like zigzags of energy going back and forth between them. It's as if they are communicating, but instead of hearing voices, I'm seeing energy. The interchange of energy is going back and forth between them. They use energy for their thought patterns.

"I'm being told that the sounds I hear—what I thought was music—are the different levels of their thought energy. It is patterns of their thoughts. As these thoughts go back and forth, they sound like music and appear as color. It's beautiful to behold. They are having what we would call a conference.

"I'm being told that I can pick up their thoughts as sound and color because I'm of a different dimension. They pick it up directly. It's like watching and listening to a symphony, like listening to the music of their minds!

"Whatever the large thing is in the middle of the group, it's alive and in a different way. It's like a large crystal, and they're doing something with it.

"All of a sudden someone else has appeared. There were five of them, and now there are six. Something that they are doing evidently brought this other being to them. Now all of the energy is coming from this being who has just appeared out of the atmosphere. Beautiful colors are shooting out of him—from his eyes and from the top of his head. He seems to be speaking to them with thought energy, but he is giving off more energy than the others. As he communicates, the ball in the middle is changing colors. This ball seems to have something to do with communication. Now the being that just arrived seems to be building something in front of the group, creating something for them. It's difficult for me to describe this scene because it's like nothing I have ever seen before. Now he is handing the others the energy form that he just created. It's pulsating. They are examining it. I'm wondering if it's a kind of food. However, I'm now perceiving that they live off the energy atmosphere and not by eating food as we know it.

"Now there is much excitement and I can hear and see the musical color exchange between them. The colors are changing rapidly and are very bright. It's laughter! The colors are so brilliant.

"I'm being told that I have been observing another dimension completely beyond our own. This dimension works strictly on a nonmaterial energy level. Everything is done with pure thought. The light, as well as everything that is created here, is brought about with the thought patterns, with the mind.

"I'm told that I am being shown this because it is what we should be doing on planet Earth. We are not using our thought patterns to the fullest, as we should be using them.

We are caught up more in the manifestation, the outer, the physical, rather than the process itself, which takes place within each human being. Humans are taught what to think, instead of how to think.

"The mind is an energy machine through which we create. We create our own circumstances. It's being explained that I'm being shown all this as an example of how the energies are used on other planes, in different areas of the universe. This is another lesson in the understanding of the energies of consciousness.

"The scene is starting to fade, and I am being taken away. I'm being lifted into the atmosphere, and I'm starting to float up. The scene is getting smaller—but it's still very, very bright. I hear the music. As I look down I see an entire city, emanating many color patterns. The music I hear is the changing, interrelating energies. There is such harmony in this dimension. The beings in this city are living in their highest potential. Everything about this universe is harmonious.

"As I float away, I'm being told that another lesson for the earth level is that of harmony. We must use our energy levels in a more harmonious way for the good of all, and not just for selfish endeavors. As we tap into the Source within ourselves, there is no end to what we can accomplish for our world. We could exist in this same harmonious level, because we create our atmosphere. Each individual soul must get his or her own energies balanced in relation to the universal energy.

"I am high up in the atmosphere, now seeing beautiful patterns below me, the great harmony of this planet of light. It's magnificent. I don't want to leave. But I know I must go back to planet Earth to do my share of the work to help make it what it can be. I have much work to do on myself. They have taken the strange goggles off me, and I am shooting back through the tunnel very rapidly."

RAM: "Count yourself back down when you are ready."

ROMC: (pause) "I think I'm back. It gets harder and harder to come back to the earth level. What would you do if I didn't come back?"

RAM: "I'd come after you."

ROMC: (chuckle) "Okay, we could play universal hide-and-seek. See if you can find me!"

RAM: "I could probably find you. I'd send your helpers out after you."

ROMC: "That's cheating."

RAM: "No, hide-and-seek is a group game."

ROMC: "I guess you're right."

The Invisibles call the earth "the emotional universe." In a later session they contrasted our emotional universe with the mental universe just described. Their way of teaching seems to involve introducing a topic experientially, and then returning to the subject again to draw comparisons and contrasts for deeper understanding. In the following session they continued their comparison of the emotional versus mental universes.

ROMC: "It's so warm in the booth today that I was going to ask you to turn off the heat, Bob. But when I thought of asking you to do that, I heard a voice say, 'Turn yourself off.' So I just pictured cool air coming in around me. And it worked!"

RAM: "That's exciting. I'll try that same technique here in the Control Room. Whose voice did you hear?"

ROMC: "My helpers are with me and I'm receiving the message that the lesson for today is: 'We can be in control of any aspect of our environment through the mind. To do this we make the adjustments internally instead of externally.'

"Everyone is a universe in and of itself. And there are memory banks of many universes within the human body. There are no outer universes. The only universes that exist are universes that are perceived from within. Therefore, there are no external universes—only internal ones.

"Souls exist in what appear to be external universes. These are only illusions. I see pictures of many other galaxies, universes, planets, and stars, and I realize that memory banks of all the outer levels are carried within the human body. History is here, but it is not here. It is in existence only in thought form. Therefore it is an internal structure. It can be perceived only through an internal process.

"The earth is here, but it is not here. In the past, it was not in physical form. In the future, it will not be in physical form. It is, in actuality, a creation from the internal structure of all who live upon it at this time. It exists only for those who experience it as existing. It does not exist for those who do not experience its existence. Therefore, it is not real, but a temporary illusion. The maps and patterns of all galaxies and universes are within the soul level of all beings and the maps differ according to the needs of each individual soul.

"If our physical bodies are universes in themselves, do they then exist in physical form? No. It is the same principle. Basically, humans are pure energy. Our physical bodies exist only for those who experience their existence. At one point, the physical body was not. The physical body only exists in relationship—as it is experienced by the soul that temporarily manifests its existence, and by other humans who perceive it to be so.

"Because we experience the physical earth, feel the physical body around our being, and observe the other planets and galaxies through telescopes does not mean that this is the reality of existence. It is not. It is only a temporary energy manifestation of the real, which exists strictly within the internal nature of the self. The outer manifestation is created by the internal structures of all souls who must experience this physical illusion for a reason of internal growth.

"The physical earth is an emotional level for those souls who need this type of physical manifestation for emotional cleansing and growth. All souls who are on the earth experience its existence through their particular need at the time of the experience. However, the earth does not exist for those who do not need to experience it.

"There are many other levels that do not exist in our internal universes, because we do not need to experience them. There will be a point in time when the earth will not exist, because it will no longer be needed for the experience. All souls, in the body or out, who experience the emotional earth level do so out of a special inner need. When that internal need is no longer there, the physical earth will not be experienced. Therefore, it will no longer exist.

"The earth is on an emotional level. But there are pure mental levels that other souls create and experience for specific purposes. The earth, then, is in the emotional memory bank of those who need to experience it. Other universes and levels of existence are in the memory banks of those who need to experience them.

"There are not, therefore, numerous 'lifetimes' upon the earth level. A soul exists in reality as a singular light being, and experiences the physical manifestations of the earth level through a projection of its light through its own internal 'cameras.' A soul has many memory banks stored within, and it projects these as an outer manifestation so that they might be experienced and released from the memory bank after being projected numerous times.

"When the soul experiences and sees these projections as no longer having validity or importance, then these images simply dissolve because they no longer have energy attached to them. Therefore reality is the pure existence of an energy being, not its outer manifestations. Humans that attach to the outer manifestations live an illusionary existence—living in the projected state and not in the soul's real energies.

"The real self is the creator and projector of the films. The films projected onto the earth screen are the outer or illusionary experiences that contain the emotional and mental memory banks that exist within each soul level. However, there are many levels of existence to be experienced *beyond* the emotional and mental levels. Each soul has different films to project from its different memory banks. This is the uniqueness of personality. Each soul writes its own scripts and plays its own roles.

"Living in the projected state means living always as an observer of life; therefore, *not being alive*. Living in the soul's pure energies means being the actor on your soul's stage of reality; thus, it is being truly alive in the light, love, and joy of your pure existence.

"For the sake of understanding, we will deal with only the emotional and mental levels in this lesson—because these are the two that have been experienced by most souls on the earth level.

"Levels relate to specific aspects of the physical body. Let me illustrate human consciousness as follows: There are five dimensions of the human self—physical, etheric-substance, emotional, mental, and spiritual. Within each of these bodies there are seven levels of energy, going from the lower to the higher universes of the self. These would be energy levels number one to seven as follows: Base of the spine, reproductive organs, solar plexus, heart, throat, third eye, and crown of the head.

"We will go into greater detail on these in a later lesson. But for now, picture the following: the five bodies laying hand-to-hand and foot-to-foot. Draw a circle around the energy centers of all of these five bodies. You will have a series of seven circles ranging from small and restricted in the center—or at the lower levels—and expanded and all-encompassing at the outer level.

"Now, picture these encircled areas of the human self as the consciousness levels of existence. The earth plane is the lowest energy level, at the very base of the physical map. Fixated at this level, those souls never get off the ground, so to speak; they exist mainly in the basic physical energies. This is the elemental consciousness. This basic existence is important for the soul growth of each individual. It is the foundation on which all other levels are built. It is grounded in the earth-consciousness. It is important to growth if one does not get stuck in this level.

"The next circle around—or the next movie projected upon the earth screen—will come from the large circular perspective. These are in the energies of reproduction, flow, and creativity. And the next circle of experience on the earth screen is in the solar plexus level. This is when the self begins to take on a stronger identity and starts to assert its ego or power. This is where greater self-expression begins to take place.

"Then we move into the heart level of energy. This is the level of emotions where the soul begins to experience more on the feeling level and moves into the experience of relationships, or the 'we' consciousness. The throat and the energies of the third eye are mental energies, where the self gets into greater control of its own existence through the mental channels.

"This moves into the higher levels of spirituality. The crown of the head is symbolic of the coming back into the Source, into the oneness of existence, and therefore it is the outer circle that encompass all other levels. It is the coming together of all into one.

"The emotional self takes in the solar plexus and heart energies, and the mental dimension of self occurs in the throat and energies of the third eye. Let's look at these more closely. I was taken into a universe of higher energies in an earlier session. I was given a glimpse of souls that exist in the pure mental levels of existence. They want us to examine more carefully what this universe represents. I'll go back into this experience.

"I can see beings sitting around what seems to be a round table, with a type of ball in the middle. The ball is lighted. I don't hear words, but I can hear sounds. They are looking at the ball, but nothing is being said. There seems to be a lot of energy in the air. I get a feeling of very heightened awareness. Strong vibrations are taking place, and it is all on a mental level.

"They are communicating and doing something together. It's a type of conference. They seem to be picking up something that is being sent to them. At the end of the table a very intense light being has just appeared. Now they are all looking at this being rather than at the ball of light in the center.

"There are still no words, but strong communication is taking place. Their thought patterns are so strong that they don't have to use words. There is nothing hidden, which is not so on the emotional earth level. There are no hidden thoughts, and there is no dishonesty. There is only a pure state of existence, and thus, attunement. There is attunement with every aspect of themselves and each other.

"This attunement is experienced because the energy is heightened to the extent that all emotions are cleansed of any hidden debris. Reality, in the emotional level, is confused with the illusion of the physical. Reality in the pure mental state is not confused with the illusion of the physical—because there is no physical, but a pure energy state of consciousness.

"Time and space are a creation of the emotional earth level. But in essence, time and space do not actually exist. They exist in the eye of the beholder, which does not make them real. Time and space are the energies manifested to project the inner picture upon the earth screen. Therefore, time and space exist only as these concepts are experienced by the soul that is projecting the experience.

"The being that has appeared to the group is a teacher, a light being who comes to them on request from another vibratory level of existence. When they seek knowledge or guidance, it comes instantaneously in whatever form they desire. (This would also be the case on planet Earth if humans would believe and accept this possibility.)

"I am experiencing something very different in this group than in group experiences in the earth emotional level. There is complete unity—thus, no sense of power, of one being over another. The ego power-structure is a part of the imbalance in the earth-consciousness.

"This is a very important factor to understand. When a being is not balanced or integrated within itself, it projects a strong ego, or power-consciousness. Thus, an emotional wall is built around the self. The ego self does not recognize the oneness of its existence with all other levels of consciousness, nor does it show appreciation or recognition of other important energy levels, including other forms of life.

"Therefore, the earth level is in a state of imbalance. Because of the imbalance of the overall emotional makeup of the ego levels of beings on the earth, the physical earth-consciousness seeks its own balance. Thus, natural disasters occur—which is the earth-consciousness shaking out the imbalance of its internal structures. This imbalance is created by the inner energies of the beings inhabiting it who make up the physical earth-consciousness.

"A power structure is not a part of the pure mental levels of consciousness. There is a powerful love energy in this level, since they have been balanced and integrated into the overall consciousness of existence. On the earth level, love is confused with emotions. Love is a pure and powerful energy expressed through the emotions. But it is *not* the emotions. There is a continual give-and-take in this type of atmosphere, with each living being recognizing its need for the others and for all other levels, thus experiencing their oneness. This need and recognition eliminates the power structure. The highest energy, which is pure love, creates overall oneness and balance.

"When you are in the presence of a being with pure love energy, the soul recognizes its own highest worth. When one is in the presence of a strong ego power, one experiences worthlessness, uselessness, and littleness, and thus falls under the control of the ego power. This is often experienced in the emotional earth level, because of the many ego barriers that have been built up by souls trying to prove themselves to be of greater value than others.

"There is no 'greater,' and no 'lesser.' Everything in the universe is to be experienced and treated with the most sacred respect, for 'All is one, and one is all.' Souls must come into the recognition of their own levels of the highest God-consciousness. Souls that come into this at-onement have the greatest reverence and respect for all that they are, and all that they are a part of. This is the highest energy, called love.

"There is no need for an ego power to project itself onto the earth screen as the 'greatest.' The purpose of the ego is to strengthen the self to bring it back into its true internal balance, and not to take control of and retard other souls in their process of growth. The ego that is into outer power rather than inner growth gets locked into playing the same unnecessary film over and over, until it realizes that it no longer needs to project such a fake image onto its screen of life. There is no greatest, and there is no least.

"All life can be experienced as pure love energy, and pure joy. Within the pure love energy levels, there is no such concept as war, because wars, struggle, and defense mechanisms exist only in areas of emotional imbalance and conflict. When all is in balance there is no need for destruction in ways that destruction is experienced on the earth level. When the emotional earth energies come into balance, conflict levels will disappear, and the earth-consciousness will shift into a state of greater harmony.

"When the earth rises to a higher rate of consciousness, its physical nature will no longer be manifest, because souls will no longer need their lower nature for the projection of their slower vibrations, their more base energy levels. When all in the earth level come unto the higher spiritual energies, their whole consciousness level will be transformed and they will exist in pure energy form—as will the earth itself, because the earth is merely a projection of the inner levels of consciousness.

"The point has been made as to the differences between the emotional and mental universes. These levels exist within each being, and are there to be tapped. At any point, all can be in touch with the highest energy levels, or beings of highest love. It is important to believe that one can break down the walls of strong ego structures that confine the soul in its own prison of singular existence. Existence is not singular, but plural. There is no loneliness or aloneness, other than that which the soul perceives.

"Souls that are locked into their inner chambers of energy cannot experience higher levels of consciousness, which are there to be tapped and released. But help comes at any time we ask. This is a universal law: 'Ask, and you shall receive.' Know that if 'All is one, and one is all,' you are never alone.

Climb out of your emotional ego prisons and experience this at-onement with all levels of life.

"You carry the keys to your own prison cells. Call upon the God-levels of your own natures, and you will know the greatest light, love, and joy, and will experience the magnificent creativity of your own true self. Be the actor on your true stage of existence and not merely the observer of old reruns."

"My helpers are indicating that it is time now to move back down into my physical body."

RAM: "Thank them for coming to share this very important lesson. Count yourself back down, and take your time coming back."

Also, I Deeply Desire Assistance [and] Wisdom . . .

~18~

Healing Assistance

One day when I arrived for my session with Bob, I was in a great deal of physical pain due to bleeding hemorrhoids. My Invisible Helpers always seemed to deal with the issue at hand. In trying to clear my energies in order to help me into the higher-vibratory dimensions, they have used some unusual "technology."

Having a technical mind, Bob was always fascinated with the technologies employed by beings in other dimensions during the out-of-body sessions of the different Explorers. He speaks about this in his second book, *Far Journeys* (Doubleday, 1985):

> *It is the display and application of a science—call it technology—which is totally absent from our human culture. We simply don't know anything about it nor do we have any accepted means by which to begin to gather information as to its nature of content. (p. 64)*

An excerpt from one of the sessions he refers to follows:

ROMC: "My body is heavy because of the physical pain I had when I woke up this morning. I feel sluggish today and not as clear as before, so they are trying to help me. I say 'they.' I feel there is someone there; but all I see are two discs and a light. I was put on one of the discs and I began spinning around. I'm still lying on the disc. The light is shining over my body, and is getting brighter. I think the light is coming from the other disc, which is up over me. It's as if I am between two energy discs."

RAM: "Ask who they are."

ROMC: "Okay. I just got the answer back. 'We are a source of light and energy, which your body needs right now.'"

RAM: "Do you feel any results from the energy?"

ROMC: "At first I was feeling out of it, but I'm starting to feel a little more energized and together now."

The Invisibles then started to work with heat and color. They sent colors through me from my head to my toes, as if I were a tube. Then they concentrated on the dark areas of my body, where the pain was, beaming in purple energy. The purple changed to blue, with an occasional flash of red. Finally they put me back into the purple light and spun me on the disc again.

The healing was not completed after the first session. At our next session a week later I still had some dark spots in my aura, and my Invisible Helpers continued working on my body. They put me on the disc again to build up my energy level and gave me instructions to tell Bob what was happening, because the vibration of my voice seemed to help keep the energy up.

I again felt the disc twirling around very rapidly. A light beam centered down on the dark area of my body that needed the healing. Some sort of energy rods were then inserted across my abdomen one by one. After that they worked with the violet and blue energies again. Another beam came from the back of me, through my spine and up through the rods.

RAM: "Report in when you feel it necessary."

ROMC: "I am to try to be aware this week of these energy rods in my abdomen. They are going to continue to send light and different types of color energy through them, especially when I'm sleeping. I was told they are also going to use heat on a couple of spots on my abdomen where I've had the pain. I was instructed to hold my index finger and thumb together in a circle over these places. I am doing this, and I can feel the heat penetrating into these areas.

"They are doing healing work. I am told that I will be aware of their presence as they work with me during the week, to clean out some of the darker areas of my physical and emotional bodies. I'm going to be taken off this disc now."

After this second session, I felt wonderful. And the next day the hemorrhoids were completely gone.

The Invisibles actually did healing work on me at the beginning of every session. Once they even gave me a good foot massage.

ROMC: "Now they are going to start working on me for cleansing and relaxation. Two of them are working on my feet. They are giving me a foot massage. As their hands touch my feet, I feel them tingle. They are energy light beings. They're very gentle and are working on my etheric body—not my physical feet, but my energy feet. They're working on my toes especially, but are barely touching them.

"I can feel lots of energy going between their hands and my energy body. It's like foot reflexology on my energy body. They're stirring up energy inside me—and it's helping me to relax.

"Now they are touching points all over my feet. It's like needles being stuck into my feet. It brings balance when they work on both feet at the same time. They're going to work like this all the way up my body. The touch of their hands is very special, and I feel an inflow of energy each time they touch an energy point on my body.

"They're starting up my legs now, and I can feel the energy moving up through my body. Now they are up to my knees, and there are some energy blocks here. They're going to break up the blockages and get the energy flowing. I get the impression that these energy blockages also create blockages in my mind, so they have to free the energy in order to cleanse my mind."

After working with me like this for some time, they put me through some exercises of deep breathing. They continually stress the importance of breathing correctly and have taught me many different types of breathing techniques during our sessions.

They also focused on Bob's health problems and questions on a number of occasions. Bob would think a question, and my helpers would often answer it without my knowing he had a question, or what it was. And they offered Bob much health advice when he openly asked for it.

On one occasion they did a diagnosis and healing for my mother, living in Dayton, Ohio, when she was not feeling well.

ROMC: "My Invisible Friends are checking on my mother now, and doing a diagnosis. They say there is something wrong with the gall bladder, and there is also some kind of poison in her kidneys. They are beaming energy rays into her. Now I'm going to try to do some healing on her myself. I am stepping into her energy body. I want to feel and experience the problem. I can feel the energy beams that are being directed into her body."

When I talked with my mother the next day, she said she was feeling much better.

Prayer and visualization also have healing power. On another occasion when my mother wasn't well, I was with a group of friends in New Jersey who prayed for her healing, and visualized her being surrounded by light. She afterward reported that she had been dozing at her home in Ohio at that moment, but was awakened with an experience of light surrounding her.

My mother, who is now in her spirit body, had a very special healing gift. When anything was wrong with any of us "kids," she would see a vision of us at the foot of her bed. Once, shortly before a disease manifested in her body, my sister Polly appeared at the foot of Mom's bed. And I appeared to her when I was in a deep depression as an eighteen-year-old in Europe—which is how she knew I was in trouble. But none of us ever remembered appearing to Mom to get help.

My mother was undoubtedly doing some important healing work during her sleep state. Since there were eight of us kids, I guess we unconsciously knew we should do something special when we needed her attention. Poor Mom—we would never let her rest!

Though I was never taught in any systematic way about the supernatural world as a child, I listened with great interest to stories of "supernatural" experiences of various relatives—not to mention hair-raising ghost stories. Thus the supernatural seemed natural to me as a child. My father was one of the last of the old-time storytellers from Jamestown, Tennessee, and we loved to sit on the porch on a summer evening and have him scare us to death with ghost stories from the mountains.

My mother was raised in Harrodsburg, Kentucky, where I was born. I vividly remember attending the wake of an aunt at my grandparents' farm outside of Harrodsburg, when I was about five. I listened, transfixed, as the adults talked about how my aunt had heard angelic music and seemed to be greeted by her deceased mother as she was dying.

I recently went back to Harrodsburg for a family reunion with all my brothers and sisters and my Uncle Matt and his children. I visited the home place where my grandparents had lived. The old house was merely a pile of bricks, though the barn was still standing. Uncle Matt told us about a picture he had of Grandma Carr. In the photograph, she was in front of the house. But about six feet from where she was standing, her "spirit body" was bending over the grave of her favorite dog, Rusty—who had once saved her life. Indeed, we are more than our physical bodies.

My Invisible Friends soon returned to the topic of healing:

ROMC: "I am being told by my friends that one very important aspect of healing is for humans to become aware of all the other dimensions within and around themselves.

"An awareness and belief in other dimensions opens up tremendous possibilities for help and revitalization. Many were healed in the Aesculapian temples in Rome and Greece because they believed in the invisible healers. We all have our own 'temples,' and this same process of healing will take place if we call upon our invisible healers for help.

"They are saying to me that healing is the process of balance in nature; there are many in their dimension who are eager to work with the earth level to help bring this balance. It is important not only to believe in the healing process, but also to ask for it. 'Ask, and you shall receive.' When they are called, teams of workers come into the earth level to help in the revitalization and healing process. So remember, belief and desire are equally important. These two, together, make up faith.

"There are situations in which healing can take place even when one is not consciously open to or aware of it. If another human acts as a mediator and establishes contact with the higher self of the person needing healing, healing can take place."

RAM: "Is there a particular place or environment that aids the healing process?"

ROMC: "Healing is a timeless phenomena and can occur at any time or place on the earth level. A group of believers asking for healing for others helps to create a very special environment for healing. The group can visualize a person in the healing light. This sets the environment for even instantaneous healing at a distance. Thus, there are helpers in both dimensions working for the healing of persons in need. A very strong vibration is built up through the thought-waves of a dedicated group, and this helps open the channels for healing.

"There is a special time on the earth level when emotional and mental healing is more effective, when the 'defenses' of the person are down. This is when a person is in the sleep state. Here, the best times for healing are shortly after the person has gone to sleep, and also when he or she has been through several dream stages, a few hours into the sleep. If a group will concentrate when the soul in need is in the sleep state, the healing energies can more easily penetrate the energy levels of the individual.

"Also, a group does not have to be together in the same place to work on healing. They can set a certain time to jointly send healing prayers and energies into the universe. This is just as effective as having the healing group gathered in one location."

RAM: "I would like to ask about aging. It seems that more and more healing is needed as we age. Why is it necessary to age?"

ROMC: "Aging is not necessary. It is an illusion of the mind that creates a breakdown in the physical form. It is completely possible for the mind to move the body outside of time, and thus keep it purified from the physical aging process. This is possible when the mind is in absolute control of the physical body. There have been those on your planet who have been able to achieve this, which is the natural state.

"Aging is the unnatural state. When the control of the physical body comes from outside, from the thought patterns and billions of energy trivia that bombard the human system, the result is aging. In the time dimension, humans perceive themselves as changing and aging, and therefore the physical body follows suit. If the body is not perceived as aging, it indeed will remain intact and always energized. You become like that which you look upon. When you see aging take place around you, then you think that this is a natural process. It is merely the power of suggestion.

"Aging is an unreal concept in the world of time. Because the higher self is not in control from the deeper levels of the reservoir of the mind, a decaying process takes place on the physical plane. As one gets in complete control of the physical from the deeper levels, then nothing from outside can penetrate.

"As you are able to gain this control, you will experience a change in perception—and your reality structure will reverse itself. What you once thought was real becomes the unreal, and what you thought was unreal becomes the real. But do not feel an urgency to accomplish this. Take it in stride, because a feeling of urgency creates a wrong environment, and anxieties create a blockage. Mental and spiritual discipline is important."

RAM: "Thank you for those thoughts. I think it is a little too late for some of us who are well on our way into the aging process. Can aging also be reversed?"

ROMC: "Everything is possible in the world of reality. Aging can be reversed because it is not real in the first place. Most humans live in the world of unreality."

RAM: "Thank you for your encouragement. Do you have more to say about the healing process?"

ROMC: "Yes, we do have another important point. We have discussed the five dimensions of the human self, and by now you realize that these dimensions are also an overall part of the consciousness of the earth dimension. All is interrelated, and perceived truly only from the inner dimensions of the human self. The outer is the unreal universe. The real can only be perceived and understood from the inner dimensions of the self.

"By now you undoubtedly have gathered that we try to introduce new concepts gently. We seek to present a concept on one level, and then return to it on another level, in more detail. Thus we bring the concepts through on various waves of energy. An energy pattern and flow has been built into these lessons that works upon the energy patterns of individuals who are ready to be opened up into various dimensions of their higher selves.

"This flow is very much like the Frequency Following Response discussed by you, Mr. Monroe. It sets up an energy pattern that keeps flowing, and in turn opens up levels into all dimensions of the human self. The very flow within the energies of this material has a healing pattern integrated within it.

"It is a healing pattern in that it will help facilitate a breakthrough in the blockages of the self. When perceptions change, energies can be transformed. When the breakthrough takes place and the flow continues in a pattern of its own, then the higher self of the individual takes over, and new levels of healing and teaching can transpire."

RAM: "Thank you. It is most interesting to learn that you have a healing pattern built into the energies that you send through to us. Can you explain a little more about how this pattern works?"

ROMC: "When individuals experience this material and come upon concepts that feel right to them at a 'knowing' level, a spiral of energy sets up a release button in their energy system that unlocks many levels of understanding that have been there but have not yet surfaced at a conscious level. The spiritual 'Ah, so!' experience helps a shift take place that goes on into infinity.

"At this point many amazing and wonderful things will happen to individuals who are released into their own higher knowing. They will also come into a much closer attunement to their own guidance system as this awakening takes place. Remember also that prayer and thanksgiving are basic keys to the process of healing in all human energy systems.

"We have said before that at the base of every human system is the principle of universal energy and knowledge. Every cell in the body is a pattern of the whole and is a universe in and of itself. All knowledge exists therein. Therefore, your bodies have a built-in healing capacity—the inner healer. But your cells must have full communication with each other in order to keep the human body functioning as it should, just as you must have full communication with each other in order to keep your planet functioning as it should. Because of the limitations in your individuals—thus on your planet—created by pollution and stress, your inner cells can have disease, with full communication blocked. Each cell in the plant life of the earth is alive with healing energy, so ingesting the earth's pure healing plants, as well as using prayer to ask for help, can stimulate your living cells to communicate with each other. When they become harmonious in purpose, healing can be instantaneous. This is all the pure God-energy that is the energy of love and the basis of all healing. Remember, the secret of life is life itself! Have reverence."

RAM: "There are many wars going on this planet at all times. Why do we continually have wars and killing of our fellow human beings?"

ROMC: "War is the manifestation of fear. The human ego is an encapsulated fear-form. Humans fear to be killed. Thus they kill out of fear, striking first before the fear turns in upon itself. The ego carries a false sense of power that manifests itself through illusory belief systems and concepts.

"The ego says, 'If you do not believe as I believe, then I shall kill you before you can change the way I think and take away from me all that I believe myself to be.' Under the influence of their egos, humans believe themselves to be nothing more than their thought-forms, which are encapsulated in fear. Fear is the only fuel that keeps your planetary wars alive. And it is only love that can transform your planet."

RAM: "So therefore, love is the only energy that will ultimately create the healing and transformation of our planet?"

ROMC: "That is indeed so. Love is a powerful energy that is to be not simply understood, but lived. The great love guardian of your planet, known as the man Jesus, came from the highest God-energy to teach the pure lesson of love. That is why all humans have come to planet Earth, to learn to love in the fullest sense of the word. The one called Jesus came to show you how this can be done. The magnitude of his love polarized the fear levels, which is what caused his physical body to be crucified.

"However, the spirit of this highly evolved energy being was released into the world to break through all fear barriers. This is known as the Holy Spirit, and has helped tremendously in the evolution of the planet. This is the energy that is helping the earth to shift into its higher levels of energy and is leading to the millennium or the 'thousand years of peace,' according to the earth-time frame."

RAM: "Thank you. It is not always easy, but we will keep trying."

ROMC: "It is time for us to leave. Thank you again for your caring attitude."

RAM: "It is our pleasure. (pause) Come back slowly, Rosie. Take your time. Count yourself back down."

ROMC: (pause) "I'm back. I was watching and listening again. That was really fascinating. I know I can go out and explore now. But it's more interesting to stay here and learn from my helpers."

RAM: "I agree. That's why I stay and listen."

ROMC: "Oh, you mean you could go out and explore with me?"

RAM: "I'm sure I could. But why go anywhere else when I can be where the action is?"

ROMC: "You're right!"

~19~

THE WISDOM AND PHILOSOPHY OF THE INVISIBLES

In the spring of 1975, David was teaching a course on World Religions at Blue Ridge Community College. As part of the course requirements, the students were to write a term paper on a world religion or religious thinker of their choice. To guide them in their research and help organize their writing, David handed out an outline of questions for the students to answer, which covered a large number of topics that most religions address—for example, "What is the nature of God?"

One of the students in the class was Leslie Moyer, a good friend of ours. Perhaps because of my background in theology, Leslie selected me as her choice of a religious thinker, and asked me to express my religious views in answer to the questions on David's outline.

As I looked over the list of questions late one evening, it struck me that it would be interesting to see how my Invisible Helpers would answer them! So at about three o'clock in the morning I sat down at my typewriter, went into the Hemi-Sync state, and waited quietly. I then typed what I received in answer to each question, just as I would speak the answers to Bob's questions in our Explorer sessions at the lab.

The answers from the Invisibles came so quickly that it seemed as though I was in this altered state for only a few minutes. But when I stopped, I had typed many pages of single-spaced material.

The following are the responses I received to David's list of questions.

1. Geographical Setting

In what country did your religious system originate?
"The religious system with which I am now involved originated within the soul, which is the true center of all religious systems. If a religious system is not based within the soul it is of man, and not of the God/man relationship. Tapping the soul is tapping the Source, which is the basis of all reality. Tapping the Source brings man into an at-one-ment with the highest reality, the true return of man to his highest nature."

What are the characteristics of the early adherents of the religion (e.g., national, cultural, racial, etc.)?
"The earliest adherent of this religion was man in his pure light form before he began to explore on his own and get caught in the lower reality, which is the slower vibration that takes in the earth plane.

"The souls on the earth plane now are mostly the souls who chose to come into this vibration and as a result could not rise above themselves, so have been reincarnating for many centuries. The enlightened souls who have lived on the earth plane are working to help raise the vibration of their fellow earth mates, and work as spiritual guides, teachers, inspirators, guardian angels, and so forth, in the body and out, and will continue to work with the earth level until the last soul is raised.

"All souls are early adherents of the true religion, which is absolute unfoldment, for all souls have as a part of their nature that highest light quality, which is the God-quality in which man was created.

"Man was created in the likeness of God; therefore, man is God. And the man who separates himself from the true God-self is an adherent to the earth religion, which is man-made and falls short of the true reality of the higher God-self."

What is the geographical distribution of the followers of the religion today?
"The universe, which is merely an atom in the soul of the Creator."

2. Historical Setting

Describe the life of the founder of the religion, if there is one.
"In the beginning there was no beginning. There merely was the light energy that was within the pulsating atom that is the very element of all life. I use the term 'atom,' for that is what the earth mind understands. It is a universe in itself. It is a universe, and it makes up the universe. Within the human form are billions of universes that have within them universes. We are a universe and are a part of a universe, just as we are God and are a part of God.

"There are many levels on which the universes operate. The universe that man can see through the microscope and telescope is the universe on the same vibration as the universe that makes up the particles of the body. Each galaxy is only a cluster of atoms operating on the same vibration.

"There is time and space in the dimension in which the outer self functions, but there is no time and space in the dimension on which the soul vibrates. The billions of universes that make up the outer human body in themselves contain the knowledge of that universe. The trillions of vibrating universes that make up the human soul are computers that contain all knowledge, because they are knowledge. They are the form of the essence of reality. There is no other knowledge. There is no other reality.

"The human body and the human soul must operate in harmony to tap into the individual's essence for the truth that is its very being. It is not necessary to look to the universes without. To tap the universes within is to tap into truth, and that is the essence of true religion. True religion is man's at-onement with his very essence. Therefore, the life of the founder is life itself."

Describe any major leaders who later influenced the development of the religion (as well as forerunners, if any).

"All souls, by the very essence of their being, are the major leaders. The only true leader is that Source within every human soul that dips into its own reservoir to drink of the water of renewal. The restless and seeking self is the true leader that eventually leads man back to his God-self. All souls will be restless until they rest in their true nature, which is the God-self.

"Many earth lifetimes are necessary to temper the spiritual restlessness which leads to the necessary unfoldment. The man and soul out of touch with itself is out of touch with the true reality. There is no other reality than true *being*. And *becoming* is the path that the soul takes through earth time to be nurtured and reawakened to its true reality.

"When the inner and outer universes come together in true harmony, there is an instant conversion into reality. The earth level is only an illusion created by the lower vibration of the many universes that are vibrating at their full capacity. Therefore, as the souls of the earth level and the souls of the surrounding galaxies and universes vibrate at their pure frequency, there will be that conversion into the non-dimensional reality of pure *light being*.

"The Aquarian Age is the speeding up of vibrations on many levels of the existing visible universe, and many dimensions of the soul level of existence. Those souls that do not go with the evolution will be burned out and put into a separate universe of like vibration to be tempered toward evolvement in a new way."

If there are no known founders of the religion, what are its historic beginnings?

"There is no beginning and there is no end. There merely

is. There are beginnings and ends to planets and galaxies only because they were created by man's slower vibrations. There are beginnings and ends to physical bodies, but these were also created by man's slower or lower self. 'Beginning' and 'end' are earth terms representing transposition from one energy form to another. Every planet and galaxy is made up of its higher aspect, which is and always will be. Every human is made up of its higher self, which is and always will be.

3. Inspired Literature

Describe the nature of the sacred books (scriptures) of the religion.
"Each being is the sacred book that contains all knowledge and all reality in and of itself."

4. Origin and Destiny of the Universe

What is the origin, and final end, of the physical universe, according to your religion? Of the earth, in particular? (That is, how and when were the universe and the earth created? How and when will they end?)
"It was created from man's need to create. Man, in experimenting with his own energy forms, split the atom of his very being, which took him away from his true essence and divided his physical from his spiritual. Therefore, in being separated from his higher self, which you call God, his dimension became unbalanced, and the physical form was created out of harmony with reality. When man gets back in tune with his true reality, there will no longer be a physical dimension, for it exists only as an illusion, man's illusion—and need for what he considers his own creation.

"The fallen angel is the self that fell from itself—that split itself into two parts to assert its individuality, but at the same time created illusion and separation from the true reality that is what man calls God. That is why there is time in the physical realm. Time is created as well by man, and is also an illusion.

"The individual soul that comes to itself in harmony lives outside of time in the true reality. There are souls on the earth that have reached this level and can at any time walk into the higher dimensions. When man and the earth and the universes come to their own harmony within and without, there will no longer be the physical. Those who fear the ending of the physical earth are the souls who are keeping the unreal as the real, and therefore are locked into untruth and illusion.

"All that is physical has a beginning and an end, and this is important on the path back to the true self. Man created the physical universe and universes, and he in turn will destroy that which he created. He must destroy the illusion in his mind's eye. However, if he destroys it with his own lower nature, there will be many souls trapped in the earth shell, locked into their own illusions.

"The earth is an entity in itself and is alive, in that it is a creation made up of the atoms of being. Just as man has a soul, the earth and all physical matter have a higher dimension. For the physical is only a shadow of the real, which is unseen to the physical eye. The great teacher said, 'Now we see through a glass darkly, but then face to face.' This is the soul of man seeing into its own true reality.

"To drop the body does not mean that man steps into reality. Reality is a dimension of existence, not a state of existence. There are many unseen beings or forces locked into the circle of their own illusion.

"The final end of the earth is merely a stage of growth into the true reality, as was stated before. The final end is only an outer illusion. The real still exists, and will always exist.

"There is only one reality and that is the God-force, as you call it. All else is an illusion."

5. Nature of Deity

Is the religion pantheistic, polytheistic, dualistic, or monotheistic?

"True religion is all of these; it is also none of these. It is all of these because it is a part of man's nature, and man's earth nature created these earth terms for his understanding. But it is not any of these because they are merely word forms to describe man's illusion of his unbeing. His being cannot be described by earth terms. It is only understood by its own higher nature.

What is the nature of God (or the gods), i.e., what is God like?

"Man creates God in his own image; therefore, this is a false god. Man's need to create God shows that he has fallen from his own true God-nature. You do not have to create that which is already there.

"God is that vital living force in all that is real. Because man has created his own unreality, he has separated himself from the true nature of his reality, which is God. God *is*. And the soul in tune with its own reality *knows*.

"Knowing is a vital part of being. The soul in tune with its higher self has no earth words to describe its true nature.

"God is experienced, not understood.

"Man's mind is a part of the physical creation, and therefore cannot comprehend the true nature of that which goes beyond itself. Experiencing and knowing God is the harmony and attunement that the released soul has with itself and all physical and nonphysical elements. *Love* is that outpouring of energy that comes from the attunement of inner and outer universes.

"Man in his own unreality knows only snatches of the energy force called love. Pure love could dissolve the need for the physical universe. The earth and universe would be enveloped in this energy form and would be automatically moved into a higher vibration, coming closer to its true nature.

"That force that is pure love and pure energy is what man would label God. There are many more dimensions that man cannot understand but can *know* by the essence of his very being and the true nature of his reality, which is God.

"There are many isolated energy sources in the invisible that have related to certain energy levels of similar vibration on the earth level. These energy beings and sources have been called God. This is the main problem that man encounters. That knowledge that is out of tune with man's nature is false knowledge. Many groups of souls feel that their knowledge source is right, and will destroy physical bodies to prove their point. This in itself is proof of its disharmony and untruth.

"Energy forms or beings that have dropped the body, but have not evolved, often join together to create new 'religions,' which merely brings man further from his true reality."

Is God (or the gods) actively involved in human affairs? How?
"Pure God-form *is* human affairs. False gods *are actively involved in* human affairs."

6. Nature of the Spirit World

What is the nature of the nonphysical spirit world?
"There is no such thing as a world outside that which man has created for his own illusion. That which is real is a dimensional existence. That which is unreal is an energy level that is locked into itself, thus slowing itself down and appearing to a soul locked into itself as a 'form.'

"True vibrating energy that does not get locked into itself does not have form. Therefore, souls and universes that drop the physical temporarily, but do not reorganize in an energy flow, create a temporary existence for the soul form. A soul in its highest form is without form. Pure light energy flow in tune with its complete being is not comprehensible to the physical mind, nor is it desirable to the physical mind, as it tries to comprehend being without form.

"As he created the physical world, man also creates the spirit world in which he desires to be enveloped. Therefore, the spirit world is that world that each soul creates. Other souls on the same vibration create a similar world. They are in awareness of and in attunement with each other, since the thought-forms are of the same essence. Thus spirit worlds that are related to earth beings are not the true reality, because they are still forms in the physical soul's eye. There are still several evolutions beyond on the soul's path to reality."

Does the spirit world include angels or demonic beings? What kinds?

"Angels and demonic beings are energy forms and are a part of the nature of earth-consciousness. There are many levels in between them.

"The angels, as they are called, being on a higher rate of atomic vibration, are aware of the presence of lower energy forms that you call demons. The lower energy forms, being a slower vibration, cannot comprehend the presence of that which transcends their own temporary reality.

"The higher forms are constantly seeking to help the slower-vibration groups, to create an atomic transposition and enlightenment. The lower form of vibration will not transcend until it is released from within the inner universes.

"Nothing stands still. All is motion that works toward its higher fulfillment. That which is the highest motion is non-motion, since it is outside of all known elements."

7. Nature of Man

What is the nature (makeup) of man?

"Man is the essence of all reality. Man is the product of his own energy field and consciousness. Man in his separateness is the self fallen from its true nature and locked into its own unreality.

"Man in his wholeness is the complete integration of all energy flow and the complete attunement of all elements with its true nature. Man locked into himself is man. Man released from himself is God.

"The only reality is the higher self released to return to its own integral consciousness."

How was man created? When? Where?

"The true nature of man is and always was, since the God-man consciousness has no beginning and no end. Man as the self fallen from itself created time, and is locked temporarily in this state until he returns to his true reality.

Is man's makeup different now from when he was first created? How?

"Man locked into his separateness from reality is the same image and record that plays over and over in time until he becomes bored with his own self-sufficiency and seeks the higher integration."

Is man involved in a cycle of death and rebirth? If so, when does this cycle end?

"Man is involved in a cycle of death and rebirth as long as he is separated from his reality, which has no beginning and no end. The cycle will end when he realizes that he has created this state of existence to fulfill his own unfulfillment. He will step off the treadmill of time and illusion when he comes into attunement with his pure being."

8. Man's Dilemma

What is man's ultimate problem or problems that the religion answers?

"There are no problems other than those which man has created for himself in separating from his pure Source. There will always be these problems until man returns to his pure Source and reality.

"Suffering is man-made. Suffering is the fire that melts the steel or turns the water into steam. Suffering is that which man has created to temper and prod himself to help work his way back to the true Source.

"Suffering is the fracture of the universes that make up the true nature of the soul and therefore in essence is good, as all that is is good. Death and rebirth are the fracture that man created for himself in falling from the flow of his own reality, and will continue until he gets back into the pure flow. Therefore, rebirth and death are good in that they will continue until the soul realizes the unnecessity of this fractured state of existence.

"All that *is* is good, in that it is all unreality working its way through time and form back to its pure state. The earth, as it rotates, is man's treadmill, which will always revolve in the same way under his feet until he realizes that he does not need to be on the earth, which was created in his own fractured state."

9. Way of Salvation

How is man's salvation, or ultimate happiness, achieved?

"It is achieved through man's attunement with his higher self, and thus attunement with the trillions of molecular universes that make up his being and exist not in time and space, but in a patterned dimension not understandable to the human mind. Once man becomes aware of his own reality, he becomes aware of all reality, thereby coming back into his own original Source."

What is the relative importance of faith versus good deeds in achieving salvation?

"Good deeds are on the physical level; faith is on the soul level. But neither lead to salvation, because they are man-made concepts and are often misinterpreted. True faith is the soul that recognizes its higher self in the higher self of the evolved being, Jesus the Christ, who came to teach pure atonement.

"Souls that are out of harmony with self bring the Christ-form down to their own unreality level. They place the Christ-light form in their own concept, which is not the real world, but of the false thought-forms that keep the world on the lower vibration.

"Those who recognize their true higher self in the Christ-God self are immediately released into their higher being. But these are few in number."

How important is the priest (ritual or ceremonial leader) in achieving salvation?

"The true priest is the higher self that helps bring man back into attunement with himself, and therefore is very important in achieving what you call salvation.

"Salvation, as man conceives of it, is further separation from the God-self, for it teaches fracture, and fracture is not wholeness.

"There is no hell other than that which the believers create and conceive of in their physical mind's eye. Hell can be considered that state of existence that man is in until he comes back into his whole being."

To what extent may the individual believer be a priest or prophet?

"All souls are the priests and prophets of their own inner universe. The true priest and true prophet is that which speaks from within the chambers of the soul yearning to reach its wholeness."

10. Mode of Worship

Are acts of worship important in the religion?

"True worship is true being in awareness of its reality. All other forms are man-made illusions that help keep man on his man-made treadmill and block the way for growth by continuing to lock man into a concept that is not in tune with his own reality.

"Throw out all forms of man-made concepts of religion, and it is at that point that true reality has the freedom to emerge from the prison cell that it has been pushed into. The soul free to be its own is the soul in the act of worship."

Are mystical experiences important in communion with God?

"A mystical experience is that which seems unreal in a real world but is actually that which is real in an unreal world. Mystical experience is the breakthrough of the soul into the truth of its reality. It is important in that it is a signpost of growth."

11. Rules of Conduct

What are the major norms of conduct in the religion (ethical rules, virtues)?

"'Being' preceded by 'becoming'! It is a soul free of ethical rules, a soul in tune with its own music and in step with its own rhythm."

12. Man's Ultimate Destiny

What is man's ultimate destiny?
"To come back into wholeness and attunement with his highest God-self."

What happens to man after death?
"Death is a soul freed of its physical body, and at that point it is attracted to its own thought-forms and energy vibrations.
"You become what you believe you are, and you will remain that until you realize and become what you really are."

Is there a belief in a heavenly existence?
"Heaven is absolute reality, and therefore it exists, but not as it is conceived in the mind's eye or the eye's mind."

Is there a belief in a purgatory state? Hell?
"Purgatory and hell represent man locked into his own unreality."

What are each of these places or conditions like?
"They are like the universes that make up each soul condition. Many souls bathe in a temporary enjoyment of their own special type of hell until they burn themselves out. Hell is a burning out of the dross that puts the blinders on the soul's true eyesight."

Can man progress or change his condition after death?
"Man's condition inside and outside the body is of his own creation and can be changed in any split second of infinity. There is nothing holding man back from true reality but himself."

Does man ever reach ultimate perfection? How? When?
"Man is ultimate perfection. But because he created an illusion around his being, he lives in fragmentation and

unreality that blind him from the truth of his ultimate being and his at-onement with all reality. Perfection is there. It is merely a matter of becoming a released state of consciousness that exists outside of man-made earth and time."

13. Attitude Toward Other Religions and the State

What is the religion's attitude toward other faiths?
"There is only one reality, and therefore only one true faith."

What is the religion's attitude toward the state or nation?
"The state or nation is merely the product of man's disillusionment and his attempt to integrate his disintegration. Man continually sets up laws, conduct codes, and so forth, through that inner-soul desire to come back into its pure perfection, to be released into the pure state.

"Therefore, the state or nation becomes a mass illusion that contributes to the soul's growth only when it realizes that it must break away from all worldly codes of conduct that imprison the soul rather than work toward its release.

"Because all is ultimate good, in that it forces man continually to see his soul's reflection, the state is important for mass growth. But it will always break down, as it is not based in reality. It has its birth and death stages, just as all thought and life forms have."

*I Ask Their Guidance and
Protection . . .*

THE NATURE OF GUIDANCE

When Bob and I first began our Explorer sessions, he asked the leader of my Invisible Helpers what his name was. The helper replied that he preferred not to be called by any name because that would tend to lock his energies into the earth plane. He added that our desire for information at the start of each session was enough to draw the Invisible Helpers to us immediately.

However, Bob continued to want to refer to the leader by some name, so he made up one. Since I had a slight Asian accent when I was repeating the leader's words while in an altered state, Bob good-humoredly started calling him "Ah, So"!

Bob did not use this name directly in conversing with the leader. But whenever he spoke to others about our sessions, he would refer to what "Ah, So" had said. Bob received so much new information from my guiding energies that whenever the head of the Invisible Helpers introduced new concepts and material, Bob would think to himself, "Ah, so . . ." (in other words, "that's what that means," or "that explains that"). So it became natural for us to call our friend, "Ah, So."

When you read the following information on the topic of the nature of guidance you may hear yourself thinking, "Ah, so!"

ROMC: "We are ready. Repeat your questions one at a time, and we will answer them as we are able."

RAM: "Very good. The first question: We perceive various methods that are being employed in our communication with you. Can we get a more accurate description of how this communication takes place, and something about the methods being used?"

ROMC: "Please hold until we are able to shift levels to answer this question." (It felt as if someone besides "Ah, So" was speaking at first, and that the helpers had to shift energies to bring him in to answer questions.)

RAM: "Very good. Time lapse: one and a half minutes. Reel time: fifteen minutes."

ROMC: ("Ah, So" begins communicating) "Dear friend, I would like to speak to you directly on the subject of methods employed in communication. I will share with you the process that takes place when I work with this energy body. Then we will shift levels and other techniques will be explained as the process itself takes place."

RAM: "Thank you very much."

ROMC: "I'm on the same consciousness level with this entity (Rosalind). We are one and the same, yet we are separate. The energies through which I work are the energies of the earth-level connections. I existed on the earth-time level many thousands of years ago in earth time. I am in contact with this entity because we were on the same level and rate of vibration.

"I say that we are one and the same because groups of souls work together on certain levels or rates of vibration. Those souls working together on a given level could be considered 'group souls.'

"This entity has been in the earth level many times. I have not existed in the earth level for many centuries. The others who work with this entity have not been in the earth vibration at all, but are on the same ray that we are on, although in a completely different energy system.

"Because of the earth contact I have had, I am able to work directly through the physical energies of this entity. This is the energy that is considered the earth level, and it stays with the souls that keep in close contact with the earth for reasons of their own growth, and of helping other souls in the growth process. The process of growing and the process of sharing is one and the same. In the process of sharing, the soul is still in a stage of its growth.

"The physical energies within this entity, and the energies that are a part of my soul-consciousness, are on the same vibratory rate. Therefore, I can speak directly through the vocal cords of this dear soul, who has worked many lifetimes helping other souls to understand their purpose and meaning.

"This soul has worked to help souls come into contact with their inner levels of existence. She has worked closely with concepts of death, helping souls to understand the nature of life and the reality of death—namely, that it does not exist. Between lifetimes she has helped to guide souls through their transition periods. She has worked in many levels in both dimensions. She and I are on the same vibration because this has been my purpose throughout the centuries of time and timelessness.

"I choose not to be identified by name because this ties my energies directly into the earth life, and I feel that I can be of greater benefit by not coming back into the earth energies with an energy identification, which is what a name is.

"It has been many centuries since I have walked the earth. Therefore, I can carry the last vibrations of my earth presence in my speaking. That is why there is a detection of an accent that would be considered Oriental. I was in the Orient many centuries ago when the vibrations of the earth were of a level of great learning and the energies were high. The souls that lived at that time were involved in lifting the energies of all who lived on the earth to a level where souls were able to communicate directly with each other.

"Let me explain further my purpose for coming through this entity. We work together as a group. I say a group, but it is a soul level. Every soul has its level and rate of vibration. As a result there are souls connecting on a direct rate of vibration—souls that have worked together closely throughout many ages of earth time and before the earth time, and who will work together beyond the earth time.

"A group soul is a part of every being and every soul. However, many souls are at a level in the earth existence where they are not aware of their oneness with other levels of consciousness. Those souls who are unaware of the other levels of their existence have chosen to come in for different degrees of personal growth. At the point where they come into the perception of their oneness with all levels of energy, this is the stage where they have grown into the awareness of their own existence and their connection to all life forms. They would then be able to get in touch with their soul group.

"There are many in the earth level at this time who are not aware of the levels of their existence and are working very much in an individual state. These are souls locked into a specific level, and they are working on their own. At least, they think they are working on their own. No one is ever really working 'on their own.'

"When a soul gets to the stage in which it is opened out to all levels of inner energies, it then becomes aware of its oneness with all energies of the universe. Now, we have chosen to work together with this entity specifically to help other souls become aware of their many levels of existence.

"This is our particular purpose at this stage of development of our personal growth and awareness. We have come to the level of awareness where we understand the nature of reality and are trying to open up other souls to this understanding. This is the very basis of the material that is going to be sent out into the universe in printed form. This material will help souls become aware of the nature of their inner energies to the extent that they will open up into unlimited levels of their own universe.

"Each soul is a universe of energies. As the levels are opened up, or there is an awakening in the mind of the soul, then there is an awareness that limitations do not exist. At this point, souls realize that they are not limited to the bodies they inhabit, and that they are much more than their physical bodies.

"Once a soul comes to this realization, there is an awakening into the higher energies. It is at this stage that the soul becomes a helping or service soul, and can help awaken other slumbering souls into this realization.

"We work with the intergroup energies specifically. The process is difficult to describe in earth terms. To understand the nature of consciousness and the levels therein is to understand the process that takes place. Because there has been a similarity in the nature of our purpose on the earth level, we work on the same vibrations.

"Souls work on many levels of vibration and can shift from one level to another depending upon the purpose and nature of the work at the time they are in direct contact. Our particular rate of vibration at this time has to do with our distinct purpose of opening up the consciousness of souls to their many levels of existence. This is why I am able to work with this entity.

"Now, there are other processes whereby entities from outside the earth level can enter into the earth. Higher-energy levels that you on the earth plane call angels work with the souls that are very much in the earth vibration and live closely connected to the earth. These souls are souls that have not awakened to any knowledge of their being and are therefore locked into a time capsule that keeps them very close to the earth energies.

"There are souls living in the darkness of their own vibrations, and because of a hunger and need for light nourishment, they try to penetrate breaks in the energy of other unbalanced souls. The lowest vibration of the soul in the earth body will attract to itself the entity that is earthbound. Like attracts like because of the similarities of the needs of both souls, in the body and out. It is very important while in the earth level to keep the energies balanced.

"Once the energy of the possessing spirit locks itself in, it becomes difficult for both souls to grow until they are able to unlock the lower aspects of their energies. The etheric-substance body of the disembodied soul can actually penetrate into the etheric-substance level of the embodied soul, and it often takes outside help to separate the souls. In many cases, there are karmic ties that have not been worked out in the proper manner.

"When we speak through earth energies such as the energies of this entity, we do not go into the energy body in the manner that possessing spirits do. We work through beams of high vibrations, called light. This is the important part of the technology of which you speak.

"All souls have all levels of energy. The opening up of the energies is what makes the difference in soul growth. Souls who are living in the earth level are there to work through their own energy levels in a very intense way. The energies of planet Earth are much more intense than energy levels of other dimensions. The earth/time frictions of duality cause more rapid growth.

"The soul can grow on several levels at one time. But earth is specifically the emotional level of the universe. Many choose earth for their emotional growth, which is represented in the body by the area of the solar plexus and heart energies. There are levels in other physical planets that are on other dimensions of energy and vibrations. When souls are in intense growth in other aspects of their energy system, they may choose other planets for this growth. At this time the earth is in a very intense level of its own growth.

"There are many souls in the vibrations around the earth, which are also the vibrations of their own being, who have dropped their physical bodies and are not aware that they are 'dead.' These are called 'earthbound' spirits. Such souls are often locked into emotional levels of their own being. They are usually not aware of anything outside themselves, and therefore cannot communicate and relate on any level other than a specific earth-time level.

"It is easier for those in the earth vibration to relate to these confused souls, since such souls are closer to the earth than the other dimension. There are those who are doing a very specialized work called 'rescue work.' Basically, they help to rescue souls from the pits of their own energies. When a soul moves rapidly from one energy level to another, if it has a strong emotional tie to the earth level, it often still perceives itself to be in the physical body, even though it is looking at its etheric-substance body.

"There are many levels of these low-vibration souls. The possessing souls are usually of a very slow vibration. The confused souls are usually on a higher rate of vibration, but because of imbalance in perception, they are locked into a time warp—and therefore still think they are functioning on an earth time/space level.

"Many of the possessing souls would be considered to be of an 'evil' nature, according to earth terms. These souls are very difficult to work with because they are so strongly embedded in their own negative energy forces. Only with the help of service souls, who understand the nature of consciousness and the level of love and understanding of all beings and all souls, can these souls be helped and released into further growth. Helpers are working from both dimensions with these lower-vibratory souls. These are angels, both in earth bodies and out of earth bodies, and they work together.

"There will be more and more work done in this area, because all souls must be released and opened into their higher levels of consciousness before the earth will transform to its higher state. Every soul that exists in the earth-consciousness, as it evolves, works for the greater good of all other souls. They are on the earth ray, and are all tied into each other's growth. As we have stressed, everything is inter-related.

"Many souls work unconsciously on different levels during their sleep state. These traveling sleep helpers work with souls in the body and out, for healing and regeneration. These are souls who work consciously with the earthbound souls; there are also those who are not aware that they work with such souls during their sleeping state.

"Many souls who are attracted to your Institute, and who are interested in raising their consciousness, work intently on many levels during their sleep state. They work with the earthbound entities, and also with physical beings who are in need and call out for help in different ways, especially through prayer.

"Therefore, many who are attracted to your Institute are often on a level of vibration of wanting to know consciously that which they do, because there is an unconscious knowledge within them that they are involved in something much beyond their own understanding. There is a desire to have a true knowledge of their consciousness levels. This very desire is a sign that a soul is in a breakthrough and in search of an understanding of its fuller nature.

"The souls that work on different levels in their sleep state can ask, while they are in a level of relaxation, what they do to help others while they are sleeping. If this question is asked before going into the sleeping state, then more awareness of the nature of the work done in this state will be received—if indeed the soul does 'moonlighting' in the true sense of the word.

"However, it is not always important to be aware of the work done, because often the souls that are involved in the awakening of other soul levels are entities who are working intensely in the earth body during the waking state. Many are in the helping professions, and many are in the helping consciousness."

RAM: "Ah, so. Very interesting. The question is, 'Why does this barrier exist within the soul?'"

ROMC: "There is no barrier. The self perceives on a very narrow spectrum. Therefore, it is a soul locked into its own narrow perceptions. Once narrow perceptions are dropped, the horizon widens."

RAM: "Thank you. How did the physical matter of earth begin in the first place?"

ROMC: "I am going to step out. There is another source that would like to speak to you now."

RAM: "Very good. Reel time: 58 minutes."

ROMC: (pause) "Dear friend, we have a very special lesson for you on the subject of how it all began. We would like for you to continue this session at the very same time tomorrow. We want to take you step-by-step through a lesson on creativity. We would like for you to have available with you some sheets of paper, a pencil, and a pair of scissors to aid in the learning process.

"Let me say that the one who was speaking before is a light being who has worked with this soul throughout many levels, in time and out. There are many others working with her, as there are many who work with every soul. I am working through the soul level of this entity as well. I am on a different dimension, and work through the mental level.

"You are interested in the process that takes place to create this communication. It is the 'like-attracts-like' law in the universe. This is where a particular energy outside the physical level is attracted to similar energy within the physical level.

"We will step aside, but say that there is much we want to talk about. We would like to suggest that as your growing energies become balanced on the earth level, you try to have more regular sessions so that the energy flow can be steady. There is so much material that is to be covered, and in the earth time there are limitations. We feel an urgency to get the material through so that it can get into written form, and thereby into the consciousness level of souls who are in need of growth and are searching for new inspiration and openings into their higher selves.

"When souls are attracted to you, remember that this is the reason that you have chosen to do this work: to help souls who are interested in awakening into their higher energy forms. This is why you have chosen to come into the earth level at this time. It is for your growth as well. As you are sharing, you are also growing.

"But you must be very careful to conserve your own energies. You must limit your activities while continuing this type of exploration work. All other types of work you can turn over to others who are capable of doing it.

"You are fulfilling the purpose for which you came, and know you must fulfill this work before you leave the earth body. You will stay in the earth body until you feel that you have accomplished that for which you came. Just remember that you are a facilitator and are helping in the facilitation of other souls into a higher understanding of themselves.

"We say that it is a privilege, as always, to be able to speak to you and to work through this energy body for this purpose. We shall step aside and will look forward to our next session with you."

RAM: "Thank you very much. We shall see you tomorrow. Reel time: one hour, twenty-two minutes. (pause) Are you back?"

ROMC: "I think so. Is it that long? Gosh, it seems as if the session was only about three minutes long! I must have been in the no-time dimension."

The Invisibles continually speak about going within to get in touch with our inner guidance, our higher self, our internal universes. They also stress the importance of asking for help. A few years ago, I read a book entitled *The Secret Science Behind Miracles*, by Max Freedom Long, published by DeVorss and Company. In this book there is an excellent example of asking for assistance and receiving guidance. The story (pp. 326-332) goes as follows:

> In Honolulu in the early twenties a large hotel was built. A man from the mainland was sent to put in the elevators. I became acquainted with him and found that he had some most unusual powers . . .
> This man's story is this: He had, at an earlier period in his life, a run of bad luck as an installation engineer for a large elevator manufacturing company. Men working on jobs under him were constantly being injured despite his care. At last the elevator company discharged him. At that time he had an invalid daughter over twenty who had been bedfast for months. His wife had died a few years earlier and his daughter had kept the house. When he lost his job the times were so hard that he could not find other employment. To make matters worse, he lost his

health, one ailment after another sending him to the doctor until he was compelled to remain in bed most of his time.

In desperation he tried Christian Science, faithfully reading the works of the founder and trying in all ways to follow the orders given him. Getting no results, he turned to New Thought, and such other religious movements as had literature on healing.

At last, running out of funds, becoming almost completely bedfast, and quite desperate, he concluded that all religious teachings were imperfect, but that there must be a higher intelligence to which man could appeal if he could only make his appeal heard. With this in mind he spent his time and strength day after day in an endeavor to reach out and find the high intelligence.

One day he suddenly sensed the fact that he had at last contacted something. He felt an electric tingling which was sharp and short, unlike anything he had ever before experienced. Immediately he cried out that he must have help at all costs, and that he was leaving his bed to demonstrate his faith by the effort.

Little by little he managed to rise from the side of the bed to his feet, praying continuously. He took one uncertain step, then another.

To his joy he found that he was growing miraculously stronger. His prayers turned to praise and in a matter of minutes he seemed to be completely cured and his full strength restored.

Triumphant and thrilled at his discovery, he went to his daughter's room and told her what had happened. He urged her to try to contact the new "Something." He tried to contact it again, himself, but seemed unable to do so.

Several days passed. He took up his life where he had left off, and tried almost hourly to repeat the mental processes which had enabled him to contact the "Something." Soon, and again with great suddenness and with the same electric tingling, the contact was made. Instantly he began to pray frantically to the "Something" to heal his daughter. He rushed into her room, still praying, caught her by the hands, and began pulling her to her feet. "Use your faith! Get up and show that you can!" The daughter responded, praying fervently and exerting herself to the utmost to leave her bed. As in his case, the needed strength was supplied. She rose, took a step, then another. The miracle of instant healing came to her as it had come to him. Voicing her thanks, she dressed and entered a new life of health.

A few days later he again made the electric contact. He had been waiting for it and had his prayer learned by heart. Instantly he voiced it. He asked to have his former job back with the elevator construction company. Confident that his prayer would be answered, he went directly to the company office and to the man who had discharged him months before. Making no explanation of any kind, he said quietly, "I am ready for work again. Where do you need me?" The man behind the desk looked at him intently for a moment, then took from his desk a bundle of papers which he held out to him, naming the city in which the installation job was to be done.

That was the beginning of an unbelievable career. He learned by practice to contact the "Something" almost at will, and never allowed a morning or evening to pass without the contact. He learned to ask to be shown any danger which lay ahead on the job, and would be warned by a strong sense of danger if there was an emergency coming up. Once having received such a warning, he would make his contact on the job and ask for guidance. Nothing came in words, but he felt urges to act in certain ways. He would find the sense of danger growing until it became almost continuous and, as he went to different parts of his jobs, the danger sense intensified around some particular place. He would station himself there, calling his trusted foreman or others to stand with him, and all would watch to prevent trouble. Accident after accident was thus caught in the nick of time and prevented . . .

This man had, for a period of several years, been drawing from the company each year a very considerable premium because no men were injured on any job which he supervised. He was given the difficult and *dangerous assignments, and he never failed. His health and that of his daughter had remained excellent.*

In this case we have an example of instant healing of physical ills, also of financial troubles, healings of body and purse. The part played by the vital force is plain to see, as is the necessity of taking time to train the lower self in the work of contacting the High Self.

Even more important, if such a thing can be, is the fact proved by this case that daily contact and hourly guidance may be had from the High Self if asked for!

~21~

THE PATRICK EVENT

The event came as a surprise to Bob and two unsuspecting Gateway participants. The session took place in the training facility on the New Land because the new lab was not yet completed. Gateway training was in session, but we slipped into a CHEC Unit during the afternoon break. Two participants remained in their CHEC Units for the break and experienced the whole session, because Bob forgot to shut off the sound system. The session was so powerful that it blew out the wiring of the CHEC Unit that I was using and the two beside it. We got through the session, but before the units could be used again, they had to be completely rewired.

Why this electrical anomaly happened, none of us knew. It was as strange as our car batteries going dead. Perhaps the technology the Invisible Helpers use is so much more powerful than our electronic systems that it simply blows ours out during particularly powerful sessions such as that of 'beaming someone in on a strong light ray,' as happened that day.

Melissa Jager—the talented director of training at the Institute for over seven years, who had contributed so much to the development and success of the Gateway training program—was in the Control Room with Bob during the session. When the Invisible Helpers told Bob that they were going to send a "lost soul" into my energies on a light beam, Melissa reported that Bob sat staring at the microphone with his mouth open and unable to speak!

In spite of the Invisibles' references to the situation of earthbound spirits around our planet, such as discussed in the previous chapter, Bob did not understand the technology of how such beings could be brought through me, and he was concerned for my welfare. The helpers assured Bob they knew what they were doing, and that he simply had to trust them and let the experience happen. Bob finally accepted their assurances, and the remarkable "rescue" session began—known thereafter as "The Patrick Event."

This exploratory session was so striking and instructive that Bob began to use it regularly in the Gateway programs, usually playing the audiotape of the session in the middle of the week's schedule. The Gateway participants often had unusual experiences of great variety following the presentation of the Patrick Event tape.

The transcript of the Patrick session follows. It began casually enough—before taking a dramatic turn.

ROMC: "Dear friend, as a continuation of our discussion yesterday, we want to say that when we work within the physical realm, we work with the mental, physical, and emotional energies. Also, we work with the vibrations of everything that surrounds the physical body of this dear entity. Natural sources help with the transmission, and in bringing through the vibrations. We work with energies surrounding the earth, the air, the sun. And we also work with fine energies that cannot be described in earth terms. Each time a session takes place, we work with levels of energy beyond the earth.

"The balance of the energies in the earth level can make a difference in the nature of the transmission. If there is static in the vibrations, the energy levels can vary. We use the term 'static' to mean that the balance is not perfect. Therefore, the transmission will not be exactly what it is meant to be.

"In the earth level, it is impossible to have a perfect transmission. Because there are always levels that are not in complete balance, one hundred percent accuracy is not possible. Also, during the transmission process, there is a continual fluctuation in the energy balance, which affects the transmission.

"Let us now speak specifically of the energy level of the physical body of this entity who is willing to allow us to transmit through her. Due to the fact that she is presently fasting, her physical level is in an inverted process at this time. It is at a good level for her cleansing, as she works on the inner healing that is very important on the earth plane.

"Fasting is a process that all physical beings periodically employ for the cleansing and regeneration of the cells. Many of the animals on the earth will fast advantageously when their bodies become ill. They instinctively know when to go into the fasting process, thus allowing the energies in their body to invert, and set up the cleansing and healing process.

"As just indicated, the energies in the physical body of this dear helper from your dimension are inverted at this time. We are, therefore, going to alter the nature of the work we will do today. An 'inverted' process means that the energies that normally extend outward into the universe have reversed, thus causing the cells to function on a different basis, in a speeded-up process. This is important for healing and cleansing, because it allows the major organs of the body to have a period of relaxation, with the exception of certain organs that are important in the fasting process.

"This process allows the organs of the body to regenerate, down to the smallest cell. The energies burst forth from each cell in a way different from normal. Food creates an outward flow of energy from the physical body. When food is not taken in, the energies are inverted and the cleansing process occurs. It is a regeneration function and an important aspect not only of healing, but of the prolongation of physical life. It also gives physical beings a chance to get into attunement with their bodies.

"We have something very special that we would like to do today. And we would like to ask this dear soul to break the fast, as of today. She has achieved that which was necessary in the fasting process. We would like to take up tomorrow what we had planned for today, which is to work with the creation process. For that session we do not want the energies to be inverted.

"Our session today is a follow-up from the last one. We were speaking to you of the souls who are still tied into the earth energies, even though they have stepped out of the physical body, and who are unaware that they are no longer in physical form. They have been called 'earthbound spirits,' and even 'ghosts.' These souls need help.

"There are many millions of souls that are in the earth vibration with the feeling that they are still in their physical bodies. They are locked into a time zone. It is necessary to penetrate their time zones, to talk to them individually and bring them into the awareness that they are no longer in physical form.

"There are different methods of approach to these confused souls. It is a special type of counseling, and the sensitivity of the person who works with them is a very important factor in this type of work. It is most important to make these souls aware of the fact that they are no longer in the physical body.

"It is important first to allow such souls to express their own personhood, and to describe their situation as they experience it—to tell their story—in their time level of reality. Then you must relate to such souls from the point of view of their present reality as they are experiencing it. They often will attempt to communicate with someone on the earth level, because they feel they themselves are still in their earth bodies.

"They commonly do not recognize the presence of anyone from our dimension—such as their guardians, or loved ones who have passed over—because they are locked into an earth-time dimension. Therefore, it often requires someone from the earth level to make them aware of their situation.

"When they see the light and realize that they have dropped the body, have 'died' in earth terms, then helpers from our dimension can take over. We then bring these souls onto a level where we can help them to adjust to their new vibrations and new reality. Thus, if you perform the task of helping such souls become aware of the reality of their situation, then we can take over from there.

"We send these souls through on a special light beam, a particular ray of energy. It is a specialized process. As a result, they can speak through this entity, and you can relate directly to help enlighten them.

"Sometimes you have to shock them into the realization that they are no longer living in the earth body. You must follow your intuition as to how to help them come to the realization that they have passed on. Each personality is unique. Each person is special. Therefore, each situation is different. You will learn through the process of working with these souls.

"Once they have realized that they are no longer in the physical body, their vibrations change, and they can begin reaching into this dimension. Ask them if there is someone that they have been close to who has passed on. If there is, ask them to look for this person, or to listen for this person.

"An alternative method is to ask them to look around and describe what they see. They are always surrounded by helpers from our dimension who are constantly trying to get into communication with them. They often become aware of our presence, once they come to the realization of the reality of their situation.

"Therefore, you perform a great service in helping to bring them through the boundaries of the earth-time level into the nonphysical level of reality. Once the breakthrough is made, the soul is able to function on a higher level of vibration.

"We are going to send a soul through to you now who has been lost in the earth-time zone. We are ready. Do you have questions before we bring in the lost entity? We want you to ask your questions now so that you will be fully prepared to work with this soul. If you have apprehensions, let us know that, too."

RAM: "I have one question. Can you remove this lost soul from Rosalind's physical body no matter what happens?"

ROMC: "We are in complete control of the energies of this lost soul. She has worked with many of these lost entities before, helping to release them. She is one who has a special ability and the strong energies needed for this type of work. There has never been a problem because we have her surrounded with a special light.

"The soul that comes in is locked into a special energy capsule. We are able to speak through her vocal cords, and the personality is able to become prominent. There has never been a problem, and we do not anticipate one, because she is of the very equal balance of energy that makes it easy for us to work in this way with the lost souls.

"There are special beings on the earth level who are the right foundation of energy for this type of work. She has strong energy because she is of the Capricorn earth energy. Strong earth energies are helpful to us in bringing in souls who are locked into the earth energies.

"We work very carefully, and there is never a problem of a soul getting caught in the aura of this dear being who is always eager to assist us in helping to raise the earth's vibrations in this way. It is a very special process and part of the lesson we are teaching you. This is not related to the 'possession' situation that we described before. What we are doing here is a completely different energy source.

"Another technique to use in assisting this lost soul is to ask it to touch what it believes is its physical body. Often this can shock such souls into the awareness that they are no longer in their physical body, as they realize that the body they are speaking through is foreign to them. The shock is an important process in awakening the soul to its true situation. When the realization process has taken place, we can relate to the soul directly.

"We work with the energy levels of these souls in many ways. But as indicated, we often cannot relate directly to them, because they will not recognize our presence. This is why we need help from the earth level. Is this understood by you?"

RAM: "Yes, thank you. As you can observe, my main concern is for Rosalind's well-being."

ROMC: "Let us say that there are many levels of souls that are lost. The ones we send through are on the threshold of enlightenment. Others are in such great darkness that we would never attempt to work with them in this way, because of the nature of their consciousness.

"There are many delightful souls who are locked into the physical universe of reality because they are imprisoned by their own thought-forms. Often it is fear that confines them, brought on by the trauma of the event of death. It is such souls that we bring through in a crying need of help, and on the verge of breakthrough.

"All souls have surrounding them many helpers. There are many levels of such helpers. That is why no soul is really lost in the universe. The term 'lost soul'—a concept that a soul can be lost for eternity in 'hell'—is not a reality in our dimension, because there is no time. Time is a creation of the earth-consciousness. Hell is actually a level of consciousness—in which a soul can exist whether in the body, or out.

"Continual work is being done to bring souls out of these lower vibrations, out of their hellish consciousness, into the higher levels of their own being. We work with souls on all levels, in the body as well as out of it. We work in a timeless level, and souls exist in a timeless level. It is a continuous process to help souls become aware of the true nature of their reality.

"And now we are ready, if you are ready."

RAM: "Yes, we will do our best to help."

ROMC: "Just be aware that the lost soul will speak through the body of this dear one who assists us. Do not be surprised by what happens. Relate to this personality the best way you know how, just as you would relate to any personality."

RAM: "I will indeed."

ROMC: "You, sir, have worked with these souls on many levels, because you have traveled out among them quite often out of the body. In fact, you might meet a soul familiar to you."

RAM: (laughter) "That will be very interesting."

ROMC: "We will have to shift energy patterns, which will take a few minutes of earth time, as we bring this soul into this capsule, this energy body."

RAM: "Thank you. We will wait." (pause)

PATRICK: "It's so cold. It's so cold in this water. Oh, my God. If you can just send someone. It seems as if I've been floating out here for so many days. It's so cold! I don't see any of my shipmates."

RAM: "But, I can hear you . . . I can hear you."

PATRICK: "Who's calling?"

RAM: "This is a friend. I can hear you."

PATRICK: "It is? Where are you? Are you floating? Are you floating on a log?"

RAM: "I'm close to you."

PATRICK: "The ship went down. It went down in the night. I've been floating . . . floating . . ."

RAM: "Yes; and I can hear you. You can talk to me."

PATRICK: "I can't hear you."

RAM: "Can you hear me now?"

PATRICK: "Where are you? It's so dark."

RAM: "It's all right. I'm close by, and I can hear you if you talk."

PATRICK: "I've been calling for help for at least twelve hours. I've lost track of time."

RAM: "What is your name?"

PATRICK: "There was an explosion . . ."

RAM: "What is your name, so I can talk to you?"

PATRICK: "Patrick."

RAM: "Patrick?"

PATRICK: "Patrick. Yes. It's so good to hear a voice."

RAM: "I am glad I can talk to you. What happened, Patrick?"

PATRICK: I was in the kitchen preparing the evening meal.1 All of a sudden it became very warm, and there was an explosion. The next thing I knew, I was floating in the darkness, and it was cold. I grabbed onto a log and have felt very alone. I haven't been able to see any of my shipmates."

---

1   A Gateway participant from Scotland, upon hearing the tape of the "Patrick Event," remarked that the galleys on small ships were referred to as "kitchens" during the era in which Patrick lived.

RAM: "That's all right. Where is the kitchen? Where is your home? When did this happen?"

PATRICK: "It was in the ship that I have worked on for several years. I am from my native country of Scotland. I have worked in the kitchen of my ship. This is my means of making a living. I spend at least nine months of my year on the water. However, I don't like to spend my time in the water. It is very cold, and I have a fear of sharks."

RAM: "Yes. I can understand that. What is the name of your ship?"

PATRICK: "My ship—it is the ship—the Laura Belle. It's a small ship. And I've been fortunate to work on this ship for several years. We transport lumber and other materials from Scotland across the bay to other countries, where there is a need for materials."

RAM: "What port did you last sail from?"

PATRICK: "The port? My mind is not clear. It seems we sailed out of Ireland the last time. Or was it Scotland?"

RAM: "What was the name of the port that you sailed out from? Where did you begin your last voyage?"

PATRICK: "It seems so long ago. My mind is not clear. We sailed . . . What year is it? It's in the year 1879. Ah, yes, we sailed from Bar Bay Harbor in Scotland."

RAM: "Patrick, what is your last name?"

PATRICK: "O'Shaunessy."

RAM: "O'Shaunessy. Yes, that's a good name."

PATRICK: "Friend, who are you? Where are you?"

RAM: "My name is Robert. And I am Scottish, also."

PATRICK: "Robert, I've been calling for help. How did you hear my call? (beginning to cry) How did you hear my call?"

RAM: "It was not hard."

PATRICK: "It . . . I'm sorry . . . " (crying)

RAM: "Patrick, I came to talk to you because you called. Now you can hear me and that is good."

PATRICK: "Where are you? It's so dark out here. I'm holding onto a log, and it's so cold. I don't see any of my shipmates; I don't see the ship. It was dark when I hit the water and I grabbed the first thing that I could. But I called and I called. And I haven't heard anyone, until I heard your voice. I am so happy that you have answered." (crying)

RAM: "That's fine, Patrick. Where were you born in Scotland?"

PATRICK: "Where was I born?"

RAM: "Uh, huh."

PATRICK: "I was born in a small village—Oban. It's a very small village."

RAM: "What is your birth date?"

PATRICK: "I was born in 1821."

RAM: "What part of Scotland was this small—"

PATRICK: "The northern part of Scotland. I was born on the water, and I have been a sailor all of my life. But I don't like to stay in the water this long. I must have been here all night—at least twelve hours. And it's so cold. I really . . . (crying) Can you help me? Please, can you help me?"

RAM: "Yes, let's see if we can get you out."

PATRICK: "Can you get me out of the water?"

RAM: "I think we can."

PATRICK: "Where are you? I can't see you."

RAM: "Now, if you just listen to me very carefully, I believe we can get you out. Wouldn't that be nice?"

PATRICK: "Oh, it's very cold! It's always so cold in December."

RAM: "First of all—"

PATRICK: "Can you get . . . are you on a boat? Can I reach for you?"

RAM: "Yes, you can reach and come to where I am. Patrick, are your mother and father still alive?"

PATRICK: "Oh, no. My mother and my father—they died of the flu when I was yet a young lad. It was quite sad, because we were such a close family. I have four brothers and sisters, and we were all quite young. To lose our parents was so tragic. Oh, to see my parents again. I've been praying for their help. I feel lost."

RAM: "Well, look around. I think if you remember how

they looked, and look above you, you might see your mother or your father—or you might hear their voices. Listen very carefully and look up over you somewhere."

PATRICK: "I can just barely lift my head out of the water. If I could just see them. I think I have been out of my head, because I've been seeing faces around me. I just know that I am still alive. I am clinging to my log . . . ."

RAM: "Well, one of the things that you have to consider is that you are like your mother and father now. You are like them now."

PATRICK: "I am like them?"

RAM: "Yes, you are like them. You have graduated. You have grown; and you are ready to move to another place."

PATRICK: "By golly. You mean that I have . . . I am . . . I am . . . ?"

RAM: "You no longer need to be swimming in the water. You can go much beyond that now."

PATRICK: "By golly. I don't need to hold onto this log?"

RAM: "No, let go of the log and see what happens."

PATRICK: "I'll let go of the log and see what happens. Okay, I just feel relaxed. I must have . . . are you saying that when the boat exploded, I died?"

RAM: "Yes, and it's not so bad. It's quite good, as a matter of fact."

PATRICK: "But I'm still alive!"

RAM: "Naturally, you're still alive. You do not die when your physical body dies."

PATRICK: "I know . . . I know . . . "

RAM: "And so, you are free now to do many, many things that you could never do before."

PATRICK: "I feel so light. I've been clinging to my log, and to my life—and my ship. I . . . I have just been clinging. Because that is all I ever had in my lifetime—my boat and my family. But I can let go . . . ."

RAM: "You can let go, because you are free."

PATRICK: "I'm free! I . . . feel as if I am floating above the water."

RAM: "You can do that now."

PATRICK: "I feel lighter."

RAM: "You are free—beautifully, wonderfully free."

PATRICK: "I see a hand. Who is reaching for me? Oh, by golly, who is reaching? Someone is reaching their hand down to me!"

RAM: "And there will be a light, and you will be able to see in a new way."

PATRICK: "It is getting lighter. The darkness is lifting. I have released the ship. I feel as if I am floating above the water. I can see.... I can see.... Is that my mother? It's my mother! It's my mother...." (crying)

RAM: "Yes, yes. And you can move on now, Patrick."

PATRICK: "It's my mother and my father reaching for me!" (crying uncontrollably)

RAM: "That's fine. Go with them."

PATRICK: (still crying) "Excuse me for crying ... I feel so happy. I don't know who you are, but you have helped me."

RAM: "I am a friend."

PATRICK: "It's so good to get out of the water ... out of the darkness. Thank you...."

RAM: "There are many friends waiting for you. Go on and away."

PATRICK: "Thank you ... thank you!"

RAM: "And good-bye.... Good-bye, Patrick!"

ROMC: (Invisible Helper speaking) "We would like to say 'thank you' for the very fine job that you have done in helping to release this soul that was locked into its own fear thought-form. We have been able to take this soul to its dearly beloved parents. There is a grand reunion taking place, and great light surrounding all of them. You have done a great service, not only for us, but for this soul. The soul has transformed into a new level of energy, and will be able to continue on from there.

"We have brought this soul as an example of the locked-in conditions of fear thought-forms. However, we do not want souls in the earth body to fear being locked into such levels for years of earth time. That fear, in itself, can create a block-age. We want souls in earth bodies to understand this process of transformation, so that the awareness will help in their transition process. They will feel the change in their physical levels, but the emotional process does not change.

"Immediately upon transformation, the soul body is in a completely different state. Dropping the body is like dropping a shell. The vibrations of the soul body are at a much more rapid rate. The mental levels are functioning at a different level—but are performing very much the same as before transition. Often it is the emotional level that locks the soul into the earth plane. Because of a very strong emotional earth attachment, it still vibrates on the slower earth level. Therefore, the complete transition cannot take place until the soul mentally and emotionally releases the earth vibrations.

"On transition, you have the same functioning capacity, but there is a change in the density of the energies. The earth is the emotional level of existence, and often souls are locked in strictly because of the emotional process. But there are also times when the mental thought-forms can lock souls in because of training that is put into the mind. For instance, there is a concept that a soul will 'sleep' until 'the last trumpet sounds.' Very strong thought-forms that can confine often come through religious training and wrong interpretations of reality.

"When a soul is programmed to believe that certain things will happen upon death, the soul will experience that strong thought-form once out of the physical body. Thus, a soul can be locked into a sleeping state, waiting for the sound of a trumpet. We often have trouble relating to these souls, because we do not sound trumpets—not wanting to reinforce other thought-forms associated with that belief.

"Sometimes, such souls will wait until they get bored—and finally open their spiritual eyes, only to realize that they are awake and alive, even though they have not heard the trumpet sound they were awaiting. It is at this stage that we can begin working with such souls.

"So, souls can be locked into the physical realm through both emotional and mental energies and sometimes for thousands of years of earth time. Of course, there is no 'time,' as we have said over and over. We say again, do not fear that upon dying you will be locked in. You can be free through the knowledge of what happens to you at the death process.

"Just as you allow yourself to be confined through your mental and emotional levels, you can free yourself by releasing fears and negative concepts. It is possible to be confined whether in or out of the body. You are exactly the same personality when you drop the body as you were before. Therefore, it is important to have continual cleansing of the emotions of fear, anger, and hostility.

"Always remember that a soul's own hostility and fear harm that soul more than anything else. But at the same time, thought-forms are very powerful and can affect others also. Therefore, you harm not only yourself, but also those toward whom the anger is directed. It is important to break into these negative thought-forms and release them. We use the term 'negative,' meaning that the energy flow is blocked.

"Work toward the higher levels of light and love. Each soul has within it the highest capacity to love. The negative energies block the love flow. Love energy is a level of energy within all life. It is the pure form of energy. Love is a pure form of energy that recognizes itself within all levels of life. It is the highest level of energy within every life form. This is the essence of love. It is that which recognizes itself.

"Ask for help in releasing the negative energies. There is always assistance for those who seek help. 'Seek, and you shall find.' There are many helpers, angels, guides, working to help you be released into your higher selves. You must learn to forgive and forget."

RAM: "Thank you very much. And we will pass along this very important event."

~22~

LOWER LEVELS

ROMC: "They are getting me prepared for another special type of experience and are going to be putting me through a cleansing and energizing process."

RAM: "Go with the flow."

ROMC: "I see a strong light beam shining down on my solar plexus. I feel energy coming into me from this light. It's flashing on and off. And now the color is changing, alternating between warm and cool colors. The contrast is energizing me. Now the beam is covering my whole body; I'm supposed to follow the light. It's pulling me up—and I am to relax and go with it.

"Now I'm up on my platform, spinning rapidly. I almost feel dizzy. It's spinning so fast that I can't see myself. I feel I'm going to disappear. I'm spinning so rapidly that I am all one. A cone of energy is building over me, and I'm floating right up through this spiral.

"I'm in a dark area, and I feel a lot of turbulence. I'm receiving the thought that on our journeys we often hit turbulence. Factors are at work outside of ourselves as well as within. I am going to be given an experience and understanding of turbulent dimensions. Sometimes we hit turbulence, but we must continue going on. We must keep moving.

"I'm now in an open space, and it is dark. I'm aware of forces around me—which are the turbulence I was just feeling. I sense these energies around me, but I can't see them.

"I'm being told that I must sensitize myself. I must be prepared for what I'll be experiencing, and put a strong energy of protection around myself. I am to visualize my light bubble around me.

"I can feel strong energies, but I can't see anything. It's a cold energy—a strange kind of coolness. I'm told that I'm in the presence of energies that are locked into themselves. My Invisible Friends are going to take me through some experiences to help me understand these energy forms, and some of the principles of what happens to the conscious self when it gets locked into certain emotional time warps.

"Many things are happening at once. I feel a coolness—and hear some sounds. I hear moans, and 'cool' voice tones. The cold is due to the energy being cut off from light and heat. These are soul forms that have shut themselves off from everything else. Now I'm being taken into further understanding of what is going on.

"As I look at consciousness, I see it as energy. These energy forms remain the same after they drop the physical body. If a soul is locked into a strong emotion, it stays in the time zone it was in when the body was dropped. In earth terms, it would be called a ghost. This is a soul that is locked into levels of its own consciousness and doesn't know how to get out.

"Another energy thought of as a ghost on the earth level is certain strong emotional energies that are locked into a time zone in the earth plane, and keep playing the same emotions over and over. Usually great emotional traumas will create these energy configurations, which are so strong that they build up a pattern of their own existence in the time realm. Other aspects of this energy self are usually in a frozen state in a different dimension. When the soul changes dimensions, its echoes usually dissolve back into its original energy patterns.

"They are taking me into a house. I can see a soul that has left the body. It's an older man. Though the body has died, the soul is exactly the same. This is a mansion. The floors are highly polished and very clean. The soul is walking around the mansion and has no intention of leaving. Much money is involved here.

"This soul has put so much into this particular home that he doesn't want to release it. He has dropped his physical body, but his mind and emotions keep his etheric-substance body in this earth/time location. There is such a coldness. Even while in the physical body, he was already cut off from everything, including himself. He was locked into his own selfishness and will remain there until he seeks help and change—or until a higher level of energy can penetrate his cold and foreboding shell of existence.

"This soul has an aura of fear around it, a fear of death. But the paradox is that this man was dead long before he dropped his physical body. His stagnant existence was death in itself, and he continues to live in stagnant nongrowth.

"Souls that are locked into their own energies are dead because they are not growing. Growth comes only with an interchange of energy. When you take in energies and hold them, not allowing them to flow through you, a stagnant existence sets in. This is why the selfish soul who only takes in and doesn't release is in a death existence. This is why I sense coldness here: it's a soul frozen unto itself.

"Now I am being taken up to get an overview of the earth. There are some dead spots in the energy levels of the earth—and large clusters of these misplaced souls seem to be gathered there. These souls seem to be gathered where there are imbalances in the earth's aura—the sick spots. It is again the like-attracts-like principle. Sick souls are drawn to the sick spots. Many of these souls are attracted to each other because of a similar consciousness.

"Now I am being guided to a level where I can hear many screams and strange sounds. This is a level of much emotional pain, a very strong feeling of pain and suffering. This is a suicide level, of souls who were in such pain that they thought that getting rid of their bodies would relieve the pain. But the pain is now much stronger than when they were in the physical body, because the pain was in the etheric emotional body. The physical helped to ground the pain; without it, the pain is more intense.

"There are many levels of consciousness where souls can be when they have taken their lives. It depends on the consciousness of the soul at the point of death. I can sense intense pain here. It is a very uncomfortable feeling. I feel a great sense of compassion because I was in this state once myself, and came close to taking my own life. I feel sure this is where I would be if I had succeeded in taking my life.

"The lesson here is that the soul, the self, is exactly the same upon dropping the body as it was prior to doing so. These souls will have to remain in this existence and work through this pain and suffering until they realize they don't have to hold onto it any longer. They have locked themselves into this level and they must let themselves out. There are many angels around to help them, if they are willing to accept help.

"There are many higher souls working with these suicides, trying to penetrate their dark and painful auras. Often the soul cannot see the light for its own darkness. It's as if they have turned off the light of their own consciousness. It appears dark, because they seem to have shut off the light, but the light is always there. I can see it—it's all around them. They can't see the light, because they have shut themselves off from that aspect of their own existence. They will stay in this state until they desire to change. Also, prayers sent from the earth level for these souls can be of great help.

"No one is alone, and there is no real aloneness in the universe. The feeling of aloneness comes from our cutting ourselves off from the reality of our light being, our higher selves. Help is there instantly when a soul desires it. 'Ask and you shall receive.'

"Souls alive in their own being go to the highest level of their energies when they drop their bodies. Souls also go through cycles of growth both within the body and without. When someone dies on the earth level, he or she goes into a new cycle of growth in another dimension. Some souls cycle back into the earth for more intense growth; some souls cycle into other galaxies or dimensions. Souls are attracted to the areas where they can receive the greatest levels of growth.

"The earth level is a very intense level of growth. In the time-space zone of the earth, friction sets up faster growth levels within souls. Lessons are often learned rapidly.

"What I was experiencing in this cold level is like a winter rhythm of a soul that is in a type of hibernation. These souls will come eventually into the spring, summer, and fall of their existence. They go through rhythms of growth in the various dimensions. Souls locked into the frozen state of existence can come into a thawing, and thus a springtime renewal, with the desire to change and grow.

"A soul never dies. There is always hope. There is not a God that punishes for eternity. There are only souls that allow themselves to be punished by themselves until they come to the realization that they don't have to remain in that existence.

"Souls are always growing toward the highest level of their own being, which is the highest form of life energies. This energy is the highest form of love."

RAM: "You mentioned earlier that everyone has an earth council that helps them decide about coming back into the earth level. Are any of these so-called lost souls sent back into earth bodies?"

ROMC: "When souls are not in a position to make decisions with their earth council, and if the earth experience would be good for their growth, they can be sent back into an earth body on a special beam of light. These souls are sent back into special situations of love so that they might learn to love themselves, and thus move out of their stagnation.

"Such souls can also be a growth challenge for the families that take them on. It is something like an adoption process on the earth plane. The child is not in a position to decide where it will go but is sent to the place judged to be best for its nurturing and growth. An immature soul would be treated in the same way."

RAM: "What about people that commit suicide—or are assisted in committing suicide—because they are dying of cancer or something of that sort and don't want to continue experiencing the pain of the body? Do these people go to a suicide level where there is a lot of emotional pain?"

ROMC: "The like-attracts-like principle is applied here as well. Often the souls that chose to leave their bodies because of physical pain rather than emotional pain are very compassionate beings. Thus, they would not go to the suicide level. They would be on the level of their highest vibration, and that could be on a plane of light. However, they often will go to a type of 'hospital' situation where they recuperate for a period of time, if the illness has put a strain on their various energy bodies.

"It is wise to live out your life and allow your body to die its natural death. An individual who is able to overcome these challenges of pain and suffering can spiritually advance very rapidly. Often those souls who take their lives because of physical pain are assigned to the suicide level, where they will work with the souls that are in great emotional pain. They go there because they are compassionate and have an understanding of the souls that took their own lives prematurely.

"When a soul takes its physical life prematurely, it often remains at this suicide level until its earth time would have expired. Time is still a part of this level, because it is so deeply embedded in the earth-time energies.

"Remember, we said that the body is an entity in and of itself; to destroy your life form before it has had a chance to drop off naturally can often set you back in your growth process. Frequently a soul comes back into a very similar situation until it has learned the lesson for which it came before.

"So nothing is ever accomplished by taking your life. It is best to pray avidly for guidance and help. You will receive help from the many 'spirit doctors' that are there to assist in any way possible. As we have said over and over, 'Ask, and you shall receive.' We must step aside."

RAM: "Thank you again for your insight and guidance. ROMC, take your time coming back."

ROMC: "Thank you. I need it. I need to warm up. I feel chilled after that experience."

RAM: "I'll warm you up with some nice music."

ROMC: "I'd appreciate that."

New Beginnings . . .

23

TRAVEL TO
THE YEAR 3000

RAM: "Reel time: 13 minutes, 17 seconds."

ROMC: "I'm having a different type of experience. I've been observing—and I'm having trouble speaking, for I'm being taken into the future!"

RAM: "Go with the flow and see what happens."

ROMC: "I can hear someone talking. What I'm seeing is so different that I'm having trouble focusing."

RAM: "What year is it?"

ROMC: "It's around the year 3000. I'm on my platform, and there seem to be many different types of platforms out in space. They are all extensions of the earth. There is so much activity out here. I'm not alone on my platform any more.

"The face of the earth has changed. There was a great need to expand, and much of the expansion went outward, away from the earth. Many changes have taken place on and around the earth.

"There is a lot of activity—and a lot of communication. The earth has expanded its levels of communication. People are flying around in different shapes of spacecraft, which seem to be coming and going from these different types of platforms. Some platforms appear to be stopping-off points for people who are traveling out to various points in the universe. People have changed in their appearance, and in physical stature. Overall, they are taller.

"Looking at the United States from this distance, it appears it is not nearly as wide as it was. There must have been some drastic changes on earth. Land has appeared in the ocean areas—as if some land has gone down, and other land has come up. It is all so completely different that it is hard to recognize things.

"Something is happening in the ocean water. At different places I can see something sticking up out of the water. I'm being told that these are exhaust pipes for cities underneath the water.

"There is also a difference in the climate. The warm and cold areas on the earth have changed. It's almost as if the north and south poles are at different places than before.

"Little circular vehicles with glass tops seem to have taken the place of automobiles. I can see a family in one. The vehicle seems to be propelled from somewhere underneath. There are landing platforms in the water where the vehicles can land and submerge right into the water. Evidently this type of vehicle can travel through water as well as in the air and on land. The family I saw flew down to the water, landed, and disappeared.

"I'm seeing many different kinds of people. I'm receiving the information that there has been communication with beings from other planets—and that the earth has become a universal melting pot. We used to just travel on the earth; but now they're traveling out into the universe as an everyday experience. I mentioned seeing people that are taller. I'm told that this is just one type; the people in the spacecraft looked very different, like beings from outer space.

"I'm being told that there was a point in the history of planet Earth when patterns of very negative vibrations built up. Then a pattern of gradual shifts took place over a period of about 200 years, beginning around the early part of the twenty-first century. It was at this point that assistance came from beings from other parts of the universe in the same way that nations come to each other's aid when help is needed.

"These extraterrestrial helpers had been observing and working with us on many different levels of communication for centuries. They are the ones that I was privileged to have some brief encounters with in some earlier sessions. They were able to come in and work out a pattern of communication to give help and pointers on how the earth could be rejuvenated. People on the earth were ready, prepared for this break-through into a new stage of development.

"I can see a thin line. I'm not sure what the line means, but it seems to start back in the late 1900s. A type of meter shows that some unusual earth activity was starting to take place at that time, just before the year 2000. A kind of needle is showing the vibration rate, the speed of the changes. There was a period during the early part of the twenty-first century when shifts took place more rapidly. Then they continued to take place a little slower for almost a fifty-year period. After this there were a lot of little shifts taking place gradually enough that people were aware that things were happening, but not as dramatically.

"Thus, in the early part the twenty-first century there were major shifts on the earth, followed by a series of minor ones. There were some major things happening throughout the universe. There were pulls on our poles. It seems there was a lot of activity in one part of the universe that directly affected our earth.

"In fact there was a major shift in the universe—something to do with black holes—that directly affected us. During the twenty-year period of major shifts there was a lot of strain upon the earth caused by outer forces in the universe. The earth is like a young child in the solar system. It's still very strong, and can endure a lot of stress and strain. It still has several growing stages to go through."

RAM: "When did the first help come from outer space? When did the first contact of communication really begin?"

ROMC: "Communication was taking place all through the 1900s, which most people weren't aware of. Direct contact was made at the point when the earth shifts were the greatest, in the early part of the twenty-first century."

RAM: "When did direct contact become public knowledge throughout the planet?"

ROMC: "For many, many years, the spaceships were in contact with the earth. Through special observation they were always aware of what was happening on earth. They are very evolved beings who see both the past and future. They are responsible for helping to bring new knowledge into the earth. It is knowledge that earth residents actually know but have not used.

"Major contact came in the 1980s. We were not as evolved at that time as we could have been. So, more mature mother planets had to come in and help planet Earth through its puberty stage."

RAM: "With whom did they make the first contact?"

ROMC: "They have been making contact on different levels for some time, including certain highly evolved souls on earth. During the 1950s, '60s, and '70s, some of these space beings were actually born on the earth in human bodies. They came in so that they could help with the contact from this end. The extraterrestrials with good intentions worked through the mental level of people with balanced energies.

"In the 1970s, this contact took place in several different parts of the earth at the same time. They had to make themselves known over a period of years in order for their presence to be believed and understood. In the 1970s, people on earth began to be more understanding and accepting of extraterrestrial contact. World governments had been aware of the extraterrestrial presence for many years but had suppressed this knowledge, mainly out of fear.

"The highly evolved space beings had taken many people onto spaceships and implanted communication devices in their brains. At a certain point in time these people remembered their contact and were immensely helpful with the communication process. Between 1977 and 1980, many more people began to believe in interplanetary contact. Beginning in 1977, spacecraft came in great numbers and hovered around our planet. Many of the smaller craft came from larger spaceships."

RAM: "From the point of view of looking back in history from the year 3000, were any such contacts made in our area of Virginia, or near where we are?"

ROMC: "Yes, contacts were made in your area, over a period of time. Contacts were made in certain power points on the earth, especially where there are no large cities, and where the vibrations are not so negative. Virginia has such power points. I also see power points in Texas, North Carolina, Alabama, and Georgia. The space brothers mapped out certain areas where they would come in. Eventually, there was even a change in the attitudes of governments of various countries.

"Now everything is shifting for me. I'm supposed to go to something different."

RAM: "Very good. Go with the flow, and I will wait."

ROMC: "The space beings who came in contact first were those who were responsible for the earth and worked carefully to map out a plan of communication. Also, we had some knowledge and energies that were helpful to our friends from outer space. After communication opened up and the work began, our whole energy system and method of using energy changed. This was when we were able to freely go into the earth, and away from it, for living and traveling.

"But there were beings from outer space that made contact with planet Earth who were not friendly and did not have the best of intentions. They also had been in contact with the earth for some time and abducted and implanted many humans. But the evolved aliens could also use these implanted devices to communicate, and did so for our greater good. We had gained enough power over our own earth that the unfriendly aliens were not able to take us over.

"It was around the year 2500 when we were involved in a space war with these beings. But it didn't last long, because a balance of power took place, with our highly evolved alien friends from outer space helping us. The evolved space brothers knew a lot about the habits of the nonfriendly aliens that they had also been tracking for many centuries. Also, we had saucers and all the space technology they did.

"One of the most important changes that took place was our use of our own human energies. We were taught how to use our energies much more fully than we had ever done before. Certain people were chosen to be taken aboard spaceships for special training. Humans were trained not only in how to conserve and use energies that come from the earth, but also in special uses of the mind. What I am doing now—traveling out into all dimensions—is something that was taught to many.

"Earth beings were given extensive training on how to use their energies from points within. There are several energy points within the human body that can be used for specific purposes—such as tapping into special knowledge and traveling into different dimensions. Much travel can be done just through using the mind. This is how space beings were first able to send communication directly to us, through the invisible wavelengths of the mind.

"Those people who received special training on energy use traveled back to the earth and began training others. We were told that if we used what we were taught in a negative way, for power or destruction, it would be taken away from us. We were also shown how to use special light-beam energies, with which we created different types of mechanisms for living and travel."

RAM: "Are all of these in common use in the year 3000? Does everyone use this energy?"

ROMC: "Not everyone in the year 3000 uses this energy—just as now, on the earth, not everyone uses the same kind of energy. Many use it, but not everyone understands it, in the same way that people drive automobiles now, but may not understand how they work. Most everyone is using the energy in some way to function.

"There are many in leadership positions who are more highly developed than others.

"The world is all one country at this point. There was a period when the whole world had to work together to survive. Some countries were completely destroyed. During the breakdown period, everyone had to help others and to combine their energies for survival. So the energies that are used in the year 3000 are used by large numbers."

RAM: "In the year 3000, what changes had taken place in terms of religious beliefs or concepts?"

ROMC: "There was a complete change in religious concepts. There is now an overall universal knowledge. Many of the old, localized concepts that separated people on earth broke down—when the helpers had to come in from other dimensions. People realized why the Christ, the highly evolved being, had stepped into history many years before. The purpose was to show the true nature of man.

"If humans use their complete potential, they will live in the higher energies that the Christ is. Therefore, they will become one with the universal energy, which is 'God' in human terms. There was also a universal understanding among religious leaders from many of the different types of religions as to humanity's purpose: to live at one's highest God-potential.

"It was just after the period of breakdown that the highly evolved Christ-like beings, with great love energies, came into planet Earth. It was then that the universal realization came that there is no being so high above others that we must worship him; rather, we all have the potential to evolve into the highest Christ-like form—which was the commission that Jesus the Christ left to the world when he said, 'Greater things will you do than I.'

"In their lower state of consciousness, humans used the term 'miracles' for what is an everyday occurrence now. When the earth changed, humans had to change their limited concepts of self and nature. There was a complete shift in consciousness, and people operated from their own inner energies. They worked with the higher universal laws and evolved into a oneness with all forms of life.

"This is when there was a breakdown of the old concepts and the emergence of the universal religion. It is a form of religion in which people are absolutely in tune with their own being, in tune with the universe around them; they are living the principles of oneness rather than just talking about them. After the breakdown period, man was forced to use all of his higher potential in order to survive on the planet."

RAM: "In the year 3000, what is man's knowledge of what we call physical death, and the hereafter?"

ROMC: "There is no fear of death—because at this point in the history of the earth, humans are traveling freely outside of their bodies. They are traveling in many forms—still using the physical vehicle for specific purposes, but traveling into many dimensions through special uses of their own energies. At this point in history there is no concept of death, because people know that there is no death, but only a transposition into higher energy forms."

RAM: "In the year 3000, is communication very common with those who have transposed?"

ROMC: "In the year 3000, there is complete communication with all dimensions at all times. There are laboratories where people work specifically with crossing the barriers of time—as you have been doing for many years in your laboratory. There are special schools and universities where people are trained in all forms of communication.

"It goes so far beyond what we know now as communication that it is hard to describe. People can travel out into all levels of universes through the body, mind, and spirit. Humans have lifted all the old barriers and restrictions that they had put upon themselves."

RAM: "How old does the average person in the year 3000 live to be? How long do they usually inhabit a physical body?"

ROMC: "The life span is over a hundred years. Because people are utilizing their energies as they should, they decide at what point they want to drop the physical body in order to work on a different energy level. The average time of leaving is well over 100. Some even decide to stay in their physical bodies, for specific purposes, up to 200 years.

"However, the whole nature and texture of the physical body has changed. It is much more highly evolved. It appears that humans have evolved from the more dense physical into the etheric-substance body.

"Eventually humans will evolve to the point, as a race, where they will not even have a physical form. Beings from many other places in the universe are living in the higher energy forms. As we evolve, we are able to get into contact with them, because we become more like them. It is the universal principle of 'like attracts like.'"

RAM: "One final thing: Is physical birth in the year 3000 the same as it is in the late twentieth century?"

ROMC: "People are born in the same manner, but again, the process is much more highly evolved. There is complete communication with the embryo from the time of conception. Schooling begins at the moment of conception. Therefore, the birth process is much simpler—because the child takes more responsibility for its entry into the physical plane.

"The child has a complete understanding of what is happening in birth. There is pure and absolute communication on the mental level. There is no pain or difficulty for the mother. The whole process of birth has evolved. Even hospitals are different, and there are no hospitals as we know them today."

RAM: "Very good. Is there a final thought you would like to give from the year 3000?"

ROMC: "Yes—that which has been shown to me is the evolution that can happen if we choose. The earth goes through growing stages. What is seen in the year 3000 is the adult level of planet Earth. This is what the earth should be, if it grows and matures properly. It is presently in the childlike stage, ready to shift into young adulthood. Mother Earth is ready to start her menstrual cycle at this stage, and the cramps and growing pains can be intense."

RAM: "Very good. Now ask your friends to return you from the year 3000 back onto your platform, and back into your normal state in the year 1976. Thank them for their help."

ROMC: "I certainly do thank them for this experience."

24

Ram's Departure

As his reading of the familiar Institute "Affirmation" came to a close, the sound of Bob's recorded voice broadcasting from the speakers was followed by a few moments of profound silence. A bird atop a tree on a nearby hill sang forth, as if delighted to have its moment in the sun to celebrate Bob's rite of passage. Then time seemed to stand still, acknowledging eternity.

A female voice followed the echo of the birdsong, as Bob's memorial service continued with a prayer. Though I could not see the speaker, I recognized the voice of my fellow Explorer, SHE. Of the Explorers Bob worked with over the years, SHE and I had remained with him the longest.

In a chapter entitled "Explorer Team I" in *Far Journeys*, Bob had written:

> *In the current Explorer group, only two remain from the original team. The tide of personal events has moved the others away from the area, their lives visibly altered by the experience. (p. 49)*

Finally SHE's ministerial studies required her to move, and I was the last Explorer working with Bob in the one-on-one sessions that had produced so much excitement and learning through the years.

SHE was eventually ordained and became the pastor of a church. I reflected on how curious it was that Bob's two longest-serving Explorers had divinity degrees. Though my master's degree work at Union Theological Seminary in New York City did not really prepare me for my exploratory sessions with

Bob, meeting David at Union and then marrying him did lead me to Virginia and to Bob.

"Interestingly, I was from Dayton, Ohio, and David was from nearby Columbus—but we had to move to a city of millions of people in order to meet. Bob was from Columbus, also. And he was living in New York City when I arrived there. What strange crisscrossing patterns destiny weaves in bringing us together!

After the prayer, Bob's family members were introduced one by one, and each offered a tribute to him. Memories flooded my mind as the words of each speaker evoked past days with Bob. I felt a warm feeling of pride come over me as I recalled the front-page article about him in the *Wall Street Journal* on September 20, 1994.

This was the kind of recognition Bob had always hoped for. Many magazine and newspaper articles had been written through the years about him and his pioneering work. But this article was special. We all could hardly believe it: "Research Institute Shows People a Way Out of Their Bodies," the headline announced. The coverage of his life and the Institute's work was well-written, upbeat, and extensive—continuing on a second page with the heading, "Some Skeptics Become Believers After They Spend a Week Learning How to Get Out of Their Bodies." That article created a surge of Gateway participants.

As I thought back over Bob's many achievements through his long and illustrious career, I concluded that the Gateway training program was his greatest contribution, helping as it did so many, many people to have extraordinary, often life-changing experiences—such as I had had in my Explorer sessions. After Bob was invited to do a weekend workshop for Esalen at Big Sur in California in the early seventies, his research had turned in a new direction, resulting in the Gateway program. After that, the Institute began receiving a growing number of requests from individuals and organizations to conduct more Gateway sessions.

He first called the program "M-5000," with the goal of running 5,000 participants through it. After the first few sessions it seemed unlikely that, logistically speaking, they would ever reach that number. But to our surprise, Bob was able to state in *Ultimate Journey:* "By 1993 over seven thousand people had experienced the evolving program, known as the Gateway Voyage." (p. 278)

In *Far Journeys*, Bob said about Gateway: "We began to recognize that we were creating for the participant a doorway, a window, a gap through which he could achieve other states of consciousness. Thus it became known as the Gateway Program." (p. 27)

Bob did little to promote the Gateway training series over the years. It proved such a remarkable and outstanding experience for the participants that it was publicized quite successfully by word of mouth. A fascinating aspect of the program was the high percentage of men who attended, possibly because of the technological thrust of the laboratory-based training. One Gateway session, much to the surprise of the Institute, ended up entirely made up of men.

As Bob was developing his Gateway program, he and I were deeply involved in our Explorer sessions. Many techniques that the Invisible Helpers were utilizing with me were integrated into the Gateway series. Bob stated that much of his inspiration for the Gateway program, and much of the information he incorporated into it, came through Explorer sessions.

Later, a new program named Guidelines was developed. It's an advanced program for Gateway graduates who want to get in touch with their guiding energies. And as a result of the Patrick "rescue" experience, Bob designed a program in 1991 called Lifeline, for communication and service to souls no longer in physical bodies. Then in October of 1996 a wonderful new program called Heartline was launched—its purpose being to utilize and use love energy more fully by exploring greater depth of self to create *heartspace:* self-love, self-trust, and nonjudgmental acceptance to move beyond feelings into the transcendental. Exploration 27 is the Institute's latest program, in which participants explore higher realms of existence, just as I have.

People come from all over the world to participate in training programs at the Institute. At first the programs were held at motels throughout the country. Then in July 1978, the maiden voyage of Gateway was held at the Institute's brand new facilities in beautiful mountain surroundings near Faber, Virginia—the New Land. Bob's dream had always been for the Institute to have its own land and facilities; this dream materialized in the attractive, functional buildings, designed to facilitate the Institute's growing programs and house Gateway participants comfortably.

Nancy Lee (Scooter) Honeycutt McMoneagle, Bob's stepdaughter, played a major role in the development of the Institute. She was one of the first Gateway trainers, and therefore helped Bob to fine-tune the Gateway program. She was also instrumental in helping to develop new programs over the years. Being good at management, Nancy Lee was one of the outstanding directors of the Institute. Without Nancy Lee, the Institute would not be what it is today.

Bob's daughter Laurie Monroe has taken over where Nancy Lee left off. She now manages the Monroe Institute and is doing an excellent job of carrying on Bob's dream as it moves into the new millennium and continues to thrive and grow. The Monroe Institute is making an impact in many countries around the world, where training programs and centers are opening rapidly.

After Bob's family members completed their tributes to him, his recorded voice again came over the loud speaker. This time he was giving instructions from his *Going Home* series, on how to deal with the death of a loved one. He urged us to release our loved ones and bless them on their soul's journey into new life and new beginnings.

Against the background of his familiar voice I recalled that just three months before, I'd had a dream about Bob. In the dream he told me that he was preparing to move his operation to a new location. When I awoke, I knew that Bob was getting ready to leave the earth plane. I discussed the dream with a study group I was in. Shortly after I received the phone call informing me of Bob's passing, I thought back over the dream.

Bob's *Going Home* program, a selection from which we were hearing over the speaker system, had just recently been completed. Bob's brother, a physician, had just received his set of the *Going Home* tapes shortly before the memorial service.

As soon as Bob's final project was completed, he was ready to leave. So he did! Bob enjoyed being involved in things; I'm sure that as he observed the memorial service from his "more-than-physical-body state," he greatly appreciated participating, even via recorded tapes, in his own celebration.

I have heard from various sources that when people die they often view their own funeral service before going to another dimension. Indeed, while I was working on this manuscript, a longtime friend of mine called to tell me about a neighbor who had died suddenly. It was a man in his early twenties. Shortly after passing on he appeared and spoke to his younger brother, who was twelve years old. He used terms that the younger brother would not know, and when the boy told his mother about the appearance, it was very moving to her.

The brother who died said that he had been at his funeral service—and wanted his younger brother to thank their mother for buying the nice, new suit that she had put on him. Then he told how he was met by his grandparents at the moment of his crossing and how great it felt in his new body and new location. He said that his physical body had been in such bad shape that he'd had to leave it. Very likely the younger brother gained a new concept of death.

When it was time for us all to say good-bye to Bob on his final out-of-body journey, the minister stated that she was sure that Nancy Penn Monroe, Bob's wonderful partner who had died two years before, was there at the celebration. Bob and Nancy had a deep love relationship.

Indeed, Bob told the *Wall Street Journal* reporter that he didn't travel out-of-body anymore. He had visited Nancy out-of-body after she died, and he'd found that being with her, free from physical trappings, was so emotionally explosive that he couldn't handle it. He stated that if he had visited Nancy again in this way, he wouldn't have been able to come back. And he knew he had more work to do before leaving.

Then the memorial service leader informed us that two white balloons, representing Bob and Nancy, would be re-leased—signifying their expansion and growth in a higher dimension. We were invited to offer our good-byes and good wishes as we released them to go on in their greater journey.

As the two balloons floated up gently, quietly, in the air, we all arose from our seats, looking up into the bright blue sky, with Roberts Mountain prominent in the background. Although the two balloons were not tied together, we watched with fascination and amazement as they floated up almost touching, as if in Hemi-Sync position, in a perfectly balanced state.

It seemed like a very long time that we watched the white balloons floating out of sight. From the corner of my eye I saw tears roll gently down the cheeks of those around me, and my eyes welled with tears at the finality of Bob's departure. But my heart leaped for joy at the thought of his new beginnings.

Within, I waved a grateful good-bye as I thought, "Thank you, Bob, for the eternal legacy that you have left behind with me. You have helped me to know beyond a doubt that I am more than my physical body! I will pass it on."

About the Author

Rosalind McKnight has always had an inquisitive mind and an exploratory nature. She gives her parents, Tim and Hester Buck, credit for helping her to get "bitten by the travel bug" early in life. Having eight children did not stop her parents from taking a yearly two-week vacation to some distant corner of the country. After she visited every state in the United States, she set her sights on Europe. She attended business college in Dayton, Ohio after high school. When she graduated, she became a volunteer for an organization that assigned her to Switzerland and Germany.

Then journeys turned to the inner vistas of the mind—education. She graduated from Manchester College in Indiana, majoring in peace studies and sociology. She became a youth fieldworker, traveling throughout Ohio for four years, working with the youth of 52 churches. Feeling that she needed further education, she attended Union Theological Seminary in New York City, where she earned her master of divinity degree. For two years she worked as a counselor at the Sloane House YMCA in New York City and then moved to Virginia, where she met Robert Monroe. This led her to a new dimension of explorations.

Robert Monroe, founder of The Monroe Institute, was doing exploration and research into practical methods of accelerated learning through expanded forms of consciousness. One of the results of his work was a method and technique for inducing relaxation and sleep. The technique employs a system of audio pulses that create a Frequency Following Response in the human brain. This technique makes it possible for the average person to maintain specific stages of sleep for any depth and duration.

The Institute also developed a way to use the same methods and techniques in the form of "binaural beats" to create synchronization of the left and right hemispheres in the human brain. The unique coherent brain state that resulted is known as hemispheric synchronization, or "Hemi-Sync." Experimenting with various sound-wave patterns offered significant gateways to new understanding and application of human thought.

Rosalind became one of Robert Monroe's Explorers in 1972 and worked with him for the next eleven years doing extensive research in his laboratory. This book is the result of that research.

During the time Rosalind was working with Robert Monroe, she was a part-time instructor at Blue Ridge Community College, Central Virginia Community College, and Virginia Western Community College. She taught courses in extrasensory perception, parapsychology, and death and dying. She also founded the Creative Living Institute and became its director, sponsoring conferences and seminars throughout Virginia on various personal growth topics. In her natural exploratory style, Rosalind also led tours to Great Britain, Europe, and Central America.

Those interested in the activities of The Monroe Institute may contact:

The Monroe Institute
62 Roberts Mountain Road
Faber, Virginia 22938
Phone: 804-361-1252
FAX: 804-361-1237
e-mail: monroeinst@aol.com
Visit The Monroe Institute website at:
www.monroeinstitute.org

Those interested in Rosalind McKnight's workshops, lectures, or other events may contact her at:

Training and Marketing Services
9516 Timberlake Road, Suite 239
Lynchburg, VA 24502

e-mail: armcknight@aol.com
Visit her website at:
www.hillcity-mall.com/romc

Hampton Roads Publishing Company

. . . for the evolving human spirit

Hampton Roads Publishing Company
publishes books on a variety of subjects including
metaphysics, health, complementary medicine,
visionary fiction, and other related topics.

For a copy of our latest catalog,
call toll-free, 800-766-8009,
or send your name and address to:

Hampton Roads Publishing Company
134 Burgess Lane
Charlottesville, VA 22902
e-mail: hrpc@hrpub.com
www.hrpub.com